'A talented madhead!'

MICHAEL JENNINGS, former WBU Welterweight champion

'Following Michael Gomez's extraordinary boxing journey was a rip-roaring roller coaster of high octane energy, huge emotion and crackling battles! Absolutely loved covering and commentating on most of the ride. What a fighter!'

ADAM SMITH, *Sky Sports*

'He was an animal before the fight and a gent after it.'

PETER McDONAGH, *former Irish Lightweight Champion*

'Michael Gomez boxed like he lived life, right in your face, a true warrior in the ring and nice guy out! It was a pleasure to cover his action packed fights.'

GLENN McCRORY,
former World Cruiserweight Champion

'Never a dull moment when Michael Gomez is around. He doesn't know what he's going to do next, so no one else has a clue what he's up to. One thing is for sure, if a fight breaks out he would be stood next to you. In fact he would be stood in front.'

THOMAS McDONAGH

'Michael was a throwback to fighters of old and a genuine world level operator. I never saw him in a bad fight. Manchester people, especially, should be very proud of him. I know all my family are. He displayed genuine fighting qualities which is rare these days.'

PETER FURY,
uncle of Heavyweight World Champion, Tyson Fury

'Michael Gomez was a terrific fighter inside the ring and crazy outside it! It was a pleasure watching him fight.'

JAMIE MOORE,
former European Super Welterweight Champion

'What can you say about Mikey Gomez. The Manchester assassin. What a great fighter! Like all the fighting travellers, he had the heart of a lion. They just keep coming at you, like a tornado. You don't win a Lonsdale belt for nothing. It's blood, sweat, tears and more blood. In 38 of his wins, 25 were by knockout. For me he was one of the best pound for pound fighters in the last thirty years. A top geezer in and out of the ring. My respect to the man. I salute him.'

CHARLES 'BRONSON' SALVADOR

'We were warriors in the ring and became good friends outside it. I was honoured to play such a huge role in Michael's story.'

ALEX ARTHUR, *former World Super-featherweight champion*

'I saw the sheer size of Michael Gomez's heart up close when I was in his corner for the epic fight against Alex Arthur in Edinburgh. A good lad, a true warrior and one of Manchester's and Ireland's finest.'

RICKY HATTON MBE

And finally…

'I am honoured to share the same name.'

WILFREDO GOMEZ,
Super-Bantamweight World champion 1977-82

GOMEZ

THE AUTOBIOGRAPHY

MICHAEL ARMSTRONG WITH JOHN LUDDEN

EMPIRE
PUBLICATIONS

First published in 2016

EMPIRE PUBLICATIONS
1 Newton Street, Manchester M1 1HW
© Michael Armstrong and John Ludden 2016

ISBN: 978-1-909360-45-7

Printed in Great Britain.

For my little sister Louise

Forever in our hearts

CONTENTS

ACKNOWLEDGEMENTS

Michael: First and most importantly, I'd like to thank my dad who came to all my amateur fights and always supported me even when his eyes got bad. Then there's Brian Hughes who made it all possible and I'm very sad to hear he's so poorly, I wish him all the best.

Next I'd like to thank Billy Graham for the best training and tactics for the Alex Arthur fight and Kerry Kayes for getting me in shape and giving me the best nutrition.

To the memory of Sam Slattery and Billy Coaty; two of the best men in my corner who have sadly passed on but will never be forgotten.

To Robin Reid for helping me catch the burglars; to John Ludden, thank you for listening to me and finally getting my story out there; Andrew Barney McHugh who got the ball rolling by writing the screenplay; Paul McCabe thanks for getting involved in the new chapter and Dawn Goddard for helping me make a fresh start. Last but definitely not least my son Mikey for taking my name and making me proud.

John: I would like to thank the following people for their help in this book. Stephen Lumb, Thomas McDonagh, Dawn Goddard, Mike Cleary, John Griffiths, Andrew 'Barney' McHugh, Ashley Ward and all of Michael's family who have been nothing but extremely helpful whenever called upon. And finally the man himself: Michael Gomez. The countless hours spent with Mike reliving his astonishing story will stay with me forever. It was an honour and a privilege to work with the Mexican Manc.

FOREWORD

MICHAEL GOMEZ has been in some difficult places. He has been a man of extremes on both sides of the ropes. Nobody will ever doubt his fighting heart. There are dozens of memories, dozens of brutal moments in terrific fights. Gomez was often fighting two opponents - one in the opposite corner and one on his shoulder calling him away. The brutal boxing reality is that he won some savage wars and lost a few of his battles. His life was a fight. And, let's tell the truth, he loved the fight. He feared nobody in the ring, nobody was a threat to him. He was fearless as a boxer. Outside the ring he was wild. His battles were different and, once again, he never turned away from confrontation. There was a lot of conflict in the life and times of Michael Gomez. I covered his big fights and a lot of the early ones. I loved the sombrero mayhem, the confidence and the action.

He was winning, impressing people but there was a dark side. I heard the early rumours about his lifestyle away from the gym and ring. It seems now that most of it was true! One night in Sheffield, at a time when his best days in the ring were over but the fighting dream was still burning, I saw the other Gomez. It was not pleasant. I would also argue that it was not Gomez that night. Gomez is not the first quality fighter to have troubles outside the ring, not the first to suffer doubts and setbacks in equal measure. The lows, the disasters, the shocks and all the great nights make his story so captivating. It could be a bad fairy tale, if only it wasn't so crazy and unbelievable.

Gomez never worked in half measures; when he lost, he really lost, when he went crazy, he went very crazy. He won well, partied hard and often lived his life like that night would be his last. And that nearly came true a couple of times!

When he started to work on this book I was sceptical. I wondered would he ever finish it? Would he put in enough of the madness? Would he remember enough of the glory? Would his co-writer John Ludden go the distance? It's all here in the raw. Michael Gomez, the fighter, and the survivor and, by his side, the writer John Ludden.

Enjoy.

Steve Bunce

SECONDS OUT

IT'S NOT EVERY DAY YOU DIE. My name is Michael Gomez. I'm twenty-four years old, of gypsy blood. Manc Irish and proud of it. But here's where my story ends. On a hospital theatre operating table. An allergic reaction to the anaesthetic has caused me to stop breathing. A surgeon explained beforehand the chance of this happening was a million to one.

A million to one? Well seconds out, this just isn't my night.

They tell me everybody loved Michael Armstrong Gomez. An adopted son of this city. The 'Manchester Mexican.'

'Never ever take a step back Michael,' said my friend old Johnny Reed in Dublin, many years ago and I never did. Not once.

I took the hits and there were many. Their best shots, both in the ring and out. Michael Gomez may have been beaten, I may have been battered, bruised and bloodied, but I never backed down. I was a fighter and as one of my heroes, Francis Albert Sinatra, sang: 'I did it my way.'

But tonight it looks like the party's over and the lights are going out. Stabbed over a stupid drunken argument by some no-mark chancer with a flick knife in Manchester. On this occasion I never wanted or asked for trouble. It was all just written in the stars.

In the operating theatre everything now is white and hazy. I see misty shadows, figures rushing around. Angels? A beeping noise. 'He's gone!' Shouts a startled voice. 'We've lost him, he's flat lining!' The seconds go past, ten. It looks like I'm counted out but I hear no bell. Twenty, thirty and suddenly I'm slowly rising to my feet. Forty, forty-eight and the referee grabs and calls me back into the centre of the ring. The Grim Reaper shakes his head and smiles. A wink to me and then he disappears. It's not been his night.

The referee looks into my eyes. He nods. 'Fight on.' I don't need to be told twice. A close call, I nearly did say hello to Elvis, but in the end dying will be simply another chapter in the crazy story of my life. And if you think this is rough, just wait until you see where it all started...

1: THE GHOST OF A SMILE

'And the caravan has all my friends.
It will stay with me until the end.'

VAN MORRISON

In 1977, far across the universe, a crater on the planet Mercury was named after the wonderful Irish poet W.B. Yeats. Back on planet Earth a small budgeted science fiction film called Star Wars was opening to stunned audiences. America was heralding Jimmy Carter as their 39th President after Gerald Ford. Whilst mourning the passing of musical idol Elvis Presley. At forty-two the King vacated his crown by heart attack. Elsewhere in New York, The World Trade Center was also finally completed and expected to stand forever. Closer to home, in England, Manchester United prevented their great rivals Liverpool from achieving a legendary treble by beating them in the FA Cup final. Whereas to the despair of anybody over forty the Sex Pistols were causing blue fucking murder with the release of their now legendary album, Never Mind The Bollocks. And as the world turned, across the sea in Ireland a future twice British and world champion was making his first public appearance in a world that for him would prove tough beyond words, but for all those lucky enough to be on board. A helluva ride. I'll let Michael take up the story...

THERE'S AN OLD GYPSY SAYING: 'After bad luck comes good fortune.' Well maybe I was just the exception to the rule. I was born in a car crash back on 21 June 1977. My expectant Mother, Mary, was being thrown around in the back of a battered old Austin Allegro, driven by my badly hungover, partially blind Father, Michael John Armstrong, in his thick rimmed glasses. It was a hereditary disease that also affected five of his brothers. He careered onwards at a crazy speed along the winding ribbon roads that sliced through the beautiful rolling fields of county Longford.

Gypsy country. Our world.

It could only be a matter of time before disaster struck.

Suddenly Dad was forced to swerve to avoid an approaching car and skidded off smashing into the signpost of an old person's nursing home. My shaken Mam's waters broke and she was going to deliver me there and then, amidst the smoking, smouldering wreck. Feeling obliged, Dad got out and cleared the cigarette butts, dirty rags and food packets from the back seats to make her more comfortable. He was good like that.

A frantic Mam was screaming. 'Michael John Armstrong, you did this to me, now get the little bastard out!'

Clearly with no idea what to do, he fumbled around trying to help and as ever wasn't short of really terrible advice. 'Come on with ya, woman. Stop ya whining and just fuckin' push will ya! By God, it isn't like you haven't done it before. Jesus, Mary and Joseph you've already got two at home. You wrote the damn book.'

Luckily for Mam, one of the staff ladies from the home came rushing out and immediately pushed him aside. 'Out of my way you useless bastard! Go and do something useful like head butt a fuckin' tree!'

And so with this good lady's help I made my way into the light, kicking and crying. Finally after a last bout of panting and pushing from Mam, I, Michael John Armstrong, only later to be Gomez, third child of Michael senior and Mary arrived. Taken inside the home I was placed over a bathroom sink and had my hair washed and the blood wiped off by my exhausted Mam. She kissed me on the forehead and sighed. 'Another fuckin' mouth to feed. Welcome to the world little one and good luck…Ya going to need it, son'.

I ask you. I mean look around. What chance did I have? I know people believe we gypsies love the great outdoors, but this to begin with was just fuckin' ridiculous. Still, things could only get better.

Seven years later: Not many people remember their first fight, but I do. I was seven and it was against a little Chinese girl the same age. She must have been mouthy to be worse than me! That was saying something. We got into a mad argument and before I could raise a fist she jumped high and karate kicked me in the mouth then ran off. Shell-shocked, I was left nursing a massive red lip and an even bigger bruised ego. No one could ever know. Luckily nobody else was around to see it, so I counted my blessings, I licked my wounds and headed home. On walking through the door my Mam was waiting and immediately went spare. 'Oh Jesus Michael, what the fuck has gone on? Have ya been fighting? Who's done this to ya?'

'Nothing Mam, I just fell. It was an accident.'

'Ah that's bollocks, away with ya Midge (my nickname sadly). That's not a fall, there's no other marks on ya face. Now who hit ya? Don't take me for an idiot. Tell me or I swear to god I'll brain ya myself?'

'Mam I swear…'

Now there was no way on this planet I was going to come clean and tell her that some little Chinese bird had done a hit and run, Bruce Lee job on me and ran off laughing. I'm still chasing a rematch. If you're out there girl? Gomez's record at this time was F1 W0 L1. Now I've come clean, on with the story.

My elder (by two years) brother Mark, more commonly known as Bones (because of his scrawny appearance) was both my best mate and partner-in-crime growing up. We were inseparable and joined at the hip. Two skinny imps, dressed in rags that had the bad habit of stealing anything that wasn't nailed down. Shopkeepers needed eyes in the back of their heads and even then we'd have stuff away; swift, sleight of hand, goods would be down the jumper or in the pocket and gone. We had the best teacher in Ireland; our Mam. She taught us so well that if I hadn't become a professional boxer, then shoplifting would have been my second career choice.

I always remember one day myself and Bones had the great idea of stealing a goat from a nearby farmer's yard. All went well at first only to hit the rocks on making our escape, when the owner appeared with a loaded shotgun and fired it into the air. The bullets flew just above our heads and to this day I'm not sure if he wasn't aiming. But I've never ran so fuckin' fast in my life. I can still see him; barefooted, half naked and screaming blue murder – 'Run ya robbing little tinker bastards, away with ya! Next time I'll be waiting and shoot ya in the fuckin' arse!' Maybe it wasn't a gift heaven sent, but somebody had blessed us.

A good thing was we rarely lived in a place long enough for locals to know what went on. If they'd ever found out we'd have been lynched. The goat story always stayed with me because I remember thinking for once 'I'll make my Mam happy by walking back through our door with something useful for a change'. I also recall at the time asking Bones if he thought our little mate had a name?

'Who cares?' He replied typically. 'Let's just call it fuckin' lunch!'

That was Bones. Only then for the little thing to jump out of my arms and bolt across a field like lightning. No matter how fast we chased, it ran like the wind. Almost as if it knew my brother's plans for the Armstrong dinner table and could smell the mint sauce. On giving up we stopped at a huge farm where I noticed four figures playing inside the gate with a football; laughing and joking, happy families.

I remember, just for a moment, watching and thinking 'haven't they got anything to worry about? Like where was the next meal coming from? Or doing a runner from the rent man?' This was something I could only ever have dreamt about. Instead of the band of thieves and vagabonds I felt blessed to call my own family. Can't live with 'em, can't live without 'em. Bones always called me a dreamer back then, but come the end of my career, when things got really tough and I really needed help, they were the ones who rallied around when nobody else wanted to know. And today, apart from one, we're closer than ever, despite fighting like cats and dogs, but what family doesn't?

It's a brave one who takes us on.

We moved on from the farm, but not before I checked for newly laid eggs in their hen pen. Nothing. Also the post box at the end of the driveway for anything useful. Again empty. Now there's a problem, because going home potless meant nothing was more guaranteed than a good hiding off the old man. Even with his badly fading eyesight he cracked a good 'un. And it was hard to duck a belt and buckle in a caravan filled with nine other kids. Not recommended. And so in times of great trouble like this we decided there was only one option. Myself and Bones turned around and went back on the rob. Because you have to understand that was how we survived to put food on the table for our sisters. Robbing and begging - another thing we excelled at. Being a pair of sad and sorry little wide-eyed, dirt-faced gypsy kids, we could always count on a couple of pennies being thrust into our hands.

'Thank ya sir, the luck will be forever with ya now. And for another couple of pennies we'll bless ya family as well!' Few ever refused us.

Besides the old tales of it being bad luck to turn down a traveller was so many times true in our case. If anyone slammed the door on myself and Bones, then we'd pick up the nearest stones or bricks and smash their house or car windows and leg it.

I messed up badly once. We'd a dog called Brandy. All animals in our family were named after booze. A chicken called Jack and another called Daniels. Best ask the old man about that. Brandy was a miserable looking dog, but I loved it. Once out begging, I managed to scratch together a pile of pennies, so being really fond of Brandy, I thought I'd treat it to a tin of dog food, only on arriving home to be almost hung upside down on the washing line by Mam. She went spare at me. 'I've got all you bairns to feed and you come back with a tin of fuckin' dog food? What's wrong with ya Midge? Where's ya fuckin' brains?' Bang, wallop! I don't think I ever ducked as much in the ring as I did from her trying to give me a good slap that day. The cupboard bare, babies screaming and she like the rest of us was forced to watch on as a tail-wagging Brandy, surrounded by the Armstrong clan, munched away on his bowl of dog food.

'Pull this stunt again Michael and I'll feed ya myself to the flea ridden mutt,' said Mam. Not my finest moment but Brandy was happy enough.

It was never boring. One night with Dad on the piss and Mam in a bad mood, myself and Bones went out and decided to go for a walk to some nearby mountains. We set off with good intentions, only to come across a huge, long, marshy bog blocking our path. Suddenly the mountains didn't look that appealing anymore. Bones being Bones never saw the problem.

'We'll just fuckin' jump,' he declared.

'No way,' I said. 'There's a reason ya all call me Midge. No fuckin' way.' Next minute he'd pushed me in! I couldn't believe it! Up to my neck in shit and mud and him laughing his head off. As I screamed and cried Bones finally pulled me out. Caked head to toe and stinking of God knows what, I stood there looking a pathetic sight. He just couldn't help himself.

'Ah Midge, you should watch what you're doing. You look a right mess. Mam is gonna fuckin' kill ya!'

And so we headed home. Bones was right. I knew I was a dead boy walking when Mam saw the state of me. Everybody else thought it was hilarious but she went mental. I was stripped bollock naked, dragged out and thrown under the old fashioned water pumps that you'd once find at the side of the road. Then still screaming abuse at me, Mam turned it on. 'I'll teach ya Michael, ya dirty little bastard!'

I've never been so cold in my life! I never did make it to those mountains.

Thanks Bones.

Double Act: I was one of ten children. The eldest, Valerie, was a second mum to us all in the dirty, chaotic and forever squabbling world of our household. Where Mam and Dad were too busy trying to kill each other, Val took over the reins and performed miracles. We were always one step away from paying a due rent. Mayo, Kerry, Galway, constantly roaming, living in slum accommodations and moth ridden bedsits before eventually landing in Dublin, Ballymun. Our home was two caravans on the side of a main road with in between a wonderful invention by Dad. An architectural work of art consisting of four poles and a roof made from black binbags.

The old man was really proud of his extension and fair play to him.

'That's a fuckin' good job if I say so myself.'

Whilst everyone else fought like mad not to sleep there, I loved it! Many a night I spent under that tent and it never leaked. For a while it worked a treat and I thought my Dad was the greatest man on the planet! He did try at times. I remember another occasion him trying to teach my Mam to drive when four of us were in the back and nearly crashing the car.

Being almost blind never doused Dad's crazy enthusiasm and when he got a mad idea in his head, it just had to come out. We'd all watch and wait for our Mam's inevitable explosion when it all went horribly wrong.

'Michael fuckin' Armstrong! I prefer ya when you're pissed

because at least then there's an excuse!'

Our problems of space returned when my sister Charlene was born and Dad in a moment of monumental, drunken madness decided to sell one of the caravans for beer money to celebrate her birth. You had to hand it to him. When he fucked up it was with style and for this escapade there was hell to pay. Mam finally dumped him.

We landed at a battered wives hostel run by the Catholic Church. Dad's drunken tempers, crazy ways and bad moods finally proving too much for her, who, growing tired of one too many fights, left him with us in tow. But like a bad penny he'd always return and we'd flock around the old man and be glad to see him. He'd be full of remorse and promising to turn over a new leaf. Dad had a way with the ladies, I'd give him that.

'I love ya Mary Armstrong. Ya rock my world!'

Mam would blush. 'Ah away with ya Michael Armstrong! Ya say that to all your tarts!'

And off we'd go again a' wandering. Playing happy families until the next time. My parents were a double act. They simply lived to love and hate each other with a passion. Most nights he'd go out on his own. But sometimes they went to the pub together and, my God, the sound of them shouting outside and then coming back in through the door. Well we braced ourselves and waited for the fireworks. All night long the swearing and cussing would fly. Plates and dishes would crash and smash as they attempted to outdo each other with the worst possible insults.

'Fuck off ya blind useless bastard!'

'Fuck ya, ya no good wasted whore'...

And these were the mild ones.

Father John: Before the return of the prodigal Dad, something occurred that changed my world forever. Whilst at the hostel I 'occasionally' attended the Holy Spirit's school. It was run by priests and nuns and rules were many. It was strict beyond words and the rules had to be respected at all times. Otherwise a crack around the head, a flying chalk brush or a whacking with a belt was guaranteed. Woe betide any kid who broke them. For some reason I was picked on more than most. An easy target, I suppose. A little tinker dressed in rags and hand me downs whose personal hygiene was never the best. At first I put up with it but then? Well I went to war with the priests and one in particular, a nasty piece of work called Father John.

When not bullying or eyeing up nuns he'd be found in the bookies or getting rat arsed in the boozer. I hated this man and made it my mission to wind him up every chance I got. This eight year-old pain in the arse finally exhausted his patience and Father John snapped and dragged me by the collar one day to nearby Finley's boxing gym. He kicked me through the door and all eyes fell upon us. The busy gym froze, the speedbag stopped being hit and the skipping ropes hit the floor. I looked around at the faces and thought, this is me.

The priest smiled. 'Now let's see if you're as fuckin' cocky Armstrong.'

The owner came over; he was huge and his face looked like it had been taking punches for most of his life. But it was so obvious, even to a blind man, that he loved this place. There was an angel's smile amidst the war wounds. It was his church and he spoke with true reverence. 'A good day to ya Father, what can I do for ya?'

'I was wondering if ya could teach this little maggot here some good manners?'

The owner looked at me and then back at the priest.

'No problem,' he replied.

Father John pushed me towards him. 'I'll teach ya to mess with a fuckin' man of the cloth, ya little shite. Do what ya have to do to teach this tinker he's nothing but dirt. I'll be back in an hour.'

As we watched him go, the owner put an arm round my shoulder. He said quietly, as Father John disappeared out the door, 'I'm a traveller myself, ignore the old fool. Now come on. I've a feeling ya were born for this.'

There I was gloved up and made to fight a much larger and bigger kid who knocked me around the ring like a spinning top. Bruised and bloodied, I was taken back to the school and it was thought by Father John that I'd surely learnt a costly but valuable lesson.

'Away with ya Armstrong and be a good fuckin' lad now!'

Know your place and if prayer doesn't work, resort to violence. This was a widely held belief amongst people like him. Father John thought he'd won by a knockout. Little did this bastard know, the tears of the little boy whose alleged sins he was trying to so hard to cleanse were simply that of rage. He had no idea of what had been unleashed in me, because I actually enjoyed getting hammered in that ring; I loved it and now all I could think about was going back to Finley's gym and getting my revenge. So I trained myself for a couple of weeks. I practised hitting anything that moved or didn't. Including my sisters.

'Midge what the fuck! Mam, will ya tell him. He's hitting things again!'

When I was ready I went back. The owner saw me coming through the door and smiled. 'I thought we'd be seeing ya again! Get gloved up little man.'

I called out that same kid from before. This time around I beat the living crap out of him. A nine-year-old scrag, knee high to a grasshopper pummelling this much bigger boy. I could feel every eye in the gym watching on in shock. I just kept punching, I never stopped until he fell to his knees crying. Only then was I dragged off him. This was the moment something clicked inside me and my mind was made up. It was a calling. The priests had sent me my vocation as if from God. I had the bug. From that day on I'd find myself waking up and walking to the gym without even thinking. I just loved it. The mists fell away and I knew my future clear as day.

I was going to be a fighter.

On becoming aware of this new found talent with my fists, Dad swiftly put me to work. Mostly outside beer gardens filled with travellers and for the price of a pint or a couple of pounds, I'd fight boys older and bigger. With the odds always stacked against me, I, or more precisely Dad, cleaned up; a little terror who, when in a fury, could cause grown men to shake their heads in disbelief by punching their boys into surrender or in most cases just knocked them flat out.

'Ya got a fuckin' mad, little one Michael.' Words heard many times by me as I did what Dad asked and went to war.

'He's a licence for printing money that little maniac.'

'You're a lucky bastard Armstrong.'

'He should be on a fuckin' lead that one.'

With a wink and a smile Dad took their money and headed off back to the bar. As for me? I never once got a word of thanks, but I wasn't bothered. Just the thought of losing and having to face my old man with his buckle and belt was always enough incentive to ensure I battered the hell out of whoever they put in front of me. The bigger they were, the harder they fell and having a quiet life meant the faster I put them down, the better. Whilst other kids were out on bikes and playing football or sat watching their favourite television programme, I was fighting, winning and loving it!

Johnny Reed: Thirty-seven-year-old Johnny Reed was a former Irish boxer of no great distinction. You've probably never heard of him. He lacked all the essential qualities to succeed in the professional game. Everything except a huge heart. Johnny's one claim to fame was sparring with the legendary Barry McGuigan. His battle scarred face bore witness to the fact that he never bothered to duck. A boxer's landscape; pug nosed, battered features with eyes that scream out the words 'I could've been a contender.'

Johnny lived in a squat that made our abode look like a palace. When he wasn't in the bookies picking losers, a drunken Johnny was in the pub reminiscing to all who'd listen, and those who wouldn't, the magnificent pissed up story of his life.

'I used to be a champion!'

Folks would shake their head and groan. 'Oh Christ, not again Johnny. Give it a fuckin' rest will ya.' There was someone, though, who adored him. Johnny Reed was my hero. I loved Johnny. Many a night I'd sleep on his moth ridden couch. I can hear his words now when I walked through the door. 'What's the craic little fella?'

The flat was a complete dump. It stank to high heaven, rubbish all over the floor, rats running everywhere, no electricity. I mean it was a pigsty but I didn't care. For it was Johnny's place. He was the one who said the words that'd stay with me forever. 'No matter what Mikey, never take a step back. Once they see fear in your eyes, it's all over.'

I'd sit for hours and listen to Johnny talk about his boxing career. There was this one trophy that he was so proud of. But on it somebody else's name was inscribed. Not wanting to upset him, I never mentioned it. Probably most of what Johnny said was bullshit, but I didn't care. I loved the man, for Johnny Reed was, and still is for me, a legend. I remember being hugely impressed by him being able to pick up a wooden chair with one leg and put it on his chest.

He also helped me with my boxing. I'd punch the man's hand.

'Are they getting harder Johnny?'

'Aye, your left is decent Mikey, but your right is still shite. Come on now, right only, no shots with your left. Jab… jab…hook.'

And God help me if I tried a left, then whack! Across the side of my face.

'Are ya fuckin' deaf lad? I said no shots with yer left!'

Johnny Reed. I've no idea what happened to him. I know Johnny and my Dad had a fight in the pub one night. Words were said and he disappeared for a while. We, as ever, never stayed in one place long enough to let the fuckin' washing dry so I lost touch.

'Any tips for me Johnny?'

'Aye Mikey, only one and don't ever forget it. In and out of the ring. Always get the first punch in.'

Fuck me, I took that advice on board over the years.

One time I was sat on a beach looking out to sea. Bones and Val were nearby playing bat and ball with pebbles and a piece of driftwood. Finally they came over to see why I was so quiet.

Val ruffled my hair. 'A penny for them little brother.'

I pointed to the water. 'I was just wondering if there was anything out there? Surely there has to be something better than this shite?'

Bones piped up as usual. 'What? Ya gonna be a sailor? Ya can't even fuckin' swim Mikey!'

I remember Val sticking up for me. 'Leave him Bones, I get ya Michael. Ya talkin' about what's over the horizon aren't ya. A better world.'

I was. Then she grabbed my hand and stared with me. We stayed there for hours.

Funny what stays in your mind.

Louise: We lost my baby sister Louise at two years old. They called it Sudden Infant Death Syndrome. When she died, none of us could take it in. We were kids for God's sake. Stuff like that happened to other people. It broke our hearts. None more than Mam who was destroyed by Louise's death. I think she blamed the old man, not for her dying, just needing someone to lash out at. I'm not too sure, but he was kicked out again and we ended up in another home for battered housewives in Rattmines, Dublin, and Dad went to live at his Mother's house nearby.

Mam was wrecked and going through a breakdown. Something had to change and so she came up with an idea that didn't include him; a fresh start for all of us across the sea. We'd go to England. Mam made it sound like she was doing this so we could all have a better chance in life, but I think she was running from what happened. But you can't get away from something like that, as I'd find out in my own life. It lives in your head, you just have to survive with the hurt. That's not easy to do.

Looking out across over the Irish Sea we gathered up our belongings. The tattered suitcases, trolleys and plastic bags and boarded a ship that'd take us to England and a new life. Louise dying is something that still haunts my family. A ghost of a smile. A bundle of joy taken from us in a too short, unholy time. But back then a sense of excitement, wonder and no little fear gripped all of us as a new adventure dawned. None more so than me, for I'd no idea what to expect. A new beginning. A new world. Or so I thought. In many ways it would be the same old story but in a different country.

The Armstrongs were coming to town and in no time at all Manchester wouldn't know what hit it!

2: SUNNY SIDE OF THE STREET

*'And we'll go where the spirits take us. To heaven or to hell.
And kick up bloody murder in the town we love so well.'*

SHANE MACGOWAN

During the eighties Manchester was as dark and grey as the bleak, dull skies above. Beneath them a city ravaged. A stark, urban landscape, raped by economic depression, all fuelled by Margaret Thatcher's right-wing Tory government that appeared determined to run Manchester and its near, unfriendly, neighbour Liverpool, into the northern dirt. A grim tale of two cities that were left to rot and die. Manchester's music matched its mood. Joy Division, later, New Order. The soulful but bittersweet laden lyrics of Morrissey and The Smiths. "I was happy in the shade of a drunken hour. But heaven knows I'm miserable now..' A soundtrack to a less than golden decade. There was though a ray of sunshine dancing like a lunatic through the clouds. The Hacienda exploded to become home to an entire new musical era.

Madchester arrived on the scene. A troublesome, but wide-eyed and willing partner to the Gunchester culture that still ran foul on the streets of the rainy city. Wretched scowls gave way to sunshine smiles. The music started up, Happy Mondays, The Stone Roses: a new vibe, People preferred to dance and not fight. Make peace and love not war. Ecstasy descended on this dirty old northern outpost and an entire generation of young Mancs danced till the sun came up. Amidst the beautiful madness arriving on these shores came a young Irish kid whom along with his family was far too busy living and surviving to notice the pills, thrills and bellyaches of an ever-changing Manchester.

A T THE FERRY PORT in Anglesey's Holyhead, a picture of
Margaret Thatcher in the arrival lounge had a Hitler
moustache scrawled upon it. An old maintenance man was
stood nearby with another of her ready to put up, he was moaning
and swearing to himself. 'Fuckin' third one today.'

The day's relative quiet in the port is rudely interrupted by a
sudden eruption of noise, arguing, shouting and screaming. I was nine
years old when we arrived on English shores. The maintenance man
watched as my clan trampled past him like an invading army carrying
our life's belongings. Myself and Bones handed him a v-sign. The
maintenance man shook his head and I could hear him grumbling.

'More fuckin' tinkers.'

After going through customs they packed us onto a bus to
Manchester. I was sat next to Val and we were both just daydreaming
and staring out the window. A real fancy expensive car came alongside
us on the motorway. Inside was an older couple; a man and a woman.
They both looked across and gave myself and Val just a real dirty look.
As if we were nothing but dirt on their shoes. Whilst he went back to
his driving her expression suddenly changed to sheer horror and we
thought what the...

Then I heard Mam's voice scream out. 'Bones fuckin' behave or
I'll kill ya, I will!' Both of us turned around and there he was mooning
them. Bones' bare arse pressed against the window. We all killed
ourselves laughing as their car switched gears and sped away. This
country had no idea what was coming their way.

As the *Madchester* music scene erupted like a supernova over the
city and far beyond, the Armstrong's exploded upon the Rosa hotel
on Clitheroe Road in Longsight, like a bad smell. A halfway house
and refuge home for Women's Aid and the homeless until more
permanent accommodation could be arranged. Amidst utter chaos
we arrived outside, throwing stones and kicking around milk bottles,
laughing, joking and hurling insults at passers by. Disgruntled

neighbours dared to peep through curtains, only to be noticed by myself and Bones and given the finger. A harassed Mam gathered us all together and Val dragged hold of Bones around his neck whilst he was halfway through pissing against a wall.

'Come on you dirty gobshite. Away with ya!'

Finally, with Mam at the helm, we piled inside to reception. The look from the woman on duty was precious. 'The Armstrongs I presume?' We all stared at her... Welcome to Longsight. It wasn't long before myself and Bones were sent to pillage the local shops by Mam but we'd already figured out a way of making money without leaving the hotel. It was Bones who came up with it. He found out that from the linen room on the top floor, there was an open hatch to the ceiling leading to the attic. From there we could balance on the wooden beams and climb down into the rooms below with a small ladder. You just had to be really careful not to slip and go through the loft insulation. It was easy pickings; we'd struck gold, but we were always careful not to get too greedy and bring suspicion on ourselves. If there was a wallet or a purse we'd only take a tenner or a twenty pound note at any one time. Sometimes, though, the urge to steal a nice watch or a ring that was lying around proved too much and we'd have them away also. It was simply in our nature.

We hadn't been there long when a familiar face showed up. Dad had made his way across from Ireland and tracked us down to Longsight. It was no surprise to me. Despite his ever-worsening eyesight, this man could find a tack in a barrel of shit. He spun Mam the same old lines about promising to become a changed man and she fell for it as ever. Hook, line and sinker. We had our Dad back. Only there was a problem. Mam gathered us all together one day.

'Right, yer Dad isn't allowed in the hotel, so from now on he's Uncle Willie to the lot of ya till I say more. Woe betides one of ya little eejits messin' up and getting us thrown out of here.'

Hardly surprising that there was more than one close shave with blowing his cover. Dad would come into the hotel for tea sometimes and you could guarantee one of us slipping up. Each 'Dad' instead of 'Uncle Willie' would be met with a swift whack across the head from whoever was nearest. We all got it at some time. Smack! Bang! Me, I was among the worst. Hit black and blue. It was good to have him back though, for you only get one Dad.

Longsight was good fun and cheap. You have to remember we'd come from Ireland where everything was so expensive. Here it was 12p on the bus to town and 38p for a bag of chips. I made friends with a couple of traveller lads my own age who were in a caravan near the hotel. They'd an older sister who really liked me, but back then I was clueless where girls were concerned. In time I more than made up for it.

More importantly for me then was our penny for the guy that we took into the dozens of Irish pubs in the area. The locals loved us because we were the real thing. Many of the regulars were just plastic Paddies singing the songs and drinking the Guinness, but most of them had never been near Ireland. Then there were the old timers who hadn't been back home for years and when pissed would get emotional about the green fields and mountains of Kerry, Mayo and Galway. They were only too happy to fill our pockets with fifty pence pieces and pound coins and buy us crisps and pop. Good times.

'Is it still the same boys? Does the auld country still make yer heart skip a beat?'

I'd smile and nod enthusiastically, whilst Bones would check what pocket his wallet was in. It couldn't last though and the council gave my Mam notice that we had to leave Clitheroe Road because they'd found us a council house in North Manchester, in a place called Moston.

I'd never fuckin' heard of it.

11 Alloway Walk was our new home, but we weren't there long. True to form, one night Mam, Dad and Val went out for a drink to

the pub and got into an argument with the wrong people, some small-time local gangsters. Dad, despite his sight, ended up fighting and gave one of them a good slap. It didn't go down well and this guy's family were not noted for letting some newly arrived Irish tinkers take liberties with one of their own. The three of them came home that same night in a state because rumours were rife a tooled-up mob were on their way round to our house intent on serious damage. And so it was a midnight flit. It was like watching worker ants as we gathered our stuff together. Practice made perfect and doing runners was something the Armstrongs specialised in. Strangely today the family whom we'd fallen out with are good friends.

Next stop was a homeless refuge in Moss Side, where we stayed for a short while until they could re-house us. It didn't take long before we were fixed up and a house was found on the Tripe colony in Miles Platting, named after a tripe factory and a stretch of housing long now demolished. Here was where our lives would take a crazy turn of events. Even for a family like ours that thought it had seen and experienced most things life could throw at us.

How wrong we were…

Thieves like us: Living next door to us in the colonies were two lesbians; Angela and Debbie. Lovely girls. In time Angela would run away with Mam and Debbie would marry Bones and have six kids by him. But that's for later. Whilst in Miles Platting we had it made with the shoplifting. There was rich pickings for thieves like us. We lived opposite a juice factory and robbed that place like you wouldn't believe. People would rip our hands off for it; pineapple, cranberry and orange juice - three cartons for a quid.

When the security guys at the factory got wise to us we moved onto a nearby chemist. 'Wash and Go' shampoo and 'Lynx Body Spray' were our main sellers and again we simply couldn't steal enough to keep up supply. Sadly the chemist clocked us one day and that line of business was closed down. But we had other avenues of finance. Next was chocolate, five packs for a quid and they lapped it up. It was like printing money. An Iceland store in the precinct was another favourite target, we almost cleaned that place out. It got so bad they hired a security guard which was unknown in those days. That never stopped us, although one day the guard spotted Mam and she dealt with it by beating the living crap out of him, whilst myself and Bones legged it. We steered well clear for a while, but went back in the end.

We had more front than Blackpool Promenade.

The Armstrongs had their own customers by this time and we'd rob to order. The family motto: *'You want it, we'd steal it.'* Including the copper boilers out of empty houses on the colonies. Nothing was safe. Oh we were very good.

Shit cakes: One day, myself and Bones got a tip off about a cake factory on Ashley Lane in Moston. If you got there early enough in the morning the trays of cakes were left unguarded in the factory yard, waiting for the delivery van to come and take them to the shops. So plans were made. After wagging school for the day we set off early and hid across the road from the factory. From there the cakes could clearly be seen stacked up on trays in the yard. They looked delicious. Whilst Bones kept look out I ran in and swiped the top tray before the pair of us made off down an alleyway and out of sight. Finally convinced nobody was following we stopped to pause for breath. The cakes made us lick our lips, but business was business. There were chocolate éclairs, cream scones, custard slices, fresh strawberry tarts. Jam donuts. It was enough to make your eyes water. Neither of us could believe how easy it'd been.

'Let's go and get another tray,' said Bones.

I hid the cakes behind a dustbin and put a piece of cardboard over them before heading back. Only to see the factory gate had been locked and two workers in their white overalls and hats were out in the yard counting the trays and looking around scratching their heads.

'I'm sure there's one fuckin' missing,' we heard one of them shout back inside to the bakery. Disappointed, but at least content with one tray, we walked back, happy in the knowledge of just how much money could be made out of our ill-gotten gains. Only to find out when I reached behind the dustbin some dirty bastard had shit all over them. I kid you not. To this day myself and Bones can't get our heads around who'd do such a thing. Run off with them, okay. But to do that!

At first shocked and heaving badly we quickly recovered and Bones decided to get back to work. He took off a shoe and then a sock to wipe off the messier bits covering our cakes. To be honest his sock smelt worse than what was on them but by the time he'd finished, they didn't look too bad. Our selling point later that morning as we knocked on to our regular customers, there was a special discount, because these were slight rejects.

Or as my brother christened them, 'Shit cakes'.

With us, you just kept going and made the best of the bad. We'd no choice. Money from shit, but somehow we always find something to smile about on the sunny side of the street.

It was around this time Mam shocked us rigid by telling the family that she was leaving to set up home with Angela. To call this a bombshell was putting it mild. Angry, confused and to be honest utterly gobsmacked, we all gathered to say goodbye as a taxi came and she left with Angela to start a new life. Later, Mam would try and get custody of us from Dad, and that moment when she stood up in the witness box and confessed to being a lesbian will stay with me forever. It broke our hearts and as for the look on Dad's face? She'd had ten of his kids for God's sake. That she failed to win the case and promised to try again was the last straw for him. He returned to Ireland with the girls to stay at his Mother's house in Dublin. Me, I wanted to remain in England and moved in with Val and her boyfriend. As for Bones? He decided to help Debbie get over her heartache at losing Angela. My brother put his heart, soul and other things into it and six kids later I think he succeeded.

I was thirteen years old when I first met Margarita. She was eighteen; exotic, black, beautiful and had two kids. For a while I thought it was Christmas every day, and then Margarita told me that she might be pregnant. Luckily it turned out to be a false alarm, but this one incident was enough to frighten me off. I quickly got over my broken heart and discovered Mandy and Lisa from the Miner's estate. Suddenly I'd a new hobby. Then it all got serious.

She Bangs The Drums: One day I was out and about in Moston causing the usual grief with my mate Steve. We were eyeing up a car stereo when suddenly I noticed coming towards us on Lightbowne Road, a small but perfectly formed, in all the right places, blonde girl. I remember saying to Steve like it happened yesterday. 'I'd love to marry that bird.'

That bird was thirteen-year-old Alison Davies. We started talking and immediately I was hooked. Alison gave as good as she got.

'Michael Armstrong, you're so full of shit it's untrue!'

But sweet with it. Her aunt Rita, who she lived with after Alison's mum Kim was killed by a drunk driver two years before, was one of my best customers. In an effort to woo her, I'd always leave sweets and stuff in a freebie bag for Alison, whilst charging Rita of course. It worked and we shared our first kiss soon after.

Nobody could get the smile off my face. This wasn't me, it must have been serious because when I went shoplifting, I found myself robbing stuff like chocolates, perfume, shampoos, women's deodorant and spot creams to give her. I'd wrap them in little bundles and hand them over as a present. I'll never forget that moment I first saw Alison walking down the road towards me. Never.

Working for God: With Bones causing a distraction by telling the girl behind the counter how much he loved her, I had the Easter egg away from the Co-op and came up with a foolproof way of making some money. Myself and Bones would go around the estate and side streets and raffle it for fifty pence a time. Whoever won got the egg and the money went to a good cause; our local church. Off we went, knocking on doors, explaining our mission for God. Older ladies would listen on with tears in their eyes as these two young scrotes waxed lyrical. Though outwardly looking like a pair of rascals, deep within, we had true hearts of gold. Into the purses they'd reach and pass us the money and sign their name on the sheet. We promised to be in touch if they won…

'God bless you love,' Bones would say, before smiling and winking at me.

Other houses were not so welcoming.

'Fuck off ya little tinker bastards and if I see ya around here again, I'll hit ya with a brick!' We'd make a note of where they lived for future reference and when our mission for the church was complete we'd go back and put their fuckin' windows in.

But mostly the chance of winning this large and delicious looking chocolate egg meant that we easily managed to get rid of all the tickets. Finally the time came for the grand raffle. All the Armstrongs were present, plus some customers who'd invested their hard earned money and for some reason wanted to be there when the draw was done. Val drew the ticket and I couldn't believe my luck.

I won the egg!

'It's a fuckin racket,' raged a neighbour and she walked off in a huff.

I split the egg with Val, my partner in crime. Of course we fixed it! As for the money? Well the girls were happy because it paid for some clothes and shoes off Conran Street market. Plus myself and Bones treated ourselves to cider, cigs and crisps. Mission accomplished. All that remained was to go and deal with the big mouth who'd made the tinker comments.

Bones threw me a brick and picked one up himself.

He smiled. 'These'll do. Come on…'

All the family were at Val's ninth floor flat playing cards on Victoria Avenue in Moston, when suddenly something large hurtled down past our window and a loud sickening thump was heard. As one we all ran out onto the landing. The old woman who lived above Val was lying dead on the concrete below. We knew she was an invalid and normally in a wheelchair and so as everybody else ran downstairs, myself and Bones went up. We saw the wheelchair still on the balcony from where she'd climbed onto and jumped to commit suicide.

'Look!' Bones pointed to a purse. 'Keep watch Midge.'

He raced over and emptied it. Twenty pounds that was all, but it was no use to her where she'd gone. Best with us. Although far too late somebody had called an ambulance and you could hear the sirens approaching. As we came out of the flats a crowd had gathered around her corpse. I couldn't stop staring at the body and the blood seeping out. How low does somebody have to get before stooping to take their own life? Years later I'd discover. Bones grabbed my arms and brought me back to reality.

'Come on, I've got an idea.'

Off we went to the chippy where the old lady's money was used to treat everybody to a bag of chips and a tin of cold drink. This, for the Armstrongs, was a feast. Moston caviar. As we all sat munching, I looked around at the smiling faces. For once nobody was speaking, just enjoying their chips. If the old lady was looking down, I'd hope she'd be happy for giving us all a brief moment of happiness.

3: PRIDE IN BATTLE

*'It's not all about throwing bombs. If you can't block a jab you
shouldn't be in here. If you can't throw a jab don't bother coming back.'*

BRIAN HUGHES MBE

I WAS ON THE ROB in a Moston newsagents. The shopkeeper
was becoming increasingly suspicious as he kept an eye on me
pretending to look at comics. 'You gonna buy anything lad? I shut
in three fuckin' hours.'

Knowing he'd rumbled me I was forced to buy a small pack of
sweets. In paying for them I noticed a flier on the counter with a
football on it.

'What's that?'

'Read it,' he replied. Only then to spot my embarrassed red face
and realise that I couldn't. The shopkeeper told me it was advertising
football trials for the local boys club on nearby Broadhurst fields. 'You
should go. It'll keep you out of mischief and my fuckin' hair.'

'I will. Thanks.' As he turned his back, I helped myself to a couple
of chocolate bars on the way out. It wasn't time wasted after all.

I went along and really enjoyed it. I had a new pastime. When I
wasn't out with Alison or fighting and robbing, I'd be playing football
for Collyhurst and Moston boys. It was run by a man called Brian
Hughes who also looked after the boxing club, based in a gym above
the Co-Op building on Lightbowne Road, in Moston. Playing
football might be pushing it a little because I wasn't much good. I had
bundles of enthusiasm and could run forever, but my short fuse and

frustration many times got the better of me and I'd explode.

In fact if I didn't get sent off every week, it was always close. Any opponent who tried to shield the ball just drove me mad and I'd lash out, no matter what size he was. One bad word back and whack! I'd go into a rage and the red card was flashed. It couldn't go on because each time I was sent off the fines were adding up. In the end the club just couldn't afford to pay them and I found myself sidelined. It got so bad, Brian sent me off himself in one game.

Although clearly livid with my behaviour I could tell he was impressed with the left hook I used to flatten the other much bigger lad.

'I'm not having that on a football pitch, Michael Armstrong. This isn't Gaelic bloody football. Off you go lad, think about what you've just done and start the bath for the other lads.'

It was another fight that changed my life, but it wasn't one that took place on a football pitch or in a ring. It was on a pavement on Lightbowne Road against a black lad called Tyson. Not long before this I'd had my nose broken for the first time when arguing with two kids wielding Chinese fighting sticks. What began as a stupid, petty set-to with Tyson, exploded when he made fun out of my nose, and it quickly escalated into a full scale scrap. I'd lost my rag and as I was busy knocking lumps out of him, I felt an arm come on my shoulder and drag me off. It was Brian and he was fuming.

'If you want to fight, Armstrong, then come to the gym tomorrow morning and learn how to do it properly. Not out on a street swinging your arms around like some yobbo annoying nice people.' These words shocked me and struck a chord. Like back in Ireland, without ever knowing, I woke up the next day and found myself walking into Brian's gym. He smiled and passed me a pair of boxing gloves.

'Here you go, son. Now let's do this properly without worrying about getting arrested.' That moment was the beginning of my career and looking back now I realise how much I owed to this man. Not only did he teach me the fine arts of boxing inside the ring, outside Brian made it his business to try and make life just that little easier. I was struggling badly in my studies. I went to Moston Brook High School and having a thick Irish brogue and not being able to read or write meant the other kids were constantly taking the mickey out of me.

'I can't understand you Armstrong, speak fuckin' English!'

The reason I struggled so much over the years was because we never stayed in one place long enough for me to settle down and actually learn anything. Myself and Bones were either sent out robbing or begging to find food or money for bills. School was never mentioned unless a social worker got involved, or a benefit was threatened. In the end I just gave up and lost interest.

One day in the gym, word got back to Brian and he pulled me aside.

'Michael what's going on? Why aren't you going to school?'

'I'm fed up with it,' I replied. 'Why should I? The others are always having a go. I've got no friends there, they just take the mickey and call me thick. I'm best here. I like it and people talk to me.'

Brian simply stared back. 'Leave it with me, young man.'

I just had to promise him that I would return to school the next day and he assured me everything would be okay. I agreed and come the following morning, I went in and noticed all the other kids looking rather nervous on seeing me enter. None of the usual nasty, sarcastic comments.

I looked up and stood at the back of the class with arms folded was Brian and the then current, undefeated European Super Lightweight champion and local legend, Pat Barrett.

'Boys and girls meet Michael John Armstrong,' said Brian. 'A very good friend of mine and Pat's. We stick together at the boxing gym. It's all for one and one for all. Everybody here would do well to remember that.'

Needless to say the piss taking stopped immediately!

There was a plaque above the ring hanging opposite the round timing clock. It said *Pride in Battle* and that summed Brian Hughes up. You were taught within those four walls not only how to inflict damage on your opponent, but more importantly how to defend yourself. That ring craft was equally important, if not more so, than just trying to spark somebody out. Brian had a saying that he'd constantly be quoting if events were getting out of hand in the gym ring.

'Lads, boxing is called the noble art of self-defence. The idea is to out-manoeuvre, out-think and of course out-punch the other fella. But that doesn't mean acting like a wild animal in the ring.'

He'd never stand for that.

There was also a picture on the gym wall depicting the sacred heart of Jesus. Brian used to point at it all the time.

'Oi you lot, he's the gaffer in here, not me!'

Good manners, discipline and behaviour were not so much asked of you, but demanded. A mob of streetwise Manc kids respected this man and not one of us dared or wanted to upset him. You listened and learned. End of.

The football banter was endless. Brian always appeared to be outnumbered, with more blues than reds in the gym, but it never stopped him giving as good as he got. Brian adored the Busby Babes and told us they had a motto. One we should always adopt both in the gym and out.

'All for one and one for all lads. Never forget it.' This was drummed into us constantly. Whenever one of the boys was fighting, we'd always be there at ringside supporting him. And away from Brian's prying eyes, outside the four walls of Collyhurst and Moston, in local pubs and clubs or on the streets, when it got equally tasty, we were always there to back each other up.

Oh you got chances with Brian but he was no soft touch. If

Brian thought you weren't dedicated enough or simply wasting his time by taking the piss, then you were out. Those he felt would simply never make a career, if they were good lads, Brian had no problems letting them stay and train in the gym. To him, character mattered as much as raw skill and toughness. Brian worked hard to make you not just a decent fighter, but also a decent human being.

We weren't allowed to swear and for me that was like being told to stop breathing. Oh we could have a laugh but God help you if Brian thought you were taking the mickey and not putting it in; twenty press ups for the slightest wrong doing. As for me, even though I trained liked a madman and listened to everything Brian said, I must have done twenty million press-ups back in those days. I got away with nothing.

'Michael Armstrong, twenty now! You didn't learn that language in here, son!'

I swear the man had eyes in the back of his head.

The best fighter at a young age I ever seen was a local North Manchester lad called Craig Dermody. He was simply in another class. When I was fifteen, I went in the ring with Craig at the gym and couldn't lay a glove on him. He tormented and teased me. I ended that session in tears such was the frustration. Craig packed in boxing well before his star truly shone because of personal problems, but I honestly believe that if he'd have carried on then Craig would have beaten Naseem Hamed and gone on to conquer the world. He was that good.

When needed, Brian Hughes could make you feel like you were a world champion. Brian had a way of getting inside your head without anybody ever knowing what was going on until he'd achieved the aim. There was always method in his wisdom and madness. I watched him one day in action and was so glad for once it wasn't me in the firing line. Thomas McDonagh would come in the gym every day with a smile and a joke and never rushed to be ready for training.

All the lads were fair game to his cruel wit. No one was safe. Funny, smiling and good as gold, but in time his laid back manner drove Brian to distraction. And so he decided to teach him a lesson!

One day Thomas was down to spar with Matthew Hall; a cracking fighter nicknamed 'El Torito' or 'The 'Little Bull', by Brian. Now Matt was the opposite of Thomas in terms of how they went about preparations. They were chalk and cheese. He'd tend to come in and within thirty seconds was either pounding the bag or in the ring ready for sparring. Whereas Thomas was as chilled as an iced beer on a summer's day!

Brian went to work. He'd been whispering in Matt's ear. 'You're the best, he's lazy. Whereas Matthew, you've what it takes son. You're dedicated and ready to go every morning. You're a champion'...

Meanwhile, unbeknown to Thomas, Brian was creating a monster, he'd happily remain sitting there still chatting, shooting the breeze and taking the piss! Finally ready, Thomas headed to the ring and stood waiting to nail him inside it. His good mate, a spitting, snarling and by now furious Matthew Hall! I'm watching all this knowing Brian's plan had worked to perfection. Thomas' face was a picture on seeing how wound up Matthew was to knock his block off.

He shook his head. 'You've been got, haven't ya?'

Matt simply nodded and growled.

Realising what'd gone on Thomas looked over to a smiling Brian. In he stepped to face an inferno! The next day Thomas arrived and got changed in world record time. Brian did this to us all when needed. It was all part of the training for life, both in the ring and out at our gym, Collyhurst and Moston under Brian Hughes and I loved it!

The vast wealth of boxing talent that came through there was breathtaking under Brian's care. Craig Dermody, Pat Barrett, Robbie Reid, Thomas McDonagh, Michael Jennings, Matthew Hall, Anthony

Farnell, David Barnes, Delroy Waul, Darren Rhodes and so many more. Each could bang but equally also, these lads were technically very good fighters. And that came through Brian Hughes.

Brian remains the finest cut man I ever saw. He learned his trade from the great Eddie Thomas who trained the legendary Ken Buchanan and Howard Winstone. His was a much-needed talent and especially in the type of ring wars I'd continually find myself in. I always kept him busy! As the years rolled on and the madness began we'd fall out, but today I retain a lot of love and respect for him; he was a true gentleman, a second Dad – a man of quality. Talking of which…

I got myself a job working in an abattoir for a man called George Buckley. Another gentleman, although George in regards to Brian, how he earned a living, meant both men existed in different worlds. George plied his trade in that strange Mancunian shadowland somewhere between night and day. One that's soundtrack consisted of police sirens, doors being kicked in and screeching cars. He was rumoured to be a member of the legendary Manchester gang, *The Quality Street Mob*. His good friends Jimmy Swords and Charlie Mason were constant visitors to the abattoir. George had a heart of gold. He bought me my first boots when I turned amateur. Sadly, I have to admit, I repaid this wonderful generosity by robbing his workplace blind. I stole enough meat from there to open up my own butchers. However, I'm certain George knew what I was up to. He had a soft spot for me being a boxer, but also more importantly and I'm sure as George was aware, something else had happened in my life which made me truly desperate for money.

Alison got pregnant.

Suddenly I had to grow up fast. At sixteen years of age and with Alison just fifteen we were going to be parents. At first I panicked and I have to admit I wanted her to have an abortion. I was a gypsy kid. I thought I knew everything but I didn't have a fuckin' clue. I was thinking only about my boxing career. But now, Jesus Christ, when I think back, I thank God she never listened to me being that young, selfish and naïve bastard. Alison was wise and old beyond her years. That little baby turned out to be Mikey. The legend. Who I love and adore like all my other kids; Jade, Louise and Brook.

We moved in together at her aunt Rita's for a while before finally landing a house in Harpurhey at 15 Vernon Road, across the way from Conran Street market. Our old landlord from the colonies sorted me out and whilst it was no palace, it was ours; somewhere to give us room to be alone, breathe and figure stuff out. I'd the job at the abattoir, I was robbing on the side and the boxing was coming on, so we didn't starve. Our first day in there and I looked at Alison and then it hit me like a crack on the head with a hammer. This was our place. I had a home, I was going to be a Dad and I couldn't stop fuckin' crying.

It was never boring living in Harpurhey. Nearby was a small farm and many a time the animals would just wander away. One morning I was in bed sleeping off a hangover when Alison shouted up.

'Mike!'

'What?' I replied, putting my head under the covers.

'There's a pot-bellied pig at the door!'

It'd been a late night and I was wrecked. I staggered downstairs and there it was, staring at me. I don't know who was more shocked; myself or the pig. I've got to be honest, the first thought in my head was how many bacon butties you could make off this big fella? And who could I sell it to? Maybe even shoot the thing myself if needed? I could easily get hold of a gun. Although what mess a sawn-off would've done to Mr Pork Scratchings didn't bear thinking about. Happily though, the pig must've read my mind, because before I could act, it disappeared. I doubt whether it got back to the farm in one piece, this was Harpurhey after all.

By this time I'd turned amateur and was loving it. I buckled down, I listened to Brian and trained like a Trojan. Every morning I'd run for ten miles. Sometimes going through the packed Conran Street market, but it wasn't like Rocky, where people threw him a drink or an apple or orange. I was more likely to get a bottle thrown at my head for grievances past. There were many of them.

'Armstrong ya fuckin' wanker, where's my stereo!'

Out of the gym I was no angel, robbing and fighting. Trouble followed me around like a bad smell, but with Alison pregnant, my head was more focused on the boxing than it'd ever been.

Brian would point to the top of the winding staircase at the gym.

'Up there is the end of your rainbow. A treasure chest of riches but you have to give everything and work hard to earn it.'

Once inside those four walls, I threw myself into the training and I was impressing. I listened to all advice and took it on board. I loved my work and I was good! To the point where Brian was putting me in championships and I wasn't just winning them, I was blowing fighters away. These were good lads, upcoming talents like myself. And when I didn't get the results, many who saw the fights always reckoned I should've had the decisions. Brian said it was political. If I was fighting cockneys, I'd have to knock them out to get a draw. Myself, I think it was because I was a traveller and didn't have the right airs and graces, the correct image. But I was a boxer, not a fuckin' posh schoolboy. I was fighting for my life and my family everyday. Not just in the ring but outside.

Although there were times it overlapped!

Just a week following Manchester United beating Liverpool in the FA Cup final, myself, Anthony Farnell and Thomas McDonagh were fighting on Merseyside. Such was the quality of our gym, Brian was having to find us fights outside the city and further afield. The reason being nobody in Manchester would take us on. And so we'd hit the road; Birmingham, Leeds and, unfortunately whilst they were still sulking from Eric Cantona's late winner only seven days before, Liverpool.

It was a crowd seething and desperate for their fighters to gain some modicum of revenge for the cup final. Sadly for them as the evening wore on myself and Arnie had already put away our opponents with first round stoppages, which hardly helped their mood, so when Thomas also won easily against a local lad called John Garvey, they erupted. Normally more laid back than a carpet, even Thomas had got fed up with the dog's abuse and gave it back to his outraged audience. It was the last straw and they snapped. Some tried getting in the ring to have a go at him and like red rags to a bull, in we went. I hardly helped matters by screaming out to the entire crowd over the ropes, 'Come on then you Scouse bastards! Who wants it?'

Happily tempers were calmed by security guards and both sets of corners. Matters settled down a little and we were ushered out of a side-door fire exit.

Brian put an arm around me. 'Bloody 'ell Michael,' he said, as we were getting in the van to head back down the East Lancs afterwards. 'I wish you'd pick your fights, son.' We drove off with Thomas still in his boxing gloves, such was the rush to get out of Liverpool, before I caused a full scale riot and possibly got us all lynched!

I wouldn't mind, but I'm a blue...

By the time I was seventeen I'd won two national titles but really should have had five or six more. A trainer called Ray Flannagan helped look after me. He was a cracking guy and like Brian, a font of boxing knowledge. It all came to a head when I got hammered on points for the second time in the ABAs (by 22-7) by a decent boxer from London called Martin McDonagh in Hartlepool. He went to the European Championships and I got left behind. I thought, what's the fuckin' point in carrying on? I went off the rails again. Big time.

Word got back to Brian and he tracked me down.

'What are you doing Michael?'

'Why bother?' I replied. 'All this training, discipline and hard work. What's the point if I'm never gonna get a fair crack?'

'These things are sent to try us son.'

I wasn't so sure and told him that if I was going to continue then I wanted to go professional and get paid for it. Otherwise I was going to turn it in. I was hardly going to be a priest or a politician, more likely a bank robber. At first he said I was too young, but Brian understood that if you took boxing out of my life, then I'd be banged up in Strangeways, quicker than it takes to boil an egg.

So he changed his mind and promised to have a word with the boxing promoter Frank Warren, who already had the 1992 Olympic Bronze medallist, Robbie Reid on his books. One of Brian's original prodigies, Robbie was soon to win the WBC Super Middleweight World championship by beating Vincenzo Nardiello. Brian told Warren that if they brought me on slowly, then I'd a real chance. Warren reluctantly agreed. He knew of my excellent amateur record and that I had real talent and could bang a bit. But he also knew I was trouble. Adding it all up, Warren decided I was worth a punt. For the first time since I was seven years old I'd be paid for doing something I loved. Only now the guy I was fighting would be the same size as me and the money was going into my pocket and not Dad's.

Johnny Reed was in my ear again. 'Never take a step back, Mikey.'

It was time to show the world that Michael John Armstrong had what it takes to survive in the ring, just as I'd done out of it. Anyone who was going to beat me would need a huge heart, large balls and an even bigger punch. If there were any out there who fancied their chances, both in and out of the ring, well bring them on! I'd never be hard to find.

4: BOTTLE OF SMOKE

'When I was young, I was fighting so much,
it was like I was born for this.'

WILFREDO GOMEZ

Frank Warren was the man: The Golden Ticket. The gravy train; Sports Network allied to Sky Sports was the aim for every upcoming young and hungry fighter to get on board. Money and fame came guaranteed so long as you delivered in the ring. Superstars were born, some manufactured. Towering above all was a cocky Sheffield kid of Yemeni heritage who ruled supreme over his division. They called him 'The Prince'. Naseem Hamed. His habit of lowering his guard and taunting opponents before knocking them off their feet was box office.

Hamed was Frank Warren's leading asset but he also promoted two fine Manchester fighters in Robbie Reid and Ricky Hatton. But there was another who possessed the potential to take on and in time outshine Naseem. Raw, ferocious and out of control. One who was as wild outside the ring as well as in it. For this kid, a gypsy Irish boy from his adopted backstreets of Moston, there were no ropes. A fight on a pavement was equally thrilling as one with Queensberry rules. Though not one to duck a challenge when it came to taming the bad habits of fighters many warned Warren this one was not worth the hassle. A cell in Strangeways they said had already been long reserved for Michael Armstrong Gomez. It was simply a matter of when.

But against all advice apart from one, Brian Hughes, Warren offered Gomez the opportunity. The chance had arisen to acquire fame, fortune and a way out of poverty. He'd been handed a golden ticket but one that came with responsibilities to behave. On signing the two shook hands and Warren delivered his one and only rule. 'Don't fuck with me Michael.' Gomez smiled and winked....Few held their breath for a happy ending.

★

'OI! WILFREDO! REIN IT IN! It's not a bloody race! Box him, son!' Words I heard many a time during sparring, where Brian would often tell me how much I reminded him of the legendary Puerto Rican Featherweight, Wilfredo Gomez. They called him 'The Bazooka'!

Gomez stood just 5 foot 5 inches and never fought above 130 pounds during his prime yet was one of the most lethal and prolific punchers in boxing history. Of his forty-four wins, forty-two came by knockout. Although technically a brilliant fighter, Gomez also possessed the power, if required, to knock opponents unconscious with either hand. Having won world titles in three weight classes, he was considered one of the all-time greats. A superstar inside the ring and out. Women loved his charisma and good looks, whilst men admired his stunning boxing skill and power. Gomez's fame spanned two decades, but when it ended, his world burned and it all came crashing down. Like me he came from poverty; a street kid who fought and clawed his way from nothing. Being compared to this legend by Brian was truly an honour. He'd give me videos of Gomez to watch. I studied his style. The way he moved and prowled like an alley cat until the chance arose and then bang! Sleep tight señor. He'd turn out the lights on his opponent.

So when Brian told me I'd have to change my surname because there was already a Michael Armstrong registered in the professional ranks, I really didn't need much persuasion. He pulled me into his little office at the gym.

'You're going to have to change your name, Michael.'

'Alright then, I'll call myself Michael McGuigan.'

Brian had something else in mind. 'I've got another idea. How does Gomez sound?'

'Yeah Gomez Armstrong sounds sweet,' I told him

'Not Gomez Armstrong soft lad,' he laughed. 'Michael Gomez.'

And so the paperwork was sorted and I became Michael Armstrong Gomez. You didn't get many of them for a pound in Moston back then.

Brian could play me like a fiddle.

'Did you get up to anything on Saturday night, Michael?'

'Not really Brian. I just had a quiet few beers.'

He stared and I always became nervous.

'Alright then,' I replied, 'a few more than a couple.'

Still Brian said nothing.

I panicked. 'Well, er… I had a skinful!'

He shook his head, clearly disappointed.

'And what time did you get in?'

'Twelve o'clock.'

Those glaring eyes!

'One o'clock?'

The death stare once more and finally my resistance collapsed.

'Okay, I give up! Four o'clock and I was hammered out of my brains!'

'Well, well' said Brian. Sounding like the cat who'd caught the rat. He'd clap his hands, 'I was only going to ask if you'd watched Match of the Day? But seeing as you've owned up? Give me twenty please young Armstrong!'

I'd been got!

One day, with time on our hands, myself, Bones, Thomas McDonagh and his brother-in-law Jamie, decided on a trip to the Lake District.

'I know the way,' slurred Bones, whilst nearly already pissed at twelve o'clock. 'Just leave it to me.'

I was driving and I'll be honest, I wasn't great at it. In fact, I'd often be told back then I was the worst driver on the planet. But it was Bones who we'd be relying on to find the place, and as he slowly kept drinking Mr Jack Daniel's, his directions became distinctly more blurred until ultimately we were truly lost when he fell fast asleep and out for the count. Trying not to panic, I just kept going, only to finally realise it was time to have a rethink when we found ourselves ten miles from Edinburgh!

'How the hell did we get here?' Asked Thomas.

I didn't have a clue. Road signs never worked for me.

On waking Bones wasn't happy. 'Where's the fuckin' lakes?'

You can imagine that went down well. We gave up, turned around and headed home. By this time I was exhausted and could feel myself falling asleep at the wheel. Then, just when we didn't need it, the sound of police sirens and the signal for us to pull over. A still drunk Bones gave them grief and so was forced to give up his details. They asked him what year he was born and being half cut he got confused and told them 1937 instead of 1973.

'That makes you seventy-three Mr Armstrong,' replied one of the policemen. 'The whiskey keeping you young, yes?' Finally, when realising we just wanted to get home and weren't up to anything dodgy, they let us go.

After a while I could feel my eyes closing.

'Mike come on,' shouted Thomas. 'Blimey mate you were nearly asleep.'

I carried on for a while, trying so hard to stay awake. Suddenly I was gone and the next thing at 110 mph the car had careered off the East Lancs, down a bank before tipping over four or five times. I remember being in some kind of crazy rollercoaster. Finally we came to a halt. Bones was next to me and we were trapped. It was Thomas and Jamie who dragged us out. Miraculously nobody was seriously hurt. Jamie and Bones had broken their collar bones, whilst myself and Thomas, though scratched and cut, were relatively unharmed. A group of people raced over to help and couldn't believe it on seeing the four of us still alive.

It was a close shave and wouldn't be the last time I'd dance cheek to cheek with the grim reaper. Two days later I went to inspect the car and there wasn't a window or panel that hadn't been smashed to pieces. Someone was keeping an eye out and finally it was time to get in the ring for real, and stay out of trouble.

11-6-95: Danny Ruegg: Eleven days before my eighteenth birthday, I stepped through the ropes at what was then the G-Mex centre in Manchester for a first professional fight. It was a Frank Warren promotion and he was paying me £1250, at that time and in my situation, it was a small fortune. Top of the bill was a bout for the vacant WBO Cruiserweight title between Carl Thompson and Ralf Rocchigiani with support fights from our own Robbie Reid and another Mancunian class act, Michael Brodie. I was much lower down the pecking order, pitched against a twenty-one year-old kid from Bournemouth called Danny Ruegg. He'd had eight fights with a patchy record, but Brian had warned me Ruegg was a decent opponent and he was right.

In a Super Bantamweight contest I fought to instructions from my corner and came through by winning on points. I enjoyed it. I was on my way and the dressing room afterwards was buzzing. It was a great atmosphere. Brian was a happy man because Robbie had also won his fight with an impressive first round knockout over the tough journeyman Martin Jolley. His seconds, Mike Jackson and Steve Goodwin, were also bubbling. Collyhurst and Moston boys had done them proud and none of us had got hurt. Frank Warren entered and came over to say well done and shake my hand. I noticed Robbie

Reid looking on in shock. When Warren had left the room, I turned to Robbie and asked, 'what's up mate?'

He started laughing. 'I don't believe it Mike! In all my time with him, Warren has never said that to me. He must really rate you highly.'

However, if I was under any delusions that this pro business was easy after just one fight came crashing down in my next two contests. I lost them both.

15-9-95: Gregg Upton: It was in Mansfield, three months on from the Ruegg fight, that I realised this business took no prisoners. Twenty-four year-old Gregg Upton had fought fourteen times before. He'd won seven, lost six and drawn one. Upton was clever and knew his way around the ring and could hit. I got cut in the second round and dropped in the third. Upton was just too strong. He had a man's strength, whilst I'd just turned eighteen. There were no arguments from me when I lost on points in a four round contest. Upton deserved it.

24-11-95: Danny Ruegg: Shortly after at Bowlers Arena in Manchester, just ten weeks after the Upton defeat, I lost again. It was a rematch against Ruegg and fair play to him, he deserved it on the night. At ringside I was disappointed to hear one of my idols, Barry McGuigan, slagging me off, saying it looked like I hadn't trained. The truth was the opposite. I'd burnt myself out. I'd over-trained. Driven like a maniac to make up for the Upton loss, I went crazy in the gym. I was so mad that come the night of the fight my legs were like bottles of smoke. Many times in the build-up Brian had warned me to slow down but I was like a man possessed and paid the price. I just kept trying to throw grenades and knock Danny out, but it wasn't happening. Three fights, one win and two losses. I was hardly setting the boxing world alight.

Salvage: Following the IRA bomb that wrecked the centre of Manchester, myself and Bones got a job working for a building contractor. It was officially classed as salvaging, but we stole more stuff than what was blown up. The word from the supervisors was music to our ears.

'Drag the job out. Don't break sweat lads.'

Talk about an invitation for trouble! And so we got stuck in... Come the end of the shift you were searched before being allowed off site, but as ever there were ways to get past this. We managed to move a load of Rockport boots. Everybody was at it, all you had to do was pass a few quid to a security guard to turn his back and you were away. One day myself and Bones were put in the Royal Exchange building on Cross Street. The place was devastated. We were amongst the first in and it was like letting a drug addict run riot in a chemist. Every drawer, cupboard and cabinet was searched. One time, Bones found five hundred quid in ten pound notes. Also we came across the keys to the Tampax and condom machines, so went around the toilets and fleeced them as well. It was easy money, but couldn't last. People got too greedy. I actually got sacked for drinking on site. For once I wasn't guilty, it was a case of mistaken identity but I think by this time they'd got wind and just wanted me out of the way. Bones followed shortly after.

Clearly, our idea of salvage wasn't what they had in mind.

19-9-96: Martin Evans: At Bowlers in Manchester there was a lot of worry and frustration in the left hook that put away the experienced twenty-nine-year-old Scouser Evans in the first round. The fight was short but sweet and it felt good but I desperately needed more fights to pay the bills.

9-11-96: *David Morris:* A big, strong lad from Wales. It was my jab that won this fight. I boxed, I hit and moved and Morris couldn't get near me. Brian was over the moon in the dressing room. 'You're learning son. Keep it up Wilfredo!'

22-3-97: John Farrell: A second round knockout at Wythenshawe Forum. Another kid who was bigger than me, but it didn't matter in the end. I hit him with a left hook that he never saw coming. Hallelujah, sweet dreams and another cheque off Uncle Frank.

3-5-97: Chris Williams: When I fought the southpaw Williams, the only people left in the Nynex arena were the cleaners, the two corners, the judges and referee. It was a stunning bill with three world title fights. Naseem Hamed and Robbie Reid were defending their crowns, whilst Salford's Steve Foster was challenging Ronald 'Winky' Wright for the WBO World Super Welterweight title. Also our own Anthony Farnell from Collyhurst and Moston was making his professional debut. A huge night for all of us and it seemed to go on forever.

I was in the dressing room growing more and more agitated as the hours went by. The roar of the crowd thundering through the walls. Finally there was a knock on the door and it was my time, only to be shocked when a show official walked in and whispered something to Brian. He nodded, the official left and Brian came over towards me. 'Your fight is off Michael, they've overrun. But the good news is you're still getting paid.'

Well I went nuts! Screaming, yelling. 'Fuck that, I don't care about the money, I'll fight for nothing.' I was in meltdown. Punching the walls, headbutting the lockers. They couldn't calm me down. Finally Brian sought out Frank Warren and he agreed to let me fight. And I got beat on points. A bad decision in my eyes, but if there's a moral to this story, I've no fuckin' idea what it is.

11-9-97: Wayne Jones: Normal service resumed at Kingsway Leisure Centre in Widnes when I ko'd Wayne Jones from Halifax with another left hook in the second round. Also on the bill that night making his professional debut was a young boxer from Hyde, for whom there were great expectations. A kid called Ricky Hatton. He did alright for himself. As for Michael Gomez, events were set to take place that would leave me reeling and a young man dead at my hands.

5: HELL'S DITCH

'There is a light that never goes out.'

MORRISSEY

I WAS DESPERATE AND WORRIED. Money was tight and we were surviving on a pittance. Alison was pregnant again and almost ready to give birth, leaving me with little choice but to go back on the rob. What else could I do? I couldn't sing or dance. Apart from boxing, this was one of the few things I excelled at. I'd shoplift in Manchester and steal car stereos to order. There were other scams... many. I was desperate. I'd also wangled a job working two days a week for a mobile butcher selling meat on Conran Street Market. I was quids in with this because I stole more than I sold. It was also a bad mistake when they gave me the day's takings to count at closing up. Again, these people were good to my family and looking back now I regret it. But times and me were different then.

I also got a call off a guy who'd brought a load of illegal booze across from France, in the back of his works van. He asked me if I was interested in moving some of it? At first the asking price was too high but a couple of mates, Chris and Steve, came in with me and we bought a load off him. It quickly proved a great investment. They loved a drink in Moston and by selling it door to door and out the back of a car boot we made a bundle. Around a fiver on every bottle sold. It was good stuff and so cheap that people couldn't get enough. It made a real change from when I was a kid and doors were just slammed in my face; now I was peddling Napoleon Brandy, Smirnoff vodka and Jack Daniel's.

I was like Father fuckin' Christmas without the beard and a sleigh. All three of us were flush with cash and couldn't wait to blow it.

Later, to celebrate our good fortune, we hit town and went clubbing. The drinking had begun much earlier. Already well-oiled by getting stuck into our own supply, come the evening thoughts turned to other things. So a quick wash and change then taxi into Manchester, where we were dropped off outside a club called Fifth Avenue on Princess Street. I nodded to one of the bouncers, Daz, who I knew from the boxing. He smiled and waved us in.

'Go on lads in you go, but fuckin' behave eh! Especially you Michael. No Rocky impressions'

This place was always busy on a Thursday evening and that night it was no exception. It was packed full of students, but there was good music, cheap drinks, two for one, and with money in our pocket we couldn't fail to pull. A small part of me felt guilty about a pregnant Alison and little Mikey at home, but to be honest also, I was that wrecked on the booze and E's it quickly passed. I had one thing on my mind and it was what Brian claimed weakened your legs in the run up to a fight. The first sight of female flesh and Gomez was on the prowl.

The reality was the three of us were so pissed, we could hardly talk, let alone chat up some out of town skirt that wasn't interested. So we ended up instead just clowning around on the crammed dance floor; annoying the uni girls who couldn't be bothered with three loud-mouthed drunken thugs from North Manchester. After an hour or so I'd gone to get a beer when I heard a scuffle break out behind me. I turned around and Chris and Steve were face to face with a gang of four lads.

Steve had picked a baseball cap off the floor, obviously belonging to one of this crew. A mouthy bastard said something to him and

Steve tried to laugh it off. They weren't having it and I thought, here we go. You could smell it. It was moody, there was an edge in the atmosphere, the look in the eyes. I can't remember who started it, there was pushing and shoving and just before it exploded, the bouncers led by Daz came over to get between the warring parties. Luckily he must have been watching and knowing what damage I'd do if seriously riled, he wisely turfed out them instead of us. That was fair as far we were concerned. All was quickly forgotten. No way were we going to war over a fuckin' baseball cap.

I thanked Daz, Chris got another round in and the night went on. This kind of hassle happened almost every time we hit town. It was nothing unusual and the desperate efforts to cop off continued. No luck! Finally we gave up and decided it wasn't our night and to head back home. Maybe get lucky at the taxi rank in Piccadilly? You never knew your luck, but Manchester was a crazy, dangerous, twilight world after twelve o'clock. All bets were off and with ready cash and a gift of the gab anything was available. Turn one corner you could get a fuck, the other cocaine. Walk straight on and get stabbed...

In this city you'd always find trouble when doing your best to avoid it. You'd find yourself in Hell's Ditch.

On walking through the main doors to leave, we see our four friends from before, waiting. Again one of them mentioned that fuckin' baseball cap. We couldn't believe it. Next second Steve was punched and his legs went beneath him. I knew he was hurt bad because the guy had whacked him with his fist and then elbow on the way down. On seeing this I lost the plot. One came for me and I floored him, another tried it and he got the same. Both backed off. There was one more.

Sam Parr came at me, so I hit him with a left hook and when he went down I could hear the crack of his head. It lasted for seconds and everything went so, so quiet. I swear on my kid's life it was in slow motion to me and I immediately knew he was in a bad place. I'd knocked countless of people out in the street and in the ring… He fell in slow motion which haunts me to this day… He fell.

In the black cab going home to Moston I sat staring out of the window as Steve and Chris were going on about who they'd punched. I said nothing, not a word, because something didn't feel right. I couldn't get the image of that kid's face out of my head as he hit the floor. It was like I saw with my own eyes the lights going out in his. Maybe it was just the booze and the drugs? But the truth was I'd never felt like this before.

I was scared.

Over the Friday and Saturday, I tried to block out what happened from my thoughts. I got wasted badly again with the lads, but come early Sunday morning there was a knock at my door. With a rotten hangover and still half-drunk from the previous night, I opened it and stood there was Daz, the doorman from Fifth Avenue. His face told me something was horribly wrong and I swiftly sobered up. I can still remember his words like it was yesterday.

'Michael, that kid you hit is in a bad way. He's in hospital.'

My stomach turned. I spent the rest of that day in a blur. I contemplated going to the hospital but decided against. Instead I just hoped and prayed the kid would pull through and this would all go away. But it just felt like dark clouds were gathering and something was telling me this wasn't going to end well.

Come the Monday I woke up late and it was nearly dinner when I came down. I made myself a bowl of cereal, switched on the television and collapsed on the sofa eating them. And then it appeared. ITV News was on and they were showing the outside of the Fifth Avenue club. A reporter was saying a young man lay critically ill in hospital and police were searching for three youths. An officer appeared on the screen.

His words cut me.

'We know who you are. Just come forward and help us with our

THE COLLYHURST AND MOSTON GYM: Brian used to say 'up these stairs walk future world champions.' He was right.

Myself and Danny Ruegg after my first professional fight, 10 June 1995. Feels like a lifetime ago now.

THE ORIGINAL GOMEZ: Puerto Rico's finest. The one and only Wilfredo Gomez! When Brian suggested a name change because there was already a Michael Armstrong he couldn't have chosen better than the unbeaten World champion at Super Bantamweight between 1977 and 1982. Here he is battling Salvador Sanchez in the 'Battle of the Little Giants' - Caesar's Palace Las Vegas, 1981.

This was my 1st British title fight and I knocked Gary Thornhill out in the 2nd round, I still count him as one of my really good friends..

4th September 1999: I'd just turned 21, and just been found not guilty of murder and knocked Gary Thornhill out at York Hall, Bethnall Green… things were looking up.

THE GEOFFREY SIMPSON AWARD
PRESENTED BY
THE BOXING WRITERS CLUB
TO THE BEST YOUNG BOXER OF THE YEAR
1999
MICHAEL GOMEZ
BRITISH SUPER FEATHERWEIGHT CHAMPION

7 wins, 4 by knockout, saw me win the Young Boxer of the Year award in 1999. Previous winners included Howard Winstone, Ken Buchanan, John Conteh, Barry McGuigan, Naseem Hamed, Joe Calzaghe and my mate Ricky Hatton.

I'm trying to psych out Lazlo Bognar before our first fight. He knocked me out in the 7th round — I was out of shape and out drinking all the time, what did I expect!

I was out in Manchester on one of my many wild nights when a fight broke out in a nightclub. Unfortunately my pal Michael Jennings got stabbed in the back and I thought I got away lightly being stabbed in the arm but things went horribly wrong when I got to hospital…

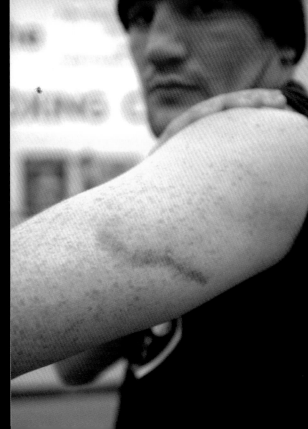

My best friend at the time, Paul Derbyshire, started bringing sombreros to my fights because he thought Wilfredo Gomez was Mexican, when in fact he was Puerto Rican. So with Farnell, Hatton and me always fighting on the same card in the early days, the fans named us The Three Amigos.

've just gone 12 rounds with
ose Manjarrez, it was a hard
ight but I beat him on points

*This was taken before the Oscar Garlindo fight at Everton Park
- I stopped him in the 11th round.*

Going to war with Oscar Galindo - Everton Park, Liverpool, December 1999.

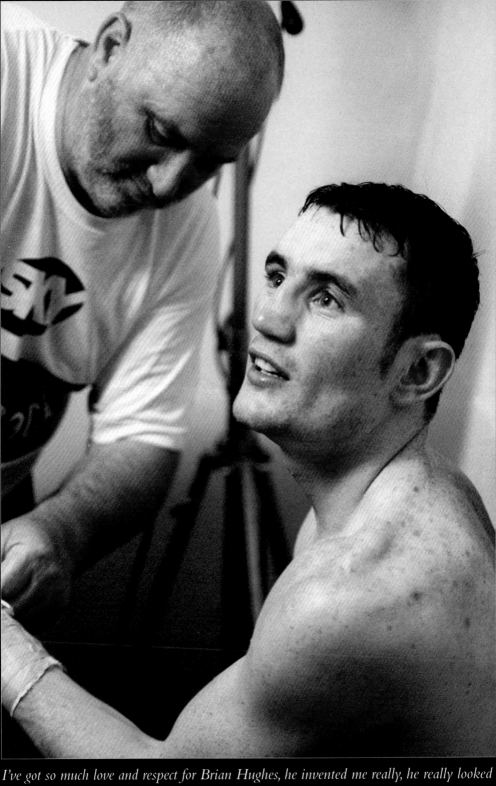

I've got so much love and respect for Brian Hughes, he invented me really, he really looked after me, I owe my career to him. Without Brian this book wouldn't exist so thank you Brian and I wish you all the best.

My fans always came with the sombreros but sadly some of them were known for kicking off after the fights.

The Mexican Manc notches up another win.

Here's me and Brian with the legend 'Smokin' Joe Frazier in Philadelphia. Normally he charged for photos but Joe liked my fighting style so we got this taken for free. But he couldn't understand me, or I him, so it ended up with Brian translating.

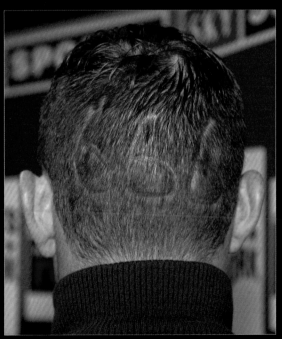

POSSESSED
I had the devil's number '666' shaved into the back of my head before my rematch with Laszlo Bognar. That night started off badly, the Three Amigos were on the same card. Anthony Farnell was up first and got knocked out in the 1st round by Takaloo, then Laszlo dropped me in the first and second rounds. Ricky Hatton was in the dressing room shitting himself because the night was going so badly for everyone. He told me afterwards thast he was delighted when I stopped Laszlo in the 3rd round.

enquiries.'

I phoned Chris's house and was told he'd already turned himself in. Same with Steve. I was panicking; I raced round to Collyhurst and Moston gym and explained all that had gone on to Brian. He kept calm, probably because of the state I was in.

'Take it easy Michael. We are going to sort this.'

Brian rang my solicitor Tom Jones who was based in Hale, Cheshire. Tom couldn't legally represent me because he was also my boxing manager and instead brought in his partner Ian Wish. Together with Ian we went to Collyhurst Police station on Rochdale Road, where I handed myself in. I explained what'd happened and before I knew, I was sat in a cell wearing a white boiler suit, being charged with pre-meditated murder. It turned out because I was a professional fighter, my fists were classed as dangerous weapons.

A search was made of our new house at Robinson Walk in Moston. The policemen who did this treated Alison like dirt and actually refused to believe she was pregnant. Alison was forced to show her hospital appointment cards as proof. They took away the clothes I wore on that night for evidence and left her confused, upset and scared to death. Meanwhile I was left to stew alone in a cell with nothing but my thoughts and quiche to eat. To this day I can't even look at the stuff.

The next morning two CID officers entered and told me in such matter of fact terms, the lad I'd hit, Sam Parr, had died and the charge was now murder. 'You're going down, Gomez' were his parting words on leaving the cell. Nobody would believe me about what really happened. My claims of self-defence were scoffed at. It was obvious, blatant even, that they thought I was simply bad news and had already made their minds up. I was trash, nothing but a tinker who got too big for his boots and was best banged up and off the streets. I was reeling. Murder? The word hit me like a jackhammer. At that moment I thought my life was over. I felt sick and dizzy and like all this was happening to somebody else. I'd been told word had already gone out in Strangeways that Gomez was coming in. I'd friends inside and even though they were good lads, I wasn't really in that much of a rush to see them so quickly again. But I was getting hints to be prepared and people close, my solicitor even, wasn't confident.

'Get your affairs in order Michael.'

It all felt like just a matter of time.

After three lousy, sickening days they gave me bail and I walked out into the Mancunian sunlight from that miserable, wretched cell into even more trouble. Before this all blew up in my face, it had kicked off with some neighbours in Robinson Walk. One of them was selling drugs for a Cheetham Hill gang and being my luck, just so happened to be the same lad I'd recently hit with a weight in a pillow. He'd been mouthing off drunk outside our house one day threatening all sorts. That same night all the windows were bricked whilst we were in bed and first thing next morning, two cars pulled up and Cheetham Hill were on my doorstep, demanding answers.

It was obvious from what they were carrying this wasn't a courtesy call. A gang of lads walked up our driveway and banged on the door. I sent everybody upstairs and answered it. I played for time and mentioned a name to them. One nodded and I was allowed to make the call. I rang Pat Barrett and he was quickly on the scene before it turned messy. For the second time in my life Pat did me a huge favour. Well respected in these parts both in and out of the ring, he managed to talk the Cheetham Hill lads around and they departed.

The word went around that I wasn't to be touched.

'Gomez is okay.'… 'For now.'

But it had been a close call. There are some battles you just can't win. Nobody can fight guns with fists.

When I was on bail, these same neighbours tried everything to provoke and make me lose my rag to end up back in jail. Before they had been wary; I had a reputation, not just because of the boxing, I was a fuckin' prize fighter for God's sake. I'd been scrapping since I was nine years old and after the last bout of trouble they'd left me alone. But not now, they'd linger outside the house. Shouting and taunting. I'd walk past them and they'd be eyeballing me and I'd have to keep my head down. It was a diabolical liberty and I couldn't lift a finger and just had to take it.

There were also family problems - nothing set me off like somebody upsetting one of my sisters. Kerry Anne had been threatened by an ex-boyfriend and it was like screw the consequences. I found who it was and chased him across the estate with a hammer and a bat. Luckily I never caught the man in question or they would've thrown away the key. At this time Alison gave birth to a beautiful little baby girl whom we christened Jade. A tiny angel born into a whole host of trouble. I could only pray that somehow when the case came to court justice would prevail and I'd be around to see her and Mikey grow up. Alison had been a rock as had my family throughout all this. All stood by me. The sisters and Bones were always there if needed.

Someone else who stepped forward to speak on my behalf was Brian Hughes. In the dock Brian spoke with typical honesty and integrity when cross examined by the prosecution.

'Mr Hughes is it not true that in your gym you train young men like Mr Gomez here to hurt people for a living?'

'No it is not sir,' replied Brian. Clearly irked by this comment. 'In Collyhurst and Moston gym we teach discipline and the art of self-defence. If, as you say, these kids come expecting to hurt people they're quickly shown the door. We train boxers not hooligans or gangsters. And with our help, hopefully decent and honest young people walk back out our gym door.'

I was later told by somebody sat behind two police officers working my case, that after hearing Brian's words, one turned to the other with a look of utter despair on his face.

'We're fucked here listening to him. Gomez is going to get off with it.'

Brian was nothing but himself in court that day; a good man speaking from the heart and telling the truth. I knew he was devastated by the loss of a life and was inwardly fuming with me for being involved in this horrific incident but Brian knew I'd not meant to kill that kid. It was indeed self-defence. Though still I remained convinced that even despite his support, I was going down.

They say you never forget your 21st birthday. On Monday 21st June 1998, the jury was out on my case. I waited in a little side room with my solicitor Ian Wish and Alison. It didn't look good. The charge had been changed to manslaughter, but Ian said I was still looking at seven years. Inside I was trying to prepare myself. However one quick glance at Alison's tear-filled face and I lost it.

Then it happened. They were out just half an hour and then against all odds, I was found not guilty. The case was turned on its head by the evidence of two people who came forward late on. A beggar woman, who'd been in a doorway opposite the club on Princess Road, said she saw everything and that I acted only in self-defence. As had a hot-dog man who was working nearby. He also spoke up after witnessing the fight. I still see both around Manchester to this day and always make sure I treat the beggar woman and shake the hand of the hot-dog man.

My immediate thoughts were of relief. I looked across to Alison and my sisters and they were all wrecked; crying and laughing, their emotions were all over the place. It had been so close. We celebrated that night and none harder than me but looking back now I shouldn't have because a kid died.

Sam Parr had died.

Not a day has gone by since when I haven't thought about him. Every time I mention his name, I bless myself and pray for him. Maybe it's unfair and selfish to say, but Sam dying ruined my life. I was never quite the same and it continues to haunt me. His parents have always been good to me and I've taken small comfort from that, but the fact remains the lights went out in Sam's eyes and self-defence or not, it was my doing.

During the trial my grandmother back in Dublin sent a Holy Mary medal and I've worn it ever since as a constant reminder to what happened. It'll always be with me. As for Sam Parr, I'll be lighting candles to him until the day I die.

R.I.P Sam.

6: ONCE UPON A TIME

'So drunk to hell I left the place, sometimes crawling, sometimes walking. A hungry sound came across the breeze, so I gave the walls a talking.'

SHANE MACGOWAN

AS MY MOTHER TRIED running away after Louise's death by taking us to England, so I boarded a plane and took flight to Gran Canaria. I was depressed, drinking heavily and taking drugs. Anything to get over the pain I felt about the court case. I was boiling over. I spoke to Brian and told him that I needed space to just train on my own. I'd been out of the ring for eight months and needed to get both my body and head back in working order.

Brian reluctantly agreed, but he wasn't happy. 'I think you should stay close Michael. Let us keep an eye on you?' I disagreed, my mind made up. The truth being I just wanted to get slaughtered every night. Smashing E's, sniffing coke. What I did during those two weeks in Spain. What I drank and took or who I went with, I can't recall. It was a daze. All was just a hazy blur but at the time it was the only way I could deal with living. People may have thought sun, birds, booze and drugs - that Michael Gomez was living some kind of young man's dream, when the truth was I just wanted to forget everything that'd happened. And this was the only medicine I had. But no matter what I did, the pain wouldn't ease.

I just couldn't get Sam Parr out of my head.

ONCE UPON A TIME

Then one evening past midnight, towards the end of the two weeks, when walking alone, along an empty beach with just a half-drunk bottle of brandy for company, I could hear the music and laughter from the resort's bars drifting and humming in the air. The stars were so bright they lit up the sand. I'd always loved the night sky. My gypsy fuckin' soul I suppose. Those evenings under my Dad's bin bags must have been good for something. It suddenly hit me that there was a place where I'd have no time to feel sorry for myself. Where if you switched off for a second, then it could be goodnight, thanks for coming and they'd turn out your fuckin' lights. Once upon a time I had been a fighter and now I knew I had to get back in the ring.

I returned to the gym and trained like a monster. Soon the weight fell off and I began to feel more like my old self. I loved the gym, the craic with the other lads, the smells and the atmosphere. I was so desperate to fight but Brian wasn't keen.

'Not just yet Michael, keep going. A little more. I need to see a little more.' And so I carried on hammering that bag, I sparred like I was possessed. But it was with a new found control. I was thinking, I was boxing. I was slick, I was sharp and almost there. I watched the videos Brian gave me of Wilfredo Gomez. The man was an incredible fighter. I studied him closely and almost wore that tape out. Then, unexpectedly one day, I was taking off from the gym and nearly out the door when Brian called me back.

'Eh Gomez.'

I turned around and he was stood there grinning. 'We've got a fight for you.'

18-4-98: Benny Jones: It was a huge bill at the *Nynex* but my name was visible once more on the posters. Gomez was back! At the top of the mountain Carl Thompson beat Chris Eubank in a war for the WBO World Cruiserweight title. Herbie Hide knocked out Damon

Reed to defend his WBO World Heavyweight crown. Naseem Hamed stopped Wilfredo Vasquez in the seventh round to party on and I beat Benny Jones on points. Jones was a much taller and more awkward opponent. Technically I was spot on and it was performances like this which pleased Brian the most. In the corner afterwards he was bubbling.

'Welcome back! You're going places Michael. The right faces are impressed.' It felt good, as did my standard rate for a fight of £1250 off Frank Warren. Whilst all the trouble was going on Warren had kept his distance but he had let it be known through Brian, that if I got my head straight, I still had a career with him.

16-5-98: Craig Spacie: I was in London, the big smoke and I loved it. York Hall, Bethnal Green. Frank Warren put me on at second billing to the heavyweight Danny Williams' fight against Juan Antonio Diaz. Brian told me beforehand to be careful because Spacie was a promising talent and could hit. He'd stopped his first two opponents and would be looking to make it three on the row.

I had a look and there was nothing to hurt me. Then in the third round his unbeaten record was over when I nailed him and stopped it. Even though it was only two fights back I felt my star was rising. I began to feel the good times were almost inevitable and that a shot at a title was coming soon. I was confident, cocky and felt like I could take on the world. Then I walked smack bang into the Nowhere Man.

7: THE NOWHERE MAN

'He's a real nowhere man, sitting in his nowhere land.

Making all his nowhere plans for nobody.'

LENNON AND MCCARTNEY

THERE WERE TIMES when I did such crazy and stupid stuff that even I had to laugh. One night we'd all gone out from the gym together to watch the Champions League final. It had been an early start and come the end of the evening everybody was wrecked. None more than me. Loud and singing and clowning around we'd all crowded into the La Mirage Indian restaurant in Moston. The staff took one look and refused to serve us. Unbeknown to me Thomas McDonagh had gone across to the bar for a word with the owner.

'We aren't gonna cause any trouble mate. What say I give you fifty quid up front?' He took the money and we settled down. The night went on, the food was demolished and the beers drunk. Suddenly I got an idea in my head. I kicked the chair away, stood up and facing the boys roared out loud.

'Come on lads, fuck it, let's do a runner!'

Off I raced out of the restaurant door and flew up Kenyon Lane. I looked around and no one was following. I thought, what the? Where are they?

I could make out Thomas still at the door waving towards me. Thinking it was kicking off with the waiters I ran back. Only for him to be grinning wide.

'What are you doing you lunatic. I paid up front!'

I walked back in and not only were the rest of the lads cracking up at me but the staff also. 'Your friend is truly mad,' one said.

None of the lads disagreed.

Even at this early stage in my career I had a decent following and courtesy of a good mate, Derby, the idea of them all wearing the Sombreros at my fight was born. I also took to having one as I entered the arena to the Mexican Speedy Gonzales-hat dancing music. The small fact Wilfredo Gomez was actually from Puerto Rico never bothered Derby. 'Fuck it Mike,' he smiled. 'They all wear these over there. We're on a winner.'

I got a few quid from this but was more grateful for Derby's help in organising the coach trips for the fans. My support came mainly from the ranks of Manchester City supporters based in Moston and Wythenshawe; Derby's City hooligan connections spreading south across town. But also I used to love looking out from the ring and seeing all my family there screaming and singing their heads off.

'There's only one Michael Gomez!'

Derby did some interesting offers to entice people onto his coach trips. For sixty quid you'd get a sombrero, a tray of Stella, a line of coke and an ecstasy tablet. Not something you'd ever be offered on British Rail. Needless to say the coaches were always packed, rocking and fuckin' wild! You'd hear them coming a mile off.

5-9-98: Peter Buckley: 'I've been around a bit, son.' The words of the hardest man I've ever fought in my life. I should have known something was coming around to bite me on the backside. Brian had sent myself, Thomas McDonagh, Anthony Farnell and Robbie Reid out running up in the hills past Oldham. We were gasping for a drink and had forgotten the bag containing our water bottles. Me, thinking on my feet, stole a pint of milk from outside a cottage in the middle of nowhere. I shared, thinking I was doing the lads a favour, but it did nothing more than dehydrate us all even further.

'Thanks for nothing Gomez,' they moaned as we staggered with our tongues hanging out before finally making it back to civilisation and a cold drink.

Sometimes you just can't do right for doing wrong.

I was in the gym on the skipping ropes when Brian came up and said I was fighting Peter Buckley. I knew the name. A twenty-nine year-old journeyman from Birmingham who seemed to be fighting every other week. When Brian told me his record I couldn't believe it. Twenty-five wins, eighty-eight losses and six draws! This is money for old rope, I thought. To me he wasn't so much an opponent, but a punch bag I simply had to roll over.

I got excited.

'I'm going to hurt this kid Brian! I'm going to knock him out!'

But Brian wasn't impressed. 'This isn't a kid Michael, he's a man. Buckley is a very educated fighter. He's been around a long time and he's been in with the best. If you put your chin out, he'll find it and hurt you.'

I nodded as if in agreement when all I was really thinking was yeah right, I'll show you! So it came to the night and we were in the ring at the Ice Rink in Telford. I glanced out across the crowd and it was my biggest turnout yet. Derby had done me proud with over two hundred screaming Mancunians in sombreros, all calling out my name. 'Gomez! Gomez!' I thought I'd made it. Michael 'The Predator' Gomez. I'm the man! I stared across at Buckley, who was just stood there. Not moving. I started ranting again. I'm worked up.

'I'm gonna knock you the fuck out!'

He doesn't say, move or do anything. Buckley's face seemed to be made of stone. Me being a cocky so and so and wrapped up in the atmosphere and the crowd singing out my name took this as fear. He's scared, I thought. Buckley knows he's soon to be in a whole lot of trouble and pain. Boy, how wrong can one traveller's son be?

In the first round I came out looking to fire bombs. I dropped my guard and he hit me with an uppercut that broke my nose! Right there and then I was almost out of the game. As wake up calls go it was deafening and from that moment on I was wary. But every time he got through it was like being hit with a slab of cement. The bell went to end round one and Brian was screaming advice at me.

'I told you, you daft sod. Now listen to me and just jab. You stick and move. Stay away from him.'

I didn't need to be told twice and from that moment on I stuck behind my jab and kept Buckley at a distance. I won the decision on points but it was a learning curve. A painful experience and one that told me don't ever get cocky in the ring and never under-estimate an opponent. Peter Buckley may have been a nowhere man; a career spanning 256 losses in 300 fights suggests as much, but he was a dangerous man. Anyone who understands and loves their boxing knows Buckley is a legend and as tough as they come. At the end I hugged him and told him he was a hard bastard. A real fighter.

'I've been around a bit, son,' Buckley replied, 'good luck to you.' And with a smile and a wink he stepped out of the ring and was gone.

Back in the dressing room I sat there cursing my splattered nose (now broken for a second time) as Brian was taking my gloves off. Frank Warren entered. He came across and nodded at Brian and inspected the damage up close. Almost under my nostrils. 'You should have stuck to your boxing,' was his prognosis.

'Oh do you think so!' I exclaimed with the blood pouring from my nose. Talk about stating the bleeding obvious..

Years later, when I bumped into Peter, he reminded me that when I was seventeen, he and a fighter called Paul Wesley came to Brian's gym and we sparred two rounds together. I'd forgotten all about it. Peter had obviously gone easy on me that day. He laughed when I told him about when we fought at Telford and how that was, up until then, the toughest fight of my life.

'I come from an Irish family also Michael,' he said, 'you were never going to knock me out.'

That was also the night I first met Stephen Lumb. His dad, owner of *Heating Spares Ltd* in Moston, was sponsoring me. A friendship began which is still strong today. Lumby has been by my side through good times and bad. It was never boring. The day after the Buckley fight I walked into a cafe in Moston and he was sat there having something to eat, just minding his own business. I asked him if he fancied going for a quick pint. One thing led to another and the rest is carnage. Lumby always said that was one bacon sandwich he regretted calling in for.

14-11-98: David Jeffrey: At the Grundy Park Leisure Centre in Cheshunt, I topped the bill and made short work of Jeffrey with a left uppercut in the first round that he never saw coming. After the fight I bumped into Barry McGuigan in a corridor. He shook my hand. McGuigan told me how impressed he was with the progress I'd made since the early days. 'You'll be okay Michael. Just keep working hard and listening to Brian. The rewards will come soon.' Suddenly my boyhood hero had me feeling like a million dollars.

19-12-98: Kevin Sheils: At the Everton sports centre in Liverpool, I fought a limited if tough kid from Cardiff that just kept coming. It was a six rounder, I gave him six pound in weight and boxed his head off. I was slick and dancing. Ducking punches and making Sheils miss constantly. The referee stopped the contest in the fourth round because he'd damaged his right arm, but it mattered little because I was so far ahead on points to be out of sight. Across the arena chants began. 'Gomez, he's from Manchester' echoed loud. I felt like something huge was just around the corner. Brian stressed to me constantly that stuff was happening behind the scenes. 'Be patient Michael, your shot will come. They can't ignore you forever.'

13-2-99: David Hinds: At the Telewest Arena in Newcastle, I won a moody contest against Hinds on points. It began as we entered the ring. He gave as good as he got and it continued early on as we butted heads returning to our corners. I also swapped insults with his fans in the crowd. All this apart, I concentrated, boxed clever and got the decision easily enough. It wasn't long after this fight that Frank Warren told me I was to be given my first shot at a major title, something I had dreamed of winning ever since I turned professional.

At this stage dreams were small (like the purses) but the higher up the ladder you moved the bigger and better both got. But at the time all that mattered to me was winning the British Central area Featherweight title, and if anyone got in the way they were going down. A sad note to the night was Robbie Reid losing on points against an unbeaten Joe Calzaghe in a contest for the WBO World super middleweight title. Personally, I thought he'd nicked it. We were a close knit crowd at the Collyhurst and Moston gym and we were all truly gutted for our mate.

8: GOMEZ TIME

'Lie down so I can recognise you.'

WILLIE PEP

WHENEVER ONE OF US had a big fight coming up, Brian was lucky in that he very rarely had to call on outsiders to come and spar at Collyhurst and Moston. Between myself, McDonagh, Jennings, Reid and Barrett, we all had totally different styles and so we were covered in all areas. When outsiders did fight in our gym, sometimes it could go horribly and painfully wrong. It was all about pride.

The red and gold colours of our gym meant everything to those who wore them. I never believed there was bad blood between us and other gyms, it was just a competitive edge and healthy rivalry. Outside we were mates and shared plenty of crazy nights out and would always have each other's backs. But when it came to the ring? That squared off arena where friendships, problems, hopes and dreams were temporarily forgotten and all that mattered was survival? It could be vicious.

27-2-99: Chris Jickells: The shorts were black with Gomez embroidered on them. The corner lads looked smart with their gold/red tops and the *Gomez/Predator* on the back. Brian, as ever, thought it a little over the top. 'Who or what is the bloody Predator?'

The shouts of 'Gomez' were smashing through the walls of the dressing room. I was ready, I was pumped and it was my time. I was going to knock Chris Jickells into another hemisphere. No way was I going to lose that night. It was already written. I stared at the Holy Mary medal sent by my grandmother during the trial that I'd tied to my boot. This was for Sam Parr. Everything I ever won would be for Sam.

He was always on my mind.

There was a smell of cordite in the Oldham arena as I got ready to enter. My supporters were screaming and clowning around, but there was others there also. Equally loud. It was a poisonous atmosphere. Jason Matthews and Paul Jones were fighting in a Commonwealth middleweight bout and their support were giving it large. Sheffield, Hackney and Moston in the same venue with most off their heads; it just didn't feel right, it felt dangerous. The Mexican dance tune started off. The corner lads gathered around and off we went. Anthony Farnell, who had already won earlier in the evening by knocking out Koba Kulu in the first round, met me on the way out. He whispered into my ear.

'Your time mate.'

My fifteenth professional fight and here I was on schedule. Jickells was experienced, he'd been around. Twenty-seven years old and like me, he had a girlfriend and two kids at home. This was his dream as well. Both of us were desperate for the vacant title. It may have meant a lot to him but it was everything and more to Michael Gomez as he soon discovered. In the opening round I had a good look at him and quickly realised he couldn't hurt me. I'd the patience and more importantly the power. Jickells could avoid me but only for so long. Not that he ever took one step back. The bell went to end the first. I eyeballed him and the referee Phil Edwards grabbed hold. 'Come on Mike, no need.'

Brian said I was doing well. 'Be patient and you'll nail him. Pick your shots.' In round two I caught and staggered Jickells straight away with two vicious right hands. I concentrated, I jabbed, I cut off the ring. Then a left hook from close in and he went down. Reeling, I saw him wince and his eyes were dazed. Jickells knew from that moment I had too much. The referee gave a mandatory eight count and he motioned to carry on. So be it.

Come round three my fans had left their seats and were down at ringside. They knew what was coming. Another left and Jickells wobbled. 'Gomez, Gomez,' was getting louder and ringing in my ears. I was catching him at will, he was panicking. I was after Jickells in that ring and there was nowhere to hide. I trapped him to a corner and let fly two left hooks, a right and then he went down again... almost through the ropes. Another eight count. I opened up and unleashed a barrage of shots but kudos to him, he came back.

Round four and my supporters were sounding increasingly confident.

'Gomez, Gomez, knock him out!' Believe me I was trying. Again I cornered Jickells with a ferocious, crashing left and once more over he went. The kid was hurting. Yet another eight count! He stood, nodded and signalled for more. Brave or stupid it mattered little, I wanted this man out of there. A slashing left just before the bell to end the fourth and I'd cut him badly under the eye. The referee again asked the question 'Do you want to fight on?' He nodded and the carnage continued.

Brian was a happy man and knew the end wasn't far off.

'Just stay calm Michael, keep this up and he's yours.'

In round five I stalked him, he was desperate. A flashing right hook and bang! For a fifth time Jickells hit the canvas. Now fuckin' stay down. But oh no, the crazy bastard unbelievably withstood another eight count! Balls of steel but sadly for him it was Gomez time. Enough; one last left uppercut and it was over. I fell to my knees with arms raised in the air. Then I stood back up, blessed myself and bent down to touch the medal. That was for you Sam.

At ringside my supporters were almost in the ring with security guards trying to keep them out. It was madness, sheer mayhem! I spotted Alison in the crowd and she was crying. All my sisters were on their feet with tears falling down their faces. Brian put a towel around me but didn't say anything. There was no need. Just the slight smile on his face spoke for how proud he was. I heard the announcement and somebody put a sombrero on my head.

'The winner and new Featherweight champion of the central area Michael Gomez!' I'd done it…

Sky Sports' Ian Darke interviewed me afterwards. I sat there on the edge of the ring beneath the ropes wearing the Sombrero, feeling higher than the world. The cheers deafening. I remember thinking does life get any better than this? When I look back now on what was set to unfold, it hadn't even started. Sadly, later that evening fighting erupted between rival supporters inside the arena and spilled outside onto the streets. A young boxing fan from Hackney was crushed beneath the wheels of a coach whilst trying to avoid the trouble. Thirty-one-year-old Dean Fisher was a father of two. What a tragedy.

9: AN IRISHMAN ON THE BOARDWALK

'Everything dies baby that's a fact. But maybe everything that dies someday comes back. Put your makeup on, fix your hair up pretty and meet me tonight in Atlantic City.'

BRUCE SPRINGSTEEN

WHEN FOOLING AROUND, my problem was the girls always knew where to find me. They'd often turn up asking for 'Midge' on the gym door steps and Brian would instantly clock them.

'Who's that Michael?'

'Oh it's one of my sisters Brian. She just needed a quick word.'

I had that many of them he always got confused and was too polite to say anything. However one time a black girl turned up. She came up the stairs, spotted me and shouted over.

'Midge?'

Brian noticed once more and came across, scratching his chin. 'And who's this?' He asked smiling.

'It's just another one of my sisters, Brian. I thought you'd met?'

'Ah right, of course. I remember you now, love. I never forget a face.'

Being too much of a gentleman to inquire further he wished her a good day and glared at me like I'd strangled his favourite kitten at birth.

'Be quick son, we've got work to do.'

Soon as she'd gone Brian came storming back across and he was raging and wagging his finger at me. 'I wasn't born yesterday Michael Armstrong. I'll be keeping an eye on you!'

Even when it was shut there was always something going on at the Collyhurst and Moston gym. One night myself and Robbie Reid were hanging out late, just sat chatting in the changing room. Both of us was deep in training for upcoming fights, so the talk was all about making the weight and the qualities of our opponents. Suddenly a loud banging noise was heard coming from the roof. We left the changing room to check it out and over the stairwell could see dust falling from the ceiling. Then, to our shock a leg appeared dangling. It was kicking a way through. This was obviously a burglar trying to break into the Co-Op store downstairs. Robbie tapped me on the shoulder and pointed towards a couple of broom handles stood up against a nearby wall in the gym.

'Keep an eye on him whilst I go and fetch them.'

I nodded but no sooner had he gone, this guy had dropped down and landed in front of me. The look on his face was precious.

'Evening,' I said, before head-butting him. As he staggered Robbie came rushing back over and cracked our new arrival with the broom handle. Lying flat on the floor we advised that to get back up could be bad for his health.

'Big fuckin' mistake lad,' I informed him.

'Welcome to Collyhurst and Moston!'

The burglar never moved a muscle. When the police arrived they asked myself and Robbie how he'd got the bruises on his face? We shrugged our shoulders and answered together. 'He fell!'

'What? On his fuckin' head?' replied the copper.

The Old Bill were no mugs and knew he'd been given a couple of digs but they let it go. Later that same week Brian called us both into his office.

'Right, Batman and Robin. Sit down.'

We did as told. Our story well-rehearsed.

'I've just had Collyhurst police station on the phone.'

We both said nothing.

'So he fell eh?'

We both said nothing.

Brian leaned back in the chair and just stared for a moment. He knew what'd gone on. Brain could read our minds.

'Well it might interest you to know that the villain in question has informed the police that he feels it would have been less painful for him to have landed in a pit of Dobermans.'

Again we both said nothing but I was dying to laugh.

Even Brian, whilst pretending to be annoyed, looked close to a hint of a smile. 'Go on get back to your training.' On walking out his office door, he fired one last parting shot. 'Oi, super heroes!'

We turned around facing him.

'From now on, leave catching criminals to the bloody police!'

29-5-99: Nigel Leake: Three months after the Chris Jickells' fight, I took on twenty-nine-year-old Yorkshireman Nigel Leake in Halifax, for the Inter Continental Featherweight title. Filled with confidence and belief, my left jab was like a machine gun. I danced and weaved and then a minute and twenty seconds into the second round, I let one fly and put him on the canvas. Once more the sombreros flew into the air. Two titles fought for and both won. Next was a date across the ocean.

An Irishman on the Boardwalk. I was off to Atlantic City.

Originally it was planned for Anthony Farnell to fight alone in America but Brian all but begged Frank Warren to take me. He told him the experience I gained over there would be priceless. At first, uncertain on whether I could be trusted, Warren finally agreed and the issue of my original passport came up.

'What passport?' I asked.

Brian shook his head and an open-mouthed Warren looked like

he'd swallowed a whale. Problems arose when I revealed that my Mam and Dad had never registered my birth back in Ireland, officially I was *persona non grata*. They needed some kind of documental evidence to prove I was who I claimed to be. That made me laugh. Who'd want to be Michael Gomez Armstrong? The fact I'd changed my name to fight hardly helped matters. It was the solicitor Tom Jones who came up with the idea of searching out my Baptismal certificate from the church authorities in Dublin. After a few frantic phone calls it finally turned up and was faxed across to England. A temporary passport was arranged and myself and Anthony were sent to represent Collyhurst and Moston gym. We'd had just one word ringing in our ears from Brian, who with Robbie Reid, was coming along to work our corners. 'Behave.'

Undoubtedly this was aimed more at me than Anthony and Robbie.

So here I was. Michael Armstrong Gomez on a plane to box in the United States of America. Myself and Arnie were fighting way down on a Showtime bill which was being staged at the Taj Majal Hotel & Casino in Atlantic City, New Jersey. Topping the same bill was a heavyweight clash between Francis Botha and Shannon Briggs and the legendary Mexican, Marco Antonio Barrera against Pastor Maurin. Six thousand people were packed into the arena with Barrera drawing huge support. It was loud, chaotic and utterly mind-blowing. I loved it and just to see my name on the poster, despite being buried near the bottom, was a real thrill.

Our time in Atlantic City had the worst possible start when myself, Arnie and Robbie went for a walk on arriving and got caught up in a mini riot. Fascinated and, to be honest, quite enjoying the spectacle, we hung around a bit, only to end up getting CS gassed by the police. We returned to the hotel coughing, spluttering and our eyes burning. Brian's face was a picture. He quickly calmed down when we told him what happened and for once it wasn't my fault.

Although I still wasn't sure he believed it.

7-8-99: William Alverzo: Brian warned me that Alverzo was a decent boxer but that I was better. If I stuck to the plan of fighting behind the jab, being patient and waiting for my moment then I'd take him without any real trouble. In the dressing room shortly before it was my turn to go on, something strange started to happen. Arnie had already fought and won by a knockout in the third round. He was buzzing but was shocked into silence by the noise coming through the walls. The shouts of 'Gomez, Gomez' could clearly be heard.

'You Armstrongs get everywhere,' smiled Brian. 'How many relatives have you got over here?'

Something wasn't right. So far as I knew I had two supporters in the crowd. There was a mate, Roger, the owner of the Kestrel pub, my Moston local, plus Arnie's dad. Perhaps these two had somehow started the chant and everyone had just joined in for the fun of it.... Or maybe they'd been bribed? I had no idea what was going on. Then it dawned on me; the name. Gomez. The thousands of Mexicans who'd come to support Barrera must have thought one of their countrymen must be up next. Oh were they in for a shock! Off we went and Brian was by now a little anxious.

'You're the whitest Mexican I've ever seen Michael. We'll have to tell them you don't go out a lot.'

My arrival in the arena with me wearing the sombrero hardly failing to curb their enthusiasm, there was an eruption of cheering! It was like a bear pit as we made our way through the newly discovered Michael Gomez Mexican fan club. They screamed out my name like a war cry. On climbing into the ring the noise level increased further. Then, as Brian removed the robe and sombrero it was like turning the noise off with a switch and one almighty silence descended upon the arena. This pale and scrawny little Irish lad stood before them shadowboxing – he was clearly not born in the backstreets of Mexico

City.

'I feel like I'm in the bloody Alamo,' muttered Brian.

Luckily this misunderstanding was swiftly forgotten because that night for six rounds I fought the best I ever had. I was slick, fast and hard hitting. I moved, I crouched and danced and bobbed. I fought like a Mexican and come the end I received a standing ovation from one of the hardest crowds in world boxing. It turned out they'd accepted me as their own after all and afterwards I was mobbed for autographs. The reaction to my performance by the American boxing journalists and insiders left me gobsmacked.

Mike Tyson's ex-manager Bill Cayton pulled Brian aside and told him he hadn't seen anyone fight like me since the forties.

'Where's this kid from Brian?'

'He's from Moston in Manchester, Bill.'

'Manchester, Massachusetts?'

'No, Manchester, England.'

'You're kidding me,' replied Cayton. 'A god damn Limey? I ain't never seen a Limey fight like that before.'

When Brian mentioned this to me this I wasn't particularly happy. 'I'm not a limey, Brian. I'm an Irish Mexican.' However the six grand I received for fighting Alverzo quickly cheered me up! With work done and away from Brian's prying eyes, it was time to party. Frank Warren's initial doubts about whether I was ready for Atlantic City would soon be turned on its head. Was Atlantic City ready for Michael Gomez?

I hit the shops with Arnie and Robbie and treated myself to a gold chain and a bracelet with the winnings from the Alverzo fight. A few drinks, then more and more. I was in heaven! The lads were urging me to calm down.

'Take it easy Mike, it isn't a race.' But I was off the leash and out of sight and mind. I wanted to party and was ready to drink Atlantic City dry! Whilst we were walking along the boardwalk I playfully slapped the backside of a very large black lady as she walked past. 'Come on girl, it's Gomez time!'

Arnie and Robbie hadn't noticed as they were out in front but she gave me a look of utter horror. I winked back at her and swiftly forgot all about it. Later, as we settled down in a bar with a few beers, two police officers approached our table and were glaring towards me in particular. Behind them stood the lady from before, pointing her finger and not looking amused. They said she was accusing me of sexual harassment. Robbie jumped to my rescue and stood to talk to the two police officers.

'You see this good looking guy here. He's a boxing champ in England. The girls love him, the boys love him. And he has a drop dead gorgeous girlfriend at home. Now, I'm not being funny, but...' with that he stared across at the still angry features of my accuser. Robbie continued on but in a whisper. 'Do you really think he'd risk everything by, with all due respect officers?' With that he motioned with his head towards the woman.

The officers glared in my direction and then hers. Finally one of them spoke. 'Okay then guys, we'll put it down to a misunderstanding.' He then pointed a finger at me. 'But you sir. Be careful. You're not in England now.' With that they left, taking the by now utterly incensed lady with them.

Robbie sat back down. 'Well this is a first Gomez,' he smiled. 'You're innocent. Obviously mistaken identity.'

'Oh no it fuckin' wasn't,' I replied, with a huge grin on my face. I won't tell you Robbie's reply but I'm sure you can guess.

Later we headed back to the hotel where Brian pulled me aside to say Frank Warren had been in touch. Warren had told him to pass word he was over the moon with the reaction to my fight and I was to be given a shot against Gary Thornhill for the Vacant British Super Featherweight Title. My dreams were coming together and there was no better place to celebrate these changing good fortunes than

GOMEZ

Atlantic City. I gathered up the lads and spread my good news. 'Now let's go and get fuckin' wasted!'

Whether through sheer luck or via a recommendation, I can't quite remember now, but we discovered the legendary Caroline Cuties strip club. I really thought I was the man. The dog's bollocks. There was me throwing fifty dollar bills at pole dancers for private shows and drinking double Jack Daniel's and coke until I fell over. A traveller's son living the dream. Like a kid in a sweet shop let loose, I just didn't know when to stop. It was truly a riot and Gomez was the man!

Towards the end of the night I'd shrunk into a drunken, dishevelled wreck. I couldn't talk or walk and then I decorated Caroline Cuties carpet. The semi-permanent fixed smiles of the working girls turned into looks of utter disgust. Luckily, taking pity, my fellow Mostonian Roger stepped in and threw me over his shoulder and carried this Irish-Mexican back to the hotel, along the boardwalk. All the time with me blabbering on and singing loud.

'You're the man Roger,' and 'Gomez, he's from Manchester!'...

The next day we flew home. Groggy-eyed, feeling sick and so ill! I was on the plane for an eleven hour flight back. Oh I was rough. All I can say is that I had to sit on the toilet to fart. My head was banging, I was sweating buckets. The journey was spent between throwing up and being lectured to by Brian.

'You have to cut the drink out Michael. It will catch up with you.'

Oh it had Brian. It had!

We finally landed in Manchester and I still had what was now turning out to be the longest hangover in history. My sisters were there to pick me up and we were giving Arnie and his dad a lift home. Then the car got a flat tyre and I was close to giving up and just sat dying in the back seat. On arriving home Alison was pissed off at the state of me but cheered up a little when I gave her some money to go shopping out of the winnings.

Back on home ground I staggered up the stairs to bed and slept for a day and a half. I'd just, for a short while, lived the American dream, even if by the end I spent it staring down the bottom of an in-flight toilet. But I'd never forget the night I fought in Atlantic City, down on the boardwalk and with thousands of Mexicans roaring out my name. 'Gomez, Gomez!'

...Not bad for a Gypsy kid born in a car crash.

10: DOWN ALL THE DAYS

'Honestly it was like a switch being turned on. From that night against Thornhill, Michael Gomez didn't just come out of his shell he exploded! He was still 'our Mike' but something had changed.'

THOMAS McDONAGH

FROM THE MOMENT I was born it'd been a struggle to survive. Nobody ever gave me anything. I had either to steal or fight for it. Down all the days, when I never gave in. I'd wronged, fell and got back up. I'd done good, bad, loved and hated. Down all the days I'd lived on my wits, lost my sister, a Mam and Dad who were never there when I needed them. But I never moaned; I fought, scratched, punched, robbed and survived. Down all the fuckin' days. And now me, Michael Armstrong Gomez, an Irish traveller, a boy from nowhere, would be fighting for the British Super Featherweight title. Down all the days they said I was dirt, jail bait and good for nothing but I fought on and kept going and my time had finally come. Down all the days.

4-9-99: Gary Thornhill: I was going to war against Gary Thornhill. It started in the press conference and just carried on. My state of mind was such that I had to hate him. In the dressing room beforehand at York Hall, Bethnal Green, I was boiling over. Head-butting lockers, punching walls and screaming like a madman. Brian and Robbie were worried I was too wired and they tried desperately to calm me down but my head was burnt out.

'For Christ sakes Michael!' shouted Brian. 'Come on now, relax.'

But I wasn't listening because Thornhill was on my mind, in my way and going down. I had my own plan. Ten grand was at stake here, so it would be the old way. Head down, arse up and keep on swinging.

Everybody who meant anything to me in this world was in the crowd and as I appeared the place went wild! Thornhill was a Scouser and he too had brought a decent following. The atmosphere was electric and you could cut it with a knife; the sombreros and the songs. The roars of 'Gomez' rang out across a packed arena. The bookies couldn't make their minds up, this was a fifty-fifty fight. Live on Sky and top of the bill. Fuckin' bring it on!

The experienced referee Larry O'Connell, who I liked, called us both together. Thornhill was slightly taller than me and he was snarling. His features set as if ready to bite my head off. I just glared at him and thought growl all you like mate, you're getting beat. O'Connell grabbed our arms.

'Now come on lads. Watch your punches at all times and good luck to both of you.'

We went back to our corners and waited to go to war in this East End cradle of boxing. Thornhill started well, he was sharp, slick and catching me early with some good body shots. But I wasn't worried, I just kept moving, going forward, trying to stay fluid and find an angle. Suddenly I caught him with a good right hand, I opened up and he was rocked. 'Gomez, Gomez knock him out' rang out from the Mancunian masses. I was in the fight.

The bell sounded to end round one and we finished up in each other's faces, touching heads. Immediately the referee jumped in to separate us. Brian was also swiftly over and escorted me back to my stool. O'Connell came across, wagging his finger. 'I'm telling him the same Mike, cut it out. Okay?'

'Keep your head Michael…' implored Brian, 'and go to work.'

Round two and he again came out fast; jabbing with his left, hit and move. The punches were sharp and accurate but I had his measure and just as he must have been thinking all was well with the world, I unleashed a left hook that he never saw coming and I'd planted him on his backside. A dazed Thornhill tried to stand but immediately fell back down to his knees.

The corner were screaming at him to take the mandatory eight count. I looked at his eyes and the signs were there. The referee said fight on and I went for him like a man possessed. A flurry of left and right hooks, all dipped with a fury to knock his fuckin' head off. I was swinging and he was hanging on by a thread. I nailed him into a corner but O'Connell stepped in to separate us.

We boxed on.

Thornhill was leaning against me; his strength sapping away, he was a desperate man. Like a tree blowing in the wind, held on only by the thinnest roots. I shrugged him off then let fly another left and his legs were almost bent over. Again he grabbed me and held on for dear life. I clipped a half decent left that caught him off balance and he fell to the floor. I stepped back as O'Connell gave him another eight count. I thought this one was a mercy call, but I wasn't going anywhere, just waiting around to finish the job.

Then after looking long into Thornhill's eyes, I held my breath and O'Connell stopped the fight. I raced to the opposite corner where my family and friends were and punched the air. What an amazing feeling. As mayhem erupted, the referee Larry O'Connell came over and put his arms around me. 'Just concentrate on your boxing Mike and you'll go far. Don't be like Naseem Hamed and all that showbusiness stuff. You're better than that.'

The next second Brian had grabbed and almost thrown me back onto the corner stool. 'You're a British Champion now, Michael Armstrong Gomez. Be proud, son and act like one both in and out of the ring.' He kissed me on the cheek and then we hugged. 'Now go and take your salute.'

Off I charged back into the centre of the ring. A sombrero came flying in and landed at my feet. I put it on. My supporters were going mad with delight. Security guards tried desperately to keep them under control, but it really was a losing battle. It was party time! It was Gomez time! There was a call for calm in the arena and then I heard those magical words over a microphone. Words I had only ever dreamt of… 'Ladies and gentlemen after one minute and forty two seconds of round two, the referee Larry O'Connell has stopped the contest. Gary Thornhill was in no position to defend himself. The winner and new Super Featherweight Champion of Great Britain. Michael Gomez!'

I stood almost in shock as the Championship belt was placed around my waist. A tap on the shoulder and it was Thornhill. I lifted his hand in the air. The man had come to fight, he was a warrior. 'You okay?' I asked. He smiled and nodded. When the fighting is over, so the bad blood should end and we wished each other all the best. Top man! After posing for a few photographs, I got the nod from Sky that they were ready to interview me at ringside. With Robbie sat alongside and Ian Darke asking the questions I prepared to do something that I'd promised myself a long time ago.

'Michael, what an amazing success story. You seemed to find that finish out of nowhere?'

I composed myself and prayed I'd hold it together. 'First of all, I'd like to dedicate this belt to a young lad who died in my company, in Manchester, two years ago. Sam Parr. This is for you Sam, I'm sorry for what happened and I love you.'

It never really hit me what I'd achieved until we got back to the dressing room. I was in a state of disbelief. The door opened and a herd of journalists came rushing in. Brian told them my entire story and they listened open mouthed. 'Come on Brian,' one said. 'That's not the kid's tale, that a bloody movie!' I watched on and thought just wow! I've made it! Michael Gomez had arrived!

I returned to Manchester on the coach with the fans and celebrated by donning a sombrero, dropping E's and drinking enough booze to sink a battleship. It was the same for weeks. Everybody sang my name, including me! We partied on and on and on…

The following night a bunch of us, the hard core, were still celebrating and we ended up in Middleton at a club called *711*. This wasn't a place for the faint-hearted. I was out of my head and throwing money around like a drunken lottery winner. The cocaine, the champagne in ice buckets, it was a riot. *711* didn't attract the type of clientele who appreciated this kind of behaviour on their patch. It didn't matter who you were - the boys from Middleton and nearby Langley started giving us daggers and hints that we were starting to get on their nerves, their patience was wearing thin. A bit of pushing at the bar ended with one of our lads pouring an ice bucket over a local and then mayhem!

Wild West time; tables and glasses hit the air and off it went! The fighting spilt out onto the pavement and came down to a stand-off between myself and a guy called Terry, a boxer himself at Lightweight level. 'He's pretty decent Mike, watch yourself,' whispered Lumby. Like days of old, both took our tops off and decided to settle it like a pair of prize fighters. Surrounded by a screaming mob of lads urging us on we circled each other, fists raised, before I looked at Terry and suddenly he smiled and I started laughing. The atmosphere immediately changed, we shook hands and the evening carried on as before. Although now I had a new drinking mate!

Bez: It was Thomas McDonagh's and Jamie Moore's professional debuts at the Bowlers Arena in Manchester. They were on the Ricky Hatton/Bernard Paul bill. Along with Lumby, Derby and a strange guy called Bez, who was in and out of mental homes, but a good laugh when relatively normal, I'd managed to obtain, from Frank Warren, four ringside tickets on the premise that whoever I brought along behaved.

'No idiots Michael.'

'No worries Frank,' I told him. 'You can trust me.' Warren's raised eyebrows spoke a thousand words.

We made a day of it and when the time came to head off for Bowlers, the four of us had seen off a skinful. Now myself, Lumby and Derby were hardly angels after a few drinks, but this Bez character was proving quite a handful. No more than in one pub when he pissed in a slot machine, so that whoever won would have to wade through it to get their winnings.

'I don't like fuckin' gambling,' he told us after doing it. The warning signs should have been flashing but seen as he'd been with us all day, we didn't have the heart to dump him. Onwards to Bowlers where I'd got myself and boys passes for the VIP bar. I spent most of the time in there signing autographs. I loved the new found fame but that evening I kept one eye out for Bez. He got me paranoid. Warren's words were ringing in my ears. By this time we were all well gone and looking forward to watching the boxing. On taking our seats one row from the front, Bez was already in spectacular form. He began yelling out. 'Go on, knock his fuckin' head off!' only there wasn't actually anyone in the ring.

Now we were really worried. Finally it was time for the fight and Thomas McDonagh was first up. This was the signal for Bez to turn it up another notch and let rip even more. 'Go on Tommy, fuckin' do him!' Suddenly Frank Warren who was sat in front turned around and glared at me.

'Lads, tone it down it eh!'

I'm thinking another black mark against my name when Bez piped up to make it infinitely worse.

'Fuck off Frank. Terry Marsh should have finished you off!'

Warren's face was priceless and I could see my career withering before my eyes. Thanks Bez.

GOMEZ

On leaving the arena we stopped on the forecourt where I spotted a mate and fellow boxer from Collyhurst and Moston. A black lad called Delroy Waul.

'Alright Del, how's it going mate?'

'All good Mike. You?'

Only for Bez to interrupt and insult Delroy in a manner and with a name that could have only one ending. We left our mate Bez lying flat on the floor after being silenced by Delroy. In all honesty he'd had it coming all day...

It was like living on a runaway fuelled by booze and drugs. I was off my head and hammered nearly every night in Roger's Kestrel pub. I also started getting into Manchester's top nightclubs with ease. The bouncers would smile and wave me through, 'come in Champ!'. The drink and the cocaine just kept piling up.

'What are you drinking Mike?'

'Have a line Gomez.'

As for the girls? I was up to my eyes with them. They no longer saw a loud-mouthed Irish Manc from Moston; a tinker – no, they saw fame and they loved it!

The same posh skirt that in the past would've looked right through me...

'Are you Michael Gomez the boxer? I saw you on the television.' That was all it took. My eyes would light up. I was getting noticed all the time. I was the man. Looking back now, it was nothing to be proud of but the fame just went to my head. I was mad for it, I was out of order, out of control and ultimately hurtling for a fall. As for Alison and the kids at home? No excuses. I'd fallen for the oldest temptation in the book and jumped in head first, thinking fuck the consequences. Or indeed anything that moved.

Even when I was on telly, I was more famous in my head than what I really was. But at the time you simply don't realise.

11: MEXICAN WARS

'I'm not an educated man. I never had an opportunity
to learn anything except how to fight.'

PANCHO VILLA

AROUND THIS TIME I received a phone call off a cousin in
Dublin telling me that my old man was in a bad way and I
should come over. He was living in a derelict flat on St
Michael's estate in Inchicore and it was a pig sty; a slum, there is no
other word. I took Alison and the kids over and remember sitting
there crying at the rotten state of the place. Two of my sisters were
still living with him at the time; Kerry Anne and Charlene. I told
them to pack their stuff because they were coming back with us. As
for Dad, he was totally blind by now. He was a mess, drinking all the
time. He was depressed, a man close to giving up but typically the
man's powers with the opposite sex hadn't waned and he'd wangled
himself a lady friend called Jaylene Alice.

'Son,' he said to me. 'The one good thing about being blind is
that the world is full of beautiful women.'

It takes a lot to finish off an Armstrong. Even one on his knees.
Dad may have been down and out but he wasn't broken.

Sisters are doing it: I'd had trouble with some mouthy kid from Blackley
in a Moston pub. I'd slapped him in an argument when playing cards
and he'd stormed out in a huff. These things happened and I thought
nothing else of it. The next day I was at home and all my sisters were

over. Another family crisis, the normal chaos, arguing and bickering was going on. I'd never get a word in but was happy to simply sit there with a hangover, a cup of tea and watch the television. For me it wasn't chat, just noise and over the years I'd learnt to just switch off. The next minute two cars pulled up outside the house and the kid I'd had words with the night before was in our garden calling me every name in the book.

'Gomez you twat! We want a fuckin' word with you!'

All the sisters are suddenly at the window staring as his mates piled out from the cars and formed up behind him. Eight in all. I thought I may as well get it over with. 'Stay here,' I told the girls as I went to open the door, only to be knocked out of the way as they charged like a mad herd with fists and feet flying into the unsuspecting lads! It was carnage. They never had a chance. I dealt with mouth almighty and the rest of his mates were simply overwhelmed. Some had girls around their necks, other were being pummelled, bit, scratched and punched. To say I was proud watching didn't do it justice. The lads were finally allowed back to their cars and they quickly sped off. Shoes, bricks and rocks, anything the girls could get their hands on, was launched as a last goodbye.

'Leave our Midge alone you bastards,' shouted one.

'And don't come back.'

…That's the Armstrongs. My sisters.

With his contacts at the club, Lumby sorted out an invitation to Manchester City's Maine Road to show off the British championship belt that I'd won against Gary Thornhill. The two of us, along with Bones, went along. They brought me onto the pitch at half time and I got a fantastic reception off the City supporters. However, already our (especially my) thoughts were turning off the football and more towards the evening's entertainment. Come the final whistle in the City boardroom, whilst enjoying a free bar, I was still stuck with the Belt and knew I couldn't risk taking it out on the town with me. That spelt disaster. So instead a stroke of luck shown itself when Emmerdale actor Jeff Hordley, who played Cain Dingle, offered to look after it until the following day. 'Not a problem Michael. It'll be an honour. I'll bring it round to your house tomorrow.'

Jeff had saved the day and so problem solved, we headed off into Manchester and utter oblivion.

The next morning I woke at Lumby's, Bones could've been anywhere and immediately I panicked over the belt. Totally forgetting I'd given it Jeff to look after. Lumby was no help and in a bigger mess than me. Thinking I was in serious trouble, I couldn't even begin to contemplate what Brian Hughes and Frank Warren would say when I told them I'd lost it. Well I could and the words 'you're sacked Gomez,' were sure to be mentioned. Then my phone rang and it was Jeff Hordley to say he was on his way round to drop the belt off.

'Jeff I love you man,' I told him.

'Love you too Mike,' he replied. 'But it was no big deal mate.'

Relief wasn't a strong enough word for what I felt at that moment.

So hard to win, but easy to lose.

6-11-99: Jose Manjarrez: The Kingsway Leisure centre in Widnes had become my second home and it was here I came up against a warrior called Jose Manjarrez, from Baja, California, down Mexico way. It was a bout for the vacant WBO Inter-Continental Super Featherweight title, and if I won, this would become my fourth belt in twelve months. Pre-fight I was up to my usual tricks to rile Manjarrez but was failing miserably. I tried pushing and head-butting him and he simply smiled. I was puzzled thinking what's going on here? Frank Warren went crazy at me. 'Michael what are you doing? You don't wind these Mexicans up. They are difficult enough characters!'

The thirty-year-old Manjarrez had been around. He was an old pro and I knew I'd have my work cut out. So it proved; for in a gruelling twelve round contest that was fought at a ferocious pace, we had a war. In the end I got the decision and proved to all that I could take a punch. At times in the ring against Manjarrez it was like going back to school. I tried everything to get under his skin but he just kept coming. By the final bell I'd huge respect for him and of the four titles I'd fought for that year and won, this was by far the hardest. They breed them tough down on the Rio Grande but then again equally so on the back streets of Moston and Dublin.

Later in the dressing room a smiling Frank Warren appeared and told me he'd just spoken to Manjarrez's trainer. It turned out that as his man entered the arena and saw all my supporters in sombreros, Manjarrez thought they were cheering for him! He couldn't understand where all those Mexicans had come from? I knew what that felt like…

11-12-99: Oscar Galindo: Just forty-three days after my war with Jose Manjarrez, I was back in the ring at Liverpool's Everton sports centre, defending that same title belt against one of his fellow countrymen. Another hard case seemingly cast from rock; a southpaw, twenty-two-year-old Oscar Galindo. Incidentally, the brother-in-law of Jose Manjarrez. He spoke tough at the press conference, telling the press I was going to be given a boxing lesson. When it was translated I just smiled. I was my usual self, nearly starting an international incident with Mexico and wanting to kick off right there and then. I was ready for him. I needed the money to put towards a new house and if you give an Irishman a fuckin' cause you've a dangerous man on your hands. Before in the dressing room there was a nice touch when Gary Thornhill came in to wish me luck and I really appreciated that.

Again I went to war with this Mexican who matched me for every punch, headbutt and sly, low dig. The early rounds were a slog, I'd knuckled down and was fit enough, but simply jaded. Too many ring hours. As the fight wore on towards its bitter end, I finally caught up with Galindo in the eleventh round. I unloaded on him and the referee Mickey Vann stepped in to stop it. I was exhausted and as the crowd roared, I fell to my knees with the thought, thank Christ that's over. Mexicans don't do rollovers.

A strange post-script took place later that evening when I bumped into Vann as we were heading home. He shook my hand and congratulated me on winning 'A great win Mike. I done you a favour there son.'

What favour? His words would stay with me and later returned to haunt me.

12: IN ALL THE WRONG PLACES

'Cause little by little we gave you everything you ever dreamed of.
Little by little the wheels of your life have slowly fallen off.'

NOEL GALLAGHER

29-1-2000: Chris Jickells: On a star studded night at the *MEN* arena with Joe Calzaghe and a revitalised Mike Tyson topping the bill, I went in against Chris Jickells for the second time in my career. We took this as a warm up fight for a forthcoming title defence against a hugely rated Dean Pithie and though you can never doubt his courage, I really could have finished this any time I wanted. Twice in the third I put Jickells down. I was catching him at will and it just didn't feel right. In the fourth round he came out swinging, caught me twice and then I thought, right, time to say goodnight.

I went on the attack and Jickells was down once more. After seeing enough, his corner threw in the towel, but unbelievably he insisted on fighting on. With both trainers screaming at the referee to call it off, I let fly a sweet left hook that brought Jickells down on both knees. The contest was finally over, but it had been brutal. This was a savage business and people like Chris Jickells were simply too brave for their own good. Thankfully he was okay. There are no postcards from the grave and too many fighters insist on going out on their shield. Sometimes we have to be saved from ourselves. But outside the ring, who was ever going to save me?

When I think back now it's clear I was being grossly underpaid and so once the last bell sounded, with no other source of income coming in, I slipped back into my bad old ways. Not that they ever went anywhere. This included selling drugs; cocaine, whizz and weed were always in great demand and I made a good few quid to top up the boxing cash. This line of business saw me back in a world I knew well but one where, if I took a wrong turn or simply got unlucky, could see my career over in an instant and banged up behind bars. There was also the old adage, don't get high on your own supply. Well that never applied to me.

Terminator: I was drunk one night in a local pub and ballooning on. I wasn't hurting anybody, just fooling around. A large guy, no less than twenty stone, took exception to being bumped into at the bar and next minute, bang! He sparked me and I hit the floor.

Customers froze whilst drinking their beers, the lads playing pool stood and stared and the card players dropped their hands. Even the fuckin' jukebox stopped playing. Gomez was out for the count. My big friend, seeing who it was he'd knocked out, took another gulp from his pint and looked extremely pleased with himself.

Suddenly I came around and by some miracle the punch had sobered me up. With senses returning I remembered what had happened and slowly I rose. I was later told it was like Dracula rising from his coffin; stiff backed, like the fuckin' Terminator. The guy who hit me put down his glass whilst mouthing the words. 'What the...' He came across only to swiftly regret it. I tore into him, just slaps really before it was broken up and my big friend called it an early night. A couple of evenings later I accidentally bumped into this guy again at the same bar. This time he turned around and just nodded. His black eye and busted lip a reminder it wasn't good manners to sucker people. Especially British boxing champions.

'Mind how you go there Mike,' he smiled.

Lesson learned.

GOMEZ

Around Manchester I was drinking and fooling around like the end of the world was just an hour away. An endless succession of booze and drug-filled evenings that always ended with another faceless girl. Thank you and goodnight. I was addicted to this new found fame. Whether I was acting up to the crowd or simply living the dream, the word went round that Gomez was spinning out of control. It couldn't go on and crazy rumours of my exploits were reaching Brian.

One day in the gym Pat Barrett had a quiet word. There I was desperately trying to work off yet another hangover by taking apart the punch bag when suddenly the big man grabbed hold of it and looked me straight in the eye. 'Listen to me. You're being seen and clocked in all the wrong places Michael. Sort it out mate, otherwise you're heading for a fuckin' fall.'

Pat was like Brian's godson. They were close and it was obvious to me where this had come from. Brian cared for all his fighters but the world outside the gym was beyond his control. Undoubtedly, if he felt they were trying to help themselves, then Brian would always go that extra mile. Nothing would be too much trouble. But when it came to hopeless causes and those who couldn't be bothered helping themselves like me, well the clock would begin to tick. I took Pat's warning on board as I knew deep down it was time to rein myself in.

Thinking of genius ways to steer clear of the demon drink and stop me blowing up between fights, I bought myself a Yamaha 80 and a Honda CR250. It became a common sight at the time to see me hurtling at death defying speeds across Moston tip, over huge mounds and bumps and dumped prams. Alongside me the railway, near to where Manchester United first began as Newton Heath. If Brian had've seen it, he'd have gone nuts. My excuses that I was trying to stay out of trouble wouldn't have cut much ice, I'm sure. Sadly, when it went dark, I reverted to type. I needed something else a little less dangerous and more time consuming. No whiskey, women or drugs.

So I took up fishing.

I bought myself some decent tackle and took off to find a quiet spot. Armed with a bagful of beers, I'd settle down on a river bank, nod to my fellow fishermen and crack open a tin. I was trying in my own way but peace and quiet wasn't for Gomez. Golf was another hobby I took up, anything to keep me out of the pubs and clubs. A lower profile, be a better boyfriend, Dad and a more professional boxer. Sadly, though, it was short lived. Fishing and golf almost inevitably led back to the pub and sessions on the lash. What I needed and desired more than anything was the incentive of another fight.

My title defence against Dean Pithie couldn't come around quickly enough.

29-2-2000: Dean Pithie: Leading up to the Pithie fight in Widnes, a meeting took place between Manchester City and Pithie's hometown Coventry City football hooligans. With me bringing around three hundred supporters and him not far behind, the potential for crowd violence inside the arena was huge, so a deal was struck between them. For the sake of myself and Pithie, they shook hands and a truce was declared. The only fighting to occur would be done inside the ring. However at the press conference I couldn't help myself. I squared up to Pithie and called him every name under the sun, but annoyingly he didn't bite.

A comment from one of his team hardly helped my piece of mind.

'You've got him rattled Dean, he's fuckin' losing it.'

This was serious stuff now. The fight for me began at the first sit down before. No bell was needed, it was simply the state of mind I had to work myself up into. I was in the zone. Rattled? No. Ready? Yes.

Come the evening and with a huge police presence in the arena expecting carnage, amazingly the opposite occurred. It was handshakes all around, beers were bought and shared and even the odd sombrero was placed on a Coventry head. Peace was declared in the arena. It was time to go to work and defend my British title against a fighter many thought would beat me including Frank Warren who didn't want me to take the fight. Pithie was hot at the time. He'd beaten Naseem Hamed in the amateurs, was durable and a banger. It was only my mad desire to win the Lonsdale Belt outright with three successive defences and Brian backing my argument, that Warren ultimately backed down and did the deal. Helped of course by the number of tickets I could shift. Due to this fact I got away with so much more than other fighters in his stable and believe me I played on this!

Only a mixture of sheer power, guts and determination not to lose got me through those twelve rounds. I was jaded, it wasn't a question of not training, I was simply suffering the effect of too many fights in a short time. Pithie had me over in the first round and I caught Frank Warren's eye as I hauled myself back up. 'I told you so Gomez,' was written all over his face. Personally I thought I'd been pushed, but the referee counted it as a knockdown and we fought on. Pithie was a tough character who had come to fight but so had I and in the fourth I levelled it up by putting him on the canvas with a crashing right.

A real scrap broke out during the eighth round and he broke his left hand and was obviously in a lot of pain. A glance to the corner for help was greeted by trainer Spencer Oliver screaming at Pithie. 'Go one handed, go one handed! You can do this Dean!' He showed real guts by not quitting and carrying on but from that moment, a few right hands apart, Pithie was a broken fighter and I won comfortably on points. Leaving me just two wins away from retaining the Lonsdale Belt - what dreams are made of.

It was a hard night's work and money well-earned but one that had left its mark. I was shattered both physically and mentally. Brian promised me a decent break afterwards. I'd also damaged my left hand and it was time to walk away from the ring for a while.

'Put your feet up Michael and do me a favour?' Brian said, 'Please stay out of trouble!'...

Yeah right, more chance of me becoming a priest.

Viva Tenerife: I was downtown with Lumby. We were both nursing our pints. Not much was happening. It was a Tuesday night and it felt like Manchester was shut. I'd more than a few quid on me. I'd just fought Pithie and thought why not? Brian did say put your feet up? A bit of the sun, the ladies and San Miguel.

'Lumby, how do you fancy Tenerife?'

'I've got no holidays left Mike. Maybe in a couple of months?'

'No I'm talking about going now, this moment.'

'You're mad Gomez! It's a Tuesday night. Nobody does this on a Tuesday fuckin' night?'

He finally agreed and we got a taxi home for the passports and then with no fresh clothes or nothing, it was Manchester airport that very same evening. Gomez had landed in Tenerife.

From getting off the plane, we went on a full session all through the day.

As evening fell the party moved onto a nightclub, drinking with not just fifty Millwall fans, but the football team who were holidaying alongside them. Somebody had explained to me that one of the players, Neil Harris, had recently had an operation to have a testicle removed. Now we'd been getting on famously. Fellow lunatics and all. Until I decided in a moment of drunken madness to jump on a table and start to sing a song that almost saw my world end that very night.

'Harris has only got one ball. The other is in the Albert Hall'...

Suddenly from laughing and joking, a deadly silence erupted.

A hundred Isle of Dogs were glaring across with a mixture of hatred and disbelief towards us. The British Super Featherweight champion and his horrified-looking mate, who was also staring at me as if to say I'd finally gone too far, were about to be taken apart, piece by piece. Luckily Harris himself just smiled and the atmosphere returned to normal. There was a small mumble and we were back in the swing. I apologised, we shook hands, no hard feelings and I bought Neil a drink.

Lumby came across to me and said only three words. He wasn't happy. 'Millwall! Fuckin' Millwall!'

The next morning, with Lumby nowhere to be seen, I woke up in a bus stop. I'd been fleeced whilst sleeping and somebody had robbed all my money and left me wearing nothing but a dodgy pair of Bermuda shorts. Skint, hungover and surrounded by a band of curious locals waiting for a bus to take them to work, I headed off in search of further adventures. Slowly, but ever so surely, it all went downhill and more crazy from there. X-rated beyond words, I don't even know where to start... So best not!

I've had easier fights than some of the sparring sessions endured with Michael Jennings. A class act both in and out of the ring. I first met Michael at the ABA championships in Crystal Palace back when we were both fifteen and I immediately liked the guy. We shared a room together and the friendship made then is just as strong today. I think Michael's first impressions of this cocky, street-wise, gypsy kid from Moston's backstreets were that I was a little crazy. He told me about a girlfriend who was four or five years older than him at the time. Rightly, he was rather proud of that. On asking if I was seeing anybody, Michael appeared gobsmacked when I told him my bird was pregnant and that I was nearly already a dad! His face was a picture. Welcome to Gomez world! Nobody was happier than me when he joined the Collyhurst and Moston gym.

Michael turned professional in 1999. He was a welterweight and a wonderfully skilled fighter, a life dedicated to boxing. His body was a temple whilst mine was a pub most of the time. Like me, he'd lost family at a young age. Two brothers, Raymond and Stephen, were tragically taken far too soon. Michael always claimed I brought out the devil in him. Not being a huge drinker, his leap into my social life was quite an eye opener. And no more than one typically madcap night down on Wigan Pier.

I splashed out on a Suzuki convertible Vitara jeep, complete with a music system and a speaker boom box. Oh, I thought I was the man back then. King of the ring and wearing the bling!

When I think back now, I cringe.

With a mate called Danny and Michael Jennings alongside me we set off for a night out in Wigan. By the time the evening came around to get into the club on the pier, we were pretty much hammered and the bouncers refused us entry. Michael wasn't having it and demanded to know why? A doorman responded by sneakily smacking him straight in the mouth and knocking his tooth out. Stunned and suddenly sobered up, he knew that being a professional fighter and hitting back could well see land him in more trouble. Instead we took it on ourselves to fight his corner. After pulling Michael away I came across a blue bin stacked high with bottles. As our mate stood nursing his bloodied mouth, myself and Danny let fly and under attack from this barrage the bouncers were forced to shut themselves inside the club. When anyone attempted to show their faces, they got it again. The sound of police sirens was a signal to retreat, content with the thought that the cowardly punch had now been sufficiently avenged as we sped off in the jeep. We were brothers-in-arms both in and out of the ring. Being the least pissed, Danny was driving but that was hardly a recommendation and he quickly careered off the road into a wall! Thankfully neither anybody else or one of us was harmed and by some miracle we finally made it back to Manchester.

After dropping Michael and Danny off I drove the last half mile home myself. Screeching to a halt, I staggered up the path and went inside expecting a furious Alison to be waiting. Then it dawned, she was in Scarborough on holiday with the kids. They were staying at a Caravan park called Flamingoland. Steaming drunk, I suddenly got the urge to go and see them, so once more I jumped back into the jeep and with a huge chunk hanging off from where we'd hit the wall, I drove off. How in God's name I made it without killing myself or anybody else is, even today, a mystery but somehow I was able to drive all the way to Scarborough and track down the caravan site. However, finding where they were staying was beyond even my drunken ingenuity and I finally collapsed in the jeep with both feet sticking out of the window. The next morning Alison was taking the kids to a playground when she noticed a familiar vehicle and even more recognisable feet. She raced across and looked on in horror.

'Mike, what the…?'

After grabbing a few hours sleep in the far more comfortable surroundings of the caravan, I awoke to find myself deep in trouble, so rather than stay and argue an unwinnable corner whilst fighting a stinking hangover, I typically disappeared out to find the nearest drinking hole, a plate thrown by Alison missing my head by inches as I went. The hair of the dog swiftly saw the old Gomez magic return and soon I was checking the holiday talent and handing out autograph cards in order to impress. It worked and I was back! Luckily, before I brought about Armageddon, Brian came up with an offer heaven sent to keep out of trouble and get me back in the ring.

And God knows I, my liver and Alison needed it.

13: CRAZY BOY

'Boxing is just showbusiness with blood.'

FRANK BRUNO

RIAN ALWAYS SAID "if you only ever get a house from boxing, then you'd won a championship belt in itself." With me making a few quid, it was no longer out of mine and Alison's reach to find a decent place to live. *'Little Beirut'* they christened the part of Moston where we'd grown up, well it wasn't going to be the home for our kids. I had good fights coming up to add money to the coffers and so we picked out a new home at 18 Mariman Drive in Crumpsall.

Myself and Alison had been too busy living, loving and fighting to ever feel sorry for ourselves. Despite all the shit life threw at us, we just kept going. Nothing was asked for or given. Alison and the kids deserved better and it was down to me to make our fantasy real. I owed this girl and it was payback time. I remember all those years ago back in Ireland robbing the farmer's goat with Bones and seeing that family playing with a football in their farmyard. Well I had my own loved ones now; Alison, Mikey and Jade. In order to give them a proper place to grow up and everything I never had, then there was business to be done in the ring. That being the only place where I seemed to stay out of trouble. I had to become the man my family needed me to be. It was time to grow up.

24-6-2000: Carl Allen: Against Dean Pithie, I'd damaged my left hand

and an opportunity to test it out in the heat of battle and make some decent cash in doing so arrived unexpectedly. Frank Warren offered me six grand to fight on his Mike Tyson v Lou Savarese undercard at Glasgow's Hampden Park. It was cash I simply couldn't turn down and a huge lump towards mine and Alison's house; a television and a sofa was bought, we were closing in. It was all coming together. However with this fight being only two weeks before I went up against the highly rated twenty-four-year-old Carl Greaves, who was coming off a three-year winning streak, it caused uproar. The Greaves camp claimed I was risking their man's payday. Arguing there was the possibility I might get injured. They should have been so lucky.

My left hand got the best possible medicine in the third of a six rounder when I dropped the journeyman Allen with a storming punch to prove I was fighting fit and ready to hand Carl Greaves a good hiding. Apparently he really fancied himself to beat me. Greaves loved a tear up and was similar to me in style. When not fighting, he was a pine furniture maker and a decent one at that. Well I had my own tools and come the 29 January they'd be put to work on Greaves, for I had a home to finish paying off. It lived in the back of my head. Each fight I had saw me build this house brick by brick and room by room. To finish it off, Greaves had to go.

I received a boost going into the fight when I was awarded the best young British boxer of the year. It was a great honour but all that mattered to me was Greaves. I'd entered into that zone where if anybody even mentioned his name I'd go spare. I snapped at his trainer on the eve of the fight when he approached me.

'Win or lose, let's all go for a meal and a drink after the fight, eh? What do you say Michael?' Well I started screaming and ranting like a lunatic.

'What do you mean you want to go for a fuckin' meal?! Do you think you're going to take my fuckin' title and then have a party? I'm going to knock you the fuck out!'

Then pointing at a shocked Greaves I raged on. 'And you, you're getting fuckin' sparked!' For me this was where I won that fight because I looked at his face and he must have thought I was a madman.

'We didn't mean it that way,' implored his trainer, in a vain attempt to calm me down. But I just went off again. 'What? You think I'm a fuckin' fool? I'm going to wipe the fuckin' floor with you!'... And on and on.

Finally Brian dragged me away and out of the room. 'What's wrong with you?' He asked.

'I just want to win, Brian,' I told him, 'I just want to win.'

A short time before, I'd given Brian a tour of our new house and when I thought of where I'd come from and what this man had done for me. Well, I just couldn't help the tears. He cried too. Back at the hotel with an arm around my shoulders Brian smiled.

'You're a crazy boy Michael Armstrong Gomez. Come on, I'll buy you a cup of tea.'

The Sky cameras were on hand to catch me in the dressing room smashing a fist into a locker with a look of sheer grim determination on my face. (I got fined £500 for that) I glared into the lens knowing that on the other side of it, all those who had written me off as nothing but a loud-mouthed tinker boy who'd got lucky with his fists, would be watching.

8-7-2000: Carl Greaves: For the entrance, I had the Manchester City mascot *Moonchester* leading me into the ring. 'Good luck Mike,' it said, 'knock his fuckin' head off.' That was a little weird. The Mexican music began and from the part of the arena where my supporters were there was an eruption of noise and the sombreros went up! No way on this earth from the moment I saw those scenes was I ever going to lose. The furniture maker was set to be dismantled.

In round one I just had a good look whilst still catching him with shots that reddened his face. Greaves was game and had come to fight but I saw nothing to worry me. Come the second my confidence was oozing and I even found time to wave at Alison in the crowd and wink towards the smiling Sky commentator Glenn McCrory, who'd always been kind to me on television. But I remained fully focused on the job at hand and as he moved in, I caught Greaves with a peach of a left hook on his temple to knock him flat out. It was similar to the one that floored Gary Thornhill. Like Thornhill, he wasn't getting up and with feet flailing, Greaves was all but dragged back to his corner.

I didn't celebrate immediately because I knew it was a bad knockout and had no intention of dancing on anybody's grave. It was a great relief on being told he was okay. Carl Greaves is a gentleman and I'm glad that today he understands my behaviour beforehand was never personal. I went across the ring and we embraced. 'You're strong as fuck mate,' he said. That was a lovely touch and just before the announcement Greaves donned a sombrero. I put my arm around his shoulders and we stood in front of my supporters who gave him a fantastic ovation. Carl had earned it. So all ended well and I was just one fight away from winning the Lonsdale Belt outright. I was on a roll, the house was ours, life was good and it was set to get even better.

14: STREETS OF PHILADELPHIA

*'Champions aren't made in the ring, they are merely recognised there.
What you cheat on in the early light of morning will show up in the
ring under the bright lights.'*

SMOKIN' JOE FRAZIER

WITH THE LONSDALE BELT in my sights, Brian arranged with Frank Warren for me to have another one-off fight in the States against twenty-six-year-old Awel Abdulai; originally from Ghana, but by then fighting out of Reno, Nevada. Brian argued the toss with Warren that after hammering Carl Greaves, I deserved the opportunity and the further exposure to American television. Plus for me, much more importantly, the six grand in cash that I'd earn over there. But after my 'adventures' in Atlantic City, Brian laid down the law.

'No partying, Michael. This trip is purely business and not pleasure.'

He vowed to watch me like a hawk. We flew to New York for five days, whereupon a Limousine supplied by the American promoters took us the second part of our journey to Harrisburg, Pennsylvania. I adored New York. As we stepped out at the airport the noise just hits you and it felt like being on a movie set; the countless yellow cabs, the crowds on the pavement, the atmosphere. New York City, as one of my idols sang, was most definitely my kind of town. Gomez in the big Apple and I was ready to swallow it up whole. All the scandal and vice would have been right up my street, but Brian was adamant…'I'm watching you Michael.' Gutted!

19-10-2000: Awel Abdulai: The fight itself against Abdulai was a straightforward points affair. We fought at a venue called The Zembo Shrine and he couldn't get near me. I outclassed him from start to finish, to the point that I was enjoying myself so much I started messing about and singing. I gave Brian a rousing out of tune version of 'Who let the dogs out' at the end of round three. A song that he hated and I used to play constantly on the ghetto blaster at the gym to wind him up. It drove Brian nuts.

'Michael behave! That's not music it's noise!'

The crowd watched on in disbelief. I was cocky, but could stand it up in the ring and they loved me! American television showed the fight and I was interviewed afterwards. The line of questioning was that that they were truly honoured to have a fighter of my class over there. A British champion. Well on hearing this my head swelled even more and I had just one thought on my mind. But oh no, Brian had me under lock and key. Again Roger had come across to watch the fight and that same night he was sat with me in my hotel bedroom. I was bored, fed up and gasping for a beer. Roger decided to go and sample the local nightlife alone and promised to tell all about it on returning. You can imagine my parting words as he left the room. The last being off.

The City of Brotherly Love: Philadelphia was a special time because here I got to meet the great Smokin' Joe Frazier at his legendary gym on the corner of North Broad Street and West Glenwood Avenue. Normally Frazier charged for photographs and autographs, but smiled to say I was an exception. He'd watched the Abdulai fight on television and said that our styles were similar. There is no higher praise. I struggled to understand Frazier and him me, so it was left for Brian to translate. His gym had the reputation for training some of the hardest bad asses in the States; spit and dirt, mean-eyed, hungry fighters who'd rip you apart if the mood arose. Well I learnt my trade in a gym on Lightbowne Road in Moston that was equal to anything I saw there.

To help us on our travels, Frank Warren had employed a local Philadelphia guy who I'd christened Apollo Creed because he was his double. Apollo acted as both minder and tour guide and was great fun to have around. We got on like a house on fire, despite him thinking I was a 'goddamn crazy Brit.' Though I still preferred Mexican Irish which confused him even more. Apollo took me to the 72 steps; a local landmark that leads up to the entrance of Philadelphia's Museum of Art. It is more famously known as the Rocky steps that Sylvester Stallone raced up in the movie. Off I flew, the theme music in my head. On reaching the top I started to shadow box. Looking out over the city there was a wonderful view of the streets of Philadelphia.

Living the dream, Gomez. Living the dream!

15: WAR

'I was able to convince my body that I could take it and nobody could hurt me. I might've gotten cut, stitches over my eyes. Broken nose. Broken hands. But I never really got hurt.'

JAKE LA MOTTA

THERE WAS A DERBY, City v United, coming up and a sports reporter from the *Manchester Evening News*, Stuart Brennan, came around the gym to do a short interview about my love of City and football. I had to confess that, although I followed them and went to matches, it was more for the craic in the pub afterwards. This was due to the fact that nearly all my mates were blues that came to the fights. In all honesty I wouldn't know one player from the next. I made the mistake of asking Thomas McDonagh, who like me was a City supporter, but hardly fanatical.

'Well you're Irish aren't you,' said Thomas. 'Just tell them Niall Quinn is your favourite player.'

Brilliant, I thought. I could easily blag the rest.

Anyway Brennan turned up and he's asking me all kinds of questions and I'm coming across like the biggest blue who ever left the shores of Ireland. I could tell the man was impressed

'Finally Mike,' he said. 'The big game on Saturday. Who'll win and what's the score going to be?

Revelling in my new role as super supporter, I stroked my chin before answering knowingly. 'City will win 2-0 and Niall Quinn will get them both.'

Brennan stared at me in disbelief and shut his notebook.

'Niall Quinn?' he repeated, appearing a little disappointed.

I nodded, being really pleased with myself.

'Absolutely, our best player.'

With that he stood up, shook my hand and left. Thomas having failed to tell me that Quinn left City six years before. I really should've stuck to the boxing.

Whether it was cockiness, over-confidence or just sheer bloody arrogance, before the next fight I went out and bought a six hundred pound cabinet to display my soon to be owned Lonsdale Belt for eternity. The last man standing in the way was Edinburgh born, thirty-one-year-old Ian McLeod. Edinburgh was a city with which I would later go to war. McLeod was a tough character with a decent record; a former IBO super featherweight champion. Two months previously, this no nonsense Scot had stood there and taken my yelling and raving and attempted head-butts at the press conference with a slight smile on his face.

Derby had driven myself and Brian down to the fight venue of Widnes in an old banger from Manchester. Following the lively press conference, the three of us went outside and got back in the car, only for the engine not to start. It ended up with Brian issuing instructions at the wheel, whilst myself and Derby attempted to bump it. Suddenly a gleaming, obviously brand new Mercedes drove up alongside. The window rolled down and it was none other than Ian McLeod. 'Alright lads,' he said grinning like the Cheshire cat. 'Having problems?'

After me spending the last ninety minutes telling the world I was going to tear his head off, McLeod was obviously loving this sweet moment of revenge. I so wanted to say something, but knew he'd wipe the floor with me. Instead I just went bright red like a traffic light. Brian smiled sheepishly and waved at him and McLeod sped off. I just went mad at Derby and started ranting.

'I can't believe you showed me up and broke down!' Derby

wasn't bothered though because him and Brian were too busy laughing at my embarrassment.

On the day of the contest Brian told me to stay in the hotel until mid-evening, as I wasn't scheduled to be on until nine o'clock. However, when he arrived in the dressing room with Steve Goodwin and Mike Jackson they found me waiting for them. 'What the bloody hell are you doing here?' asked Brian.

I told him I was so wired, I was close to smashing up the hotel room. Just to be in the building made the fight seem nearer.

'It's the Lonsdale Belt, Brian. Please let me stay?' On cue an official walked in carrying a long black case. I looked and, as if reading my mind, he opened it and there was the Belt. 'Get that thing out of here now!' snapped Brian. 'He's got to win it.' The red-faced officials swiftly apologised but before him shutting the case, I managed to touch and plant a quick kiss on it. As he left I shouted after the official, 'you keep that baby safe, mate. It's going on my wall!'

11-12-2000: Ian McLeod: It was a night when three of the lads at Collyhurst and Moston came out to fight with me. The brilliant Michael Jennings, Darren Rhodes and Thomas McDonagh all won their bouts in style. One was left. I entered to an unbelievable reception with more supporters than ever from Manchester. The sombreros flew into the air! I loved these people.

They were dancing and singing like lunatics. It was hysterical. A sense of Mancunian madness had descended upon the arena. But if you shut your eyes it could've been Mexico City! I daren't lose! I daren't!

McLeod, in tartan, was already in the ring. A face of granite, his eyes met mine from the moment I climbed through the ropes. Something was telling me it was going to be a long night. So it proved. A ferocious twelve round contest that I finally won but had to go through hell before I get there.

WAR

I blazed away with everything I had at McLeod but this was a warrior and one tough bastard. After a confident start, I swiftly found myself in a war. He was docked a point in the second for holding and I cut him in the third. By the fourth I was well on top and McLeod's corner were clearly worried about the bleeding over his eye. I was faster and hitting harder but he just kept coming forward. This man wanted a tear up and I was never going to duck a brawl. That was a big mistake because in the fifth McLeod gained a second wind and caught me close in. For the first time in my career I was cut; a bad one over the left eye. This was new territory and I was entering the fuckin' twilight zone.

Round six and he came out firing. I was in big trouble and struggling to keep him off. So many were screaming advice from my corner but I heard Brian most of all. 'Weave. Move your head from side to side Michael. Side to side!' Anthony Farnell also. 'Concentrate Mike, use your head.' Pat Barrett. 'Box him Mike!' Michael Jennings was almost in the ring. 'Come on Gomez, fight your fight!' But instead I stood toe to toe, it turned into a slug fest; like a Rocky movie without the fuckin' music. Rounds seven, eight, nine, ten and eleven were just brutal. I hurt like hell but I was certain he felt worse. Referee Richie Davies' shirt dripped in blood. Our blood. I out-punched McLeod but he wouldn't go away. By the final round Brian told me just to stay away from him; box and jab, I had it on points by a mile. We touched gloves, huge respect in both our eyes and then went hell for leather again.

At the last bell Davies raised my hand and the arena erupted. That night was savage. I had never suffered so much to win a fight. Sombreros flew into the ring and I noticed McLeod putting one on. We embraced. I always thought the Mexicans were a special breed, but that man put them in the shade. Finally, they handed over the Lonsdale Belt. It felt beautiful and once fastened around me had a new home for life. Today it sits under my bed. Priceless. One for the kids, a reminder that once upon a time their dad was a fighter. It was a hell of a night

Afterwards in the dressing room, as the doctor was treating my cut, I started to think 'who next?' Time was starting to run fast. I was twenty-three years old and had promised myself that I'd retire at twenty-six. To do this, I needed bigger fights and purses. Naseem Hamed was by far the biggest star we were all aiming to knock out but there were other world champions out there that were more beatable in my eyes; notably Brazilian Acelino Freitas and Hull's Paul Ingle. I was confident of my chances against both, although Brian wasn't so sure. I'd heard on the boxing grapevine that Frank Warren was eager to push me onwards but Brian simply wasn't having it.

'I decide who Michael fights, not you,' Brian allegedly told him. He was utterly determined to keep me on a short leash until he was one hundred percent certain I was ready for that world title shot.

'Not just yet son. Just a couple of more fights and then we go after the big boys.' I had to trust him because this man had done me proud so far.

I got another scare afterwards when I started pissing blood in the shower. I mentioned this to Brian on the quiet and got advised to have a cold shower, a rub down, stay warm and drink lots of water. If this didn't work, he'd take me to hospital the following morning. Happily it went away but served as a reminder that this was a vicious sport and I couldn't afford to be in too many more wars. Ultimately boxing is cruel and takes no prisoners. If you're not careful it will just spit you out.

I thought for a moment of Johnny Reed and though I loved Johnny dearly, I'd no intention of ending up like him.

16: IN THE HANDS OF ANGELS

'To see a man beaten not by a better opponent
but by himself is a tragedy.'

CUS D'AMATO

SUDDENLY, COCAINE WAS EASIER to get hold of in Moston than chips and gravy, and any thoughts I had of travelling the right road disappeared with every line and double Jack fuckin' Daniel's I sank. If you wanted to stay pissed in Manchester on my side of town, well, come for a ride with me. From the back street brothels of Ancoats to the big shot nightclubs on Deansgate, I was your man. Paradise, a snort, a drink and a fuck were always under a fiver away on the taxi meter.

'Hey Gomez, how are you doin' mate?'

A knowing wink by smiling doormen who ushered me through.

While most people were waking up and going to work, I was falling headfirst into oblivion without a parachute. But I don't want pity, I was enjoying myself. Good or bad, life had to be lived. How could anyone ever tell me what's right or fuckin' wrong? I'd a Mam and Dad who were never around and when they did their advice was hardly parental, so what chance Brian Hughes, a priest or a policeman? I wasn't a poet or a politician, I was a fighter. A gypsy lad earning a living with his fists. I never stop. I just drank, got high and fucked. Onwards and fuckin' upwards, I had no morals or scruples, my head was so far gone nothing else mattered.

They called it living the dream.

Any thoughts of Alison and the kids were mere postcards from holidays in a past existence. Every night was a dip into Mancunian Valhalla. It was the fame that drew the crowds; a free pint, a girl's phone number and then more. So much more. I was someone who'd never been anybody. But now I was Michael fuckin' Gomez, I was no longer the kid running from a farmer with stolen eggs in his pockets and praying they wouldn't break so I never get a belt off the old man. God forbid the yoke broke because then the fuckin' joke was on me.

'Anyone seen Gomez lately?' Asked Brian in the gym. The silence was deafening. He knew. Everybody did. And then it was time to fight again. Put another line on the table.

Hey, that's entertainment.

I rose from a drunken slumber back to reality and the day job. It was announced that I'd defend my WBO Intercontinental super featherweight title in Widnes against a well-travelled, thirty-two-year-old Hungarian southpaw called Lazslo Bognar. A tough character with thirty fights, twenty-five wins, three losses and two draws, Bognar was a step up in class. He'd been around and if I wasn't careful I'd end up in serious trouble. Five weeks before, I turned up at the gym in a right mess; shattered through lack of sleep, horribly overweight and bloodshot eyes.

Brian didn't say a thing. He didn't need to. Nobody did. And even though I knuckled down and trained like a madman, the excess body fat proved hard to shift. I lived in the gym; I ran, sparred and skipped. There were endless saunas and swimming sessions. I sweated buckets that went over the brim. I strained every sinew and muscle but the nine stone four pound weight limit felt like over the hills and very far away.

Even up to a week before the fight I was drinking and taking drugs. I just had no self-awareness and couldn't help myself. It was just a disaster waiting to explode in my face. I was falling to earth and would land with one almighty, horrible, fuckin' bang.

IN THE HANDS OF ANGELS

It was coming.

I was scared to death of the consequences of defeat. As the bout drew nearer I started to panic. I became obsessed with the colour of my piss. I was eating tiny mouthfuls of baby food then making myself sick. I was training to make the scales and not the fight. It was a ticking bomb; it was so dangerous because I was worried that when I got in the ring there'd be nothing left. I'd spent the night before the weigh-in dressed in a sweat suit in the sauna. Come the morning I felt drained. I knew I was still well over, around nine stone, seven pounds. Brian knew this and the old pro thinking on his feet came up with a solution. As I got on the scales he quickly pushed me off. 'That's it he's under,' said Brian. We got away with this because of a mix up behind the scenes. Instead of an official Inspector it was supervised instead by a British Boxing Board of Control referee. Unsure of the proper procedure, he took his eye off the ball for one moment and that was all it took. No one, not officials or anybody in the Bognar camp, noticed what had gone on.

I'd made the weight and didn't know whether to laugh or cry.

I was in no condition to do twelve rounds but there was twenty grand on offer. I'd already promised Alison a new kitchen. God knows she deserved it for putting up with my antics. I was convinced Alison knew what I was up to, just not the extent of it. Also, if by some miracle I came through this, I was number one contender for a shot at Acelino Freitas' WBO world title.

I was in turmoil.

Part of me thought if I just went hell for leather to get Bognar out of there early, then everything would be okay. I knew I'd the power and so that was my only plan. If it didn't work then I was in the hands of angels. What other option did I have? I was desperate, my head was spinning and I decided to come clean.

'Brian I can't do this, I'm fucked mate.'

He wasn't having it. 'What do you mean you can't fight? That's a defeatist attitude.'

'But Brian, I'm'…

'Michael, listen to me. If you pull out of the show now you won't get paid and you'll never get another fight. Now you can do this. You need to do it, so come on!'

And that I swear to God is how it went.

As for the fight…

10-2-2001: Lazslo Bognar: The night before I got into a scuffle in the hotel foyer with another boxer, Tony Mulholland from Liverpool and his brother. Words were had but it was quickly broken up. Neither of us could risk getting injured. Not that I could feel any worse.

The legendary announcer Jimmy Lennon Junior was the evening's Master of Ceremonies he delivered his famous catchphrase. 'It's Showtime!'

It felt like anything but for me as I stood in the ring glaring at Bognar who seemed a real cool character. Two of our lads had already fought and won. Michael Jennings and Thomas McDonagh and both were now at ringside cheering me on, as were Robin Reid and Anthony Farnell. I caught Michael's eye and I think he knew I was in trouble. My supporters were, as ever, there in force wearing sombreros, out of their heads. Cheering and utterly convinced I just had to turn up to win. 'Gomez, Gomez' thundered out across the arena and I was so afraid of letting them down. All my family and friends. Live on Sky and on Showtime American television with delayed coverage. What the fuck was I doing in there?

Boos greeted Bognar's name, but he didn't seem to care. The referee Dave Priest brought us together. Here we go, top of the bill, live around the world and I was a shell of my normal self. We touched gloves and prepared to fight. I crossed myself and reached down to touch the medallion on my ankle. The bell sounded and I went for Bognar from the off. Nothing felt right, my timing and movement were all over the place and though I was on the front foot, I was hardly catching him with anything of note. I had to take Bognar out early, there was no other choice. Otherwise I'd simply grind to a halt and become a punch bag. Round one ended.

Brian was trying to calm me, 'Take your time and don't panic. You've got all night.'

Oh no I hadn't because I was an Irishman in a rush.

In round two I went after him again but I was getting hit myself on the counter. I was wide open and he was catching me at will. I'd charge and get picked off. Bognar was confident and a left hook hurt me badly. The bell rang and back on the stool Brian was right into me.

'Will you stop pushing, what's the matter with you? You're taking too many shots and you're out of control, now pack it in! You're going to get stopped here, so come on now. Listen! Box, pick your shots and slow down.'

I was already ragged. Bognar sensed it and was gunning for me. A good left hook staggered him, but only for a second. Oh, he was sharp. A sweet combination rocked me. I wasn't so much fighting as a Mexican Irishman, but more a Moston madman at last orders. Like a drunk staggering towards a bar I kept going forward, trying like hell to find just that one punch to end it.

'This fella is blowing already,' said Brian, but it never felt like that to me.

Round four began and I heard a muted 'Gomez, Gomez' rise almost reluctantly from the crowd. More a cry of desperation than a roar of victory. I also noticed a lot of concerned faces through the ropes, Frank Warren's most of all. He looked paler than me. Bognar was smart, he'd come in close peppering shots then withdraw. I just went after him on a swing and a prayer. Desperate to get close but I simply couldn't throw enough punches. My crowd were all murmurs now. There would be no fiesta that night, it felt more like a wake. I heard familiar voices calling out: Derby, Murph, Lumby. 'Come on Mike,' 'Sort it Mike.' 'You can do it Mike.'

Suddenly I nailed Bognar with a right hand body shot and I could tell it hurt him. I'd finally broken his rhythm and this man wasn't quite so cocky now. He was saved by the bell though and the opportunity had passed. Again Brian was going mad. He was confused and had no idea just how spent I was. 'Michael just relax, son. You're brawling, not boxing.'

I was breathing heavily and I could tell from his face he was already worried. Though I tried to tell him pre-fight that I wasn't ready, I truly believe he didn't realise the state I was in. If he had Brian wouldn't even have allowed me in the arena, never mind the ring.

It was over now, I had to forget it. I caught him again with a left uppercut, but he shook it off and hit back with a volley of shots that almost put me down. I went in low and swinging wildly. The clock on my legs was ticking. I got inside, hooks and upper cuts. A right hand drove Bognar back. A left hand body shot and finally I dropped him! There was fifteen seconds left. A final chance, please God stop the clock, but it wasn't to be. Bognar was also cut after we clashed heads. Sadly that was it. The bell sounded. 'He's yours now Michael,' said Brian. 'Relax, pick your shots and go after him.'

Go after him with what?

In round six, Bognar came out firing. He was off-loading fast jabs that rocked me rigid every time. I took one last gasp and went chasing him with body shots but the power was almost gone. The lights nearly out. Bognar caught me with a left uppercut, then another. He was snapping my head back and I couldn't do anything about it. Just one punch. Please God give me that one. No style, class or technique by now, this was street fighting.

I was flat, jaded and exhausted, just fighting from memory. Each one of his many punches that landed put me in a different place; a club, a bar, a pub, a brothel - echoes and scattered memories of my crazy nights out, flashing images, the drink and drugs, the countless girls. What the fuck was I thinking?

Bognar appeared a little weary himself. He'd probably just grown tired of hitting me. Still I hung in there. Through sheer exhaustion I was making every mistake in the book and all I had was an instinct to keep going. A last left hook from him almost felled me, but I survived and as the bell rang, I staggered back to the corner…

'I'm going to stop it,' he said.

'No Brian don't.'

'Michael you're acting like a beaten man, now get your head up.'

'Brian, I'm fucked.'

'I know you're tired, but we either have to stop the fight or you carry on.'

I knew it was my choice. Whether it was pride, stupidity or just sheer stubbornness, I wouldn't let him stop it. I'd get one more round.

'Get control of it now. One really good shot to the body and you've got him. Now come on Mike, you look beaten. Remember he's as tired as you.'

I said a silent prayer for a miracle.

By round nine, it was like come on hit me. I stood there waiting with nothing left to give. Hoping beyond all senses he'd drop his guard and from some mystical place, I'd find the strength to end it. But this was a foolish dream. The curtains finally came down when Bognar caught me with a fierce combination and I felt like I was floating. Over I went. The referee grabbed me and stopped the fight.

I clung on to him for dear life before being placed on a stool with the doctor and Brian right on top of me. It was dreamlike. I heard the silence and felt the shock in the arena. Bognar's trainer picked up a sombrero that had been thrown in and placed it upon his fighter's head. He stood in the middle with arms raised shouting 'champion!' Then ran to the three corners of the ring to salute the crowd. Good luck to him, but he never beat Michael Gomez. It was just a ghost he smacked around that night for nine rounds.

It was my first defeat in four years. Brian said they were going to take me back to the dressing room on a stretcher but I wouldn't have that. 'No way Brian! No fuckin' way!' He nodded. I may have been beaten, but I wouldn't give Bognar the satisfaction of seeing that. I was going to walk out of the fuckin' ring, no matter how unsteady and nobody was going to stop me. Myself and Bognar had unfinished business and I'd catch up with him again soon.

Brian caught sight of Frank Warren who was stood close by outside the ropes, checking on me. 'Honestly it's stupid this,' he shouted over to him.

'You'll get somebody killed, I'm telling ya.'

Warren looked perplexed. To this day I've no idea what Brian was so irate about. But at that moment tempers were raised and passions high. Everybody was upset but none more than me. I was devastated and had nobody to blame but myself. Anthony Farnell leaned in and grabbed my arm to see how I was… Totally wasted and embarrassed. Shamefaced at letting everyone down. It felt like the end of everything. Okay maybe I could've stood my ground and not taken the fight but nobody forced all that booze and drugs down me.

In this game if you don't live the life, then you pay the price.

And my God I paid a heavy price that night.

The fallout from this loss was felt not just by me. Brian came under fierce criticism for not stopping the fight after round eight. Sky commentators and online forums went for him with a ridiculous vengeance. It was cruel and unfair.

It all stemmed back to Paul Ingle being seriously injured two months before the Bognar clash in December 2000. Ingle was defending his IBF World Featherweight title in Sheffield against South African Mbulo Botile. Rumours had been rife he'd been struggling to make the weight after a series of postponements. In an absolute war with Botile, Ingle was down in the eleventh and then again in the twelfth. After being dropped for the second time he remained on the canvas for several minutes, before being removed from the ring on a stretcher. An unconscious Ingle was taken to the hospital, where he underwent surgery to remove a blood clot from the brain and was forced to spend several weeks in intensive care. This cast a dark cloud over boxing once more over whether it should be banned.

Brian Hughes just so happened to get caught in the firing line.

Nobody cared more about their fighters than this man. Come the Monday morning, Brian walked into the gym, called us all together and obviously upset, said that he was ready to pack it all in and let us go elsewhere. Well, nobody was having that and we quickly changed his mind. This was the Collyhurst and Moston gym mindset; all for one and one for all. Brian Hughes was going nowhere. If you took away Brian from that place it'd miss not only his vast boxing knowledge that was second to none but you'd also lose the heart and soul of the place. The gold dust would simply vanish.

As for Michael Gomez?

What shortly lay in wait would rock me more than any punch in the ring could ever achieve. My boxing career may have stalled, however for my next trick on the streets of this fair city, I was set to make a comeback to not just rival any of Muhammad Ali's, but leave him in my wake

I was going to rise from the dead.

17: FORTY-EIGHT SECONDS

'Then the door was open and the wind appeared.
The candles blew and then disappeared.'

BLUE OYSTER CULT
Don't Fear the Reaper

S O MUCH FOR LEARNING A LESSON. In typical Gomez style I decided to get over the Lazslo Bognar fight by smashing the booze and cocaine in a manner that would have put Tony Montana to shame. For a time I wanted nothing to do with the gym and just went off the rails in spectacular style. Losing to Bognar cut me deep. Many got a crack who dared to try taking the piss. It was a closed subject unless somebody fancied a smack in the mouth. Looking back now, I wasn't a decent person to be around at that time. I could be a bully and look for a slight when none was meant.

I ignored the phone calls from Brian and soon they stopped all together. Did I feel I was letting him down after all he'd done for me? Of course but I knew no different. My head was all over the place. I cared for people, I just had a rotten way of showing it. I pushed them to the edge and sometimes over. Undoubtedly stories were reaching Brian of what was happening. The lads in the gym were clued up. They couldn't fail to be and although he quizzed them regarding my whereabouts and actions, none were forthcoming. It was my business and my choice. As hopeless cases go, for Brian Hughes, I was up there with the best.

I staggered from one brawl and piss-up to another. I always felt something was brewing. A nasty surprise lurking just around the corner, the truth was I never had to go looking for trouble, it magically found me easily enough. Allied to the fact my family were never ones to just enjoy a quiet life, there was always a crisis or feud simmering. As soon as one flame was extinguished, another flared up. It was like trying to put out a fuckin' bonfire with a water pistol. One of my sisters always appeared to have some kind of traumatic love affair occurring in their lives. Bricks, bottles and glasses were constantly flying. The Armstrongs were an emotional lot. I had to admit I was over protective but that was just my nature. If one word was said or fist raised against any of them, I'd be on the warpath. I couldn't help it. My blood, a clan that stuck together and even though at times we nearly killed each other, God help an outsider who upset one of us.

There was a murder in Moston. A lad was stabbed and one of my sisters got arrested because her boyfriend at the time was involved. I'd never liked him. A small time, no good waster who sold a little weed and thought he was a big-time gangster. Furious at her being pulled in, I found out his address and slapped him around a little, only to be arrested for it. But what brother wouldn't have done the same? In my mind I did it for the right reasons. I was looking after my family. It was boiling over. On a separate occasion another sister got pregnant by someone I considered beneath her. An argument blew up between them and she got really upset and phoned me. That was all it took. I asked around for his whereabouts, found out, but only to then crash my car chasing him with bad intentions and a hammer in the boot.

At one time or another I was involved in gang warfare, up for an affray charge, on bail and banned from Manchester city centre. It was never boring.

In a quieter moment I rang Michael Jennings and asked if he fancied a night out? Michael was a little dubious after our last lively escapade down on Wigan Pier but I quickly talked him round. 'This is Manchester Michael, not Wigan. People love me around here. I'm a living local legend!'

Despite the banning order, we set off into town. At first all was sweet, but as the night wore on and I got more of a taste. Things changed. At the time behind Alison's back, I was seeing two other girls, Dion and Mandy. I'd text them throughout the evening as they were both out and about in different clubs. I was keeping my options option. Michael thought I was mad.

'You've got a beautiful girl at home in Alison, Mike, and you play around like this. I don't understand. You'll regret it one day.'

He was right but at the time I didn't give a flying fuck. Wrong I know, but that was me back then. We finished in Piccadilly 21 club where Dion was in with her mates. However beforehand I'd nipped away to meet Mandy who was out partying on Oxford Road; Gomez was spreading the love.

Then everything started to go pear-shaped. It began in 21 when I noticed two lads who I knew belonged to a Cheetham Hill crew chatting to Dion, being over-friendly and coming onto her. I immediately saw red, went across and was straight in their faces.

'I don't give a fuck who you are. She's with me.' My reputation was such they backed off and I thought that was the end of it. Everything seemed sorted.

Later myself and Michael left the club to find something to eat. We were walking down Oldham Road just chatting. Michael was trying to talk some common sense into me.

'Come back to the gym, Mike. Don't throw it all away.' Suddenly we heard an engine noise, turned around and two mopeds appeared behind us. What happened next was all over in a blinding flash with no time to think, act or realise what was going on. Two lads jumped off them, one stabbed Michael in the back and I got slashed by the other on the arm. As we lay on the floor they got back on the mopeds and rode into the night. It was done, quick as that.

We'd been had.

Michael was bleeding badly. I immediately rang an ambulance and within ten minutes it arrived. Already we were surrounded by a crowd of curious, pissed-up onlookers. I felt fine, it was just a scratch. How little did I know! Swiftly the word went across town that Gomez had been stabbed. I was sat on the back of the ambulance when Dion turned up. Then out of the corner of my eye, I noticed Mandy walking towards us. She saw Dion, guessed the rest and immediately tore into her.

'Who the fuck are you?' She screamed.

'Never mind that,' replied Dion. 'Who the fuck are you?'

I tried backing away only to get a mouthful off the pair of them.

'Gomez, get back 'ere ya fuckin' bastard!'

'You're a piece of work, Michael!'

So much for spreading the love!

Myself and Michael were taken in the ambulance to Manchester Royal Infirmary on Oxford Road. The immediate concern was for him due to the amount of blood lost. But luckily he was okay and just needed a handful of stitches.

Whilst waiting for news on Michael, a nurse entered the waiting room and asked me if I'd had my arm seen too? At first I told her it wasn't worth it for such a small wound, but she insisted on taking a closer look and then almost screamed. A genuine look of panic cut across her face. I'll never forget it. Before I could complain I'd been thrown into a wheelchair and it was explained to me in a very matter of fact manner that if they didn't act fast, due to the arterial damage, I'd lose my arm.

The next morning I wasn't allowed food or drink because of the upcoming operation. I lay there in shock unable to take in what was going on. Hungover and dehydrated, I felt terrible. I was transferred to Withington hospital and a place on a ward was found whilst being prepared for surgery. Everything was happening so quick, I didn't have time to think. I still refused to believe that this was serious.

There was a guy in the bed opposite called Adam, the victim of a motorbike accident. He was a boxing fan who immediately recognised me. Another lad who had been hit by a forklift truck was also welcoming. Michael and Robbie Reid came to visit as did my Dad, Bones and sisters. Alison was on holiday but one of my mates drove down to Scarborough to bring her and the kids home. A fuming Bones and others wanted to know who did it, but I told them I'd handle it. In time nothing happened. I heard names and rumours but ultimately it all just melted away.

The police arrived. Two CID officers grilled me, but I said nothing. I was already in trouble because I'd broken my banning order from being in Manchester. 'Just wise up Gomez and get back in the fuckin' ring,' one of them said. 'Carry on like this and you'll be dead before you're thirty.' The man was psychic as well as Old Bill. Everybody wanted to give me advice. But at that moment other things were on my mind that were much more pressing.

When alone with the other patients I was ballooning on about how I'd a bad feeling something terrible was going to happen. That I was absolutely dreading going under the knife. 'Fuckin' seconds out lads.'

'Give over,' replied Adam. 'Mike, you're a boxing champion. Yours is a simple, standard procedure. It'll be over and you'll be back in your bed before you know it.' I wasn't having it. When the time came to be wheeled away, I was all but convinced the end was nigh. Even on the operating table as they placed the mask over my face and I was told to count down from ten, I was still panicking. So much I ripped it off and the surgeon had to calm me down.

'Michael, look, I have done this many times before. The odds of it going wrong are a million to one. Please, just try and relax. Take deep breaths, put the mask back and start counting down from ten. I promise, you'll be fine.'

And so rather than being counted out from one to ten, I did it the other way around. Only then as panic swept the operating theatre, I, in typically dramatic Gomez fashion caused utter carnage and flat-lined. An extremely rare allergic reaction to the anaesthetic caused me to die for forty-eight seconds.

I'd stopped breathing, my body shut down and I was dead.

End of.

People still ask me if I remembered anything about those moments I was gone and I joke that I saw Elvis naked. The truth was more prosaic, there was nothing. I woke up in intensive care surrounded by machines and wires and a beautiful blonde nurse staring at me like I was a ghost.

'Welcome back Michael,' she smiled

'Why? Where have I been?' If I didn't feel like death warmed up, I'd have had a real go at getting her telephone number. The shock to my body from this incident had caused it to blow up massively. When I stared in the mirror it was like somebody had been at me with a pump. If being a Mr Blobby double wasn't bad enough, the burn marks on my chest from the electrodes they'd been hammering to bring me back felt like somebody had been stubbing out cigarettes on it. All in all I was a mess.

A bit like the ward.

Whilst recuperating it was like staying on a building site. They had me on severely strong drugs and at times I thought surely I must be hallucinating? But I wasn't. The hospital was in the midst of a major re-fit and our ward was being taken apart piece by piece. It was nothing strange to wake up in the morning and see workmen walking past carrying a door. Or a window that had been ripped out. 'Morning Gomez,' they'd smile up on recognising me. 'Get well soon you mad fucker!'

Many a time pigeons would just fly in and land on my bed. I'd have staring contests with them. It was surreal and in a way reminded me of living back in Ireland. If myself and Bones had been on this job, the potential would have been endless.

At last, the surgeon came to see me on the ward. Mr 'One in a Fuckin' Million'.

He explained exactly what'd gone on. How I'd died then been brought back from the dead. 'We've also put twenty-six stitches on the outside of your arm. Seven on the inside of your muscle, seven on the outside and a plastic plate in your arm. You're a very lucky young man, Mr Gomez.'

Unable to believe what I was being told, that last line brought me straight back down to earth.

'Lucky? Are you kidding me? I came in to have some fuckin' stitches and you kill me! And you call that fuckin' lucky?'

Val was there. She'd never left my side all the way through. When I complained to her that I was bored and fed up she just laughed.

'It's alright for you, Midge. At least you got to leave for forty-eight seconds. I've been stuck here without a break!'

I was in hospital for ten days and the usual carnage that followed me around continued unabated even in a hospital ward. During my early days, whilst being given morphine and away with the fairies, I blurted out to Alison every dirty little secret I was hiding from her. She went spare. Alison always tried hard to live with my misdemeanours, but the playing away with other women was beyond the pale.

'I'll put up with a lot Mike, apart from the messing around' she warned me in the past.

And yet here I was confessing to a line of conquests that could have stretched twice around Piccadilly Gardens. Convinced she'd throw me out, a broken hearted, numb and shocked Alison gave me one last chance instead.

But there were new rules. I couldn't go to the corner shop or be half an hour late from the gym without her throwing me daggers and accusing eyes. Here I was, back from the dead, where they didn't even want to let me through the door on the other side. But some things just refused to change. Facing facts, miracle or no fuckin'miracle, I was more on my arse than ever.

18: BURNING BRIDGES

'It don't matter, as long as he can count up to ten.'

SONNY LISTON
when asked about a referee

I HAD BRIDGES TO BUILD. It wasn't a question of seeing the light after my brief flirt with the other side. There were no angels with harps, no pearly white gates and no all-knowing guy with a big white beard telling me I couldn't come in because I was barred (although it would've been interesting to have been read the charge sheet). No, for me dying and coming back was simply another page in the crazy book of my messed up life. As for building bridges? I could kid myself I was capable, when everybody else who once cared about me knew only too well that I'd just burn them down again.

My unfortunate confession to Alison in a state of delirium meant one more fall from grace and my bags were well and truly packed. The suitcase had come down off the wardrobe and was at the end of the bed.

As for Brian? He welcomed me back into the gym but I felt a coldness that wasn't there before. Somehow I'd developed a mindset that if I could get a rematch with Bognar and beat him then everything would be okay. Just like the old days with Brian. A second Dad I could once more confide in; a playful slap around the head when I was messing around in the gym, a laugh and a joke, the boxing stories of past heroes - I missed all that badly.

As for Alison? From the winnings from this fight I'd take her and the kids to Spain; a beach, some wine and the sun and sea would work wonders. A romantic holiday and all sorted. She'd love me again. Sentimental claptrap and a pipedream maybe but that was the only plan I had.

First though, I had to get back on side with Frank Warren. I was called down to London and he gave me a dressing down that almost stripped the paper off his office walls. I was left in no doubt that my career was on the line. The abattoir and market work was calling again followed, undoubtedly, by Strangeways.

'Mike you've nearly gone down for manslaughter, you've been shot at, stabbed, died and come back. Done for drunk driving, causing an affray and God knows what else. This will only end up one way unless you fuckin' wise up, son.'

Frank was right apart from the shooting. Not yet guilty on that one. I wasn't so much burning the candle at both ends, I'd set fire to the church and razed it to the ground. I begged him for another fight with Bognar, but he told me I first had to prove I was serious and prepared to buckle down. 'This is last chance saloon, Michael,' he declared, 'don't fuck it up!'

And so I hit the gym with a fury. I was in a permanent rage, Bognar's face forever on my mind wearing that sombrero and screaming out 'champion!' I must have been impressing, even if nobody was speaking up, because Brian got me a gig on an Anthony Farnell undercard. Arnie was defending his WBO intercontinental Super Welterweight title at the Wythenshawe Forum. For me it was only an exhibition match against Michael Jennings, whose opponent had pulled out late, but it was a start and a way back in.

Michael had a great following and we kept it quiet from them that it was me who was filling in. On the night I turned up, changed quickly, walked into the arena and they went mad! I got in the ring doing push ups and fooling around. Telling them all over the ropes what I was going to do to their hero!

'Jennings is in big trouble. I'm gonna spark the fucker out!' Lumby came along donning a sombrero and was busy receiving a pile of friendly dog's abuse for doing so.

Now myself and Michael were good mates, although once in the ring all that went right out of the window. Both of us went for it but come the end we embraced and all was forgotten. Taking this bout at short notice must have helped me get back in Frank Warren's good books but not straight away. For that night in Wythenshawe I truly realised how far my star had fallen in the Warren camp. Later in the evening as I sat down for Anthony's fight, one of his people came over. He tapped me on the shoulder.

'You can't sit there Mike, it's reserved mate, you'll have to move.'

Now before the Bognar loss they'd have made a point of letting me stay and relocate the other person. But not now, I was a nothing again. There were two ways I could have dealt with this. Either smack him in the mouth and kiss everything I'd worked so hard for goodbye, or just take it on the chin and walk away. I did the latter, it upset me and I'll admit I was nearly in tears but it was the right call.

One morning soon after at the gym, whilst pummelling the speedbag, I got called into Brian's office. I stood before him sweating from the work out, my eyes never leaving his and he gave me the news I'd been praying for.

'It's a rematch, Michael. In five weeks' time you're back in against Lazslo Bognar, on 7 July, at the Manchester Velodrome. Frank's putting on a huge show called Mad4it. All the Manchester lads are fighting. Anthony's defending his title, Ricky Hatton is topping the bill and you're third. You've got five weeks, now off you go, son.' With no time to waste I headed off back to continue training, only to hear him shout … 'And Michael.' I turned around to facing Brian once more. His face first serious, only for him to break into a smile.

'It's Gomez time!'

Hearing those words was like a rocket going off in my head.

From that moment on until the start of the fight I turned into a spitting, snarling maniac. I lived to smash Bognar and whipped myself into decent shape. No booze, women or drugs. This had nothing to do with fitness, it was more a state of mind and I was going to nail him no matter how long it took. Bognar would have to kill me to win this fight and as I'd just proved, even then that never meant I was down and out.

Five weeks.

I'd be ready.

Meanwhile, I was up before the court for the affray charge but escaped with a fine, another last warning from a surprisingly lenient judge and luckily not a custodial sentence. I thanked him and got out of that courtroom quickly before he changed his mind. And so, free from worry, all my thoughts turned towards the fight. For the press conference I was acting like a crazed lunatic. I'd had a blood-red 666 shaved onto the back of the head and I had the devil in my heart that day. Bognar glared at me like I should've been committed. He smiled and outwardly remained calm but inside a part of him must have thought what the hell is going on here?

All I could think about was getting right in his face and staring him out. Looking in the eyes and seeing if he was ready to go to the same places I was to win this fight. Twice I was physically pulled away as I attempted to head butt him. I wasn't so much wired as teetering on self-combusting.

'Calm down Michael,' yelled Brian. 'Save a little for the ring.'

He'd no need to worry. Bognar was mine.

7-7-2001: Lazslo Bognar: The Mexican music blasted out across the arena, the noise level of 5500 people inside the Manchester Velodrome was deafening as I stepped out once more to do battle. I'd remained of the state of mind that all the crap in my life was down to him and he was going to pay. Not true I know but it worked for me. Once inside the ropes, amid the applause and the roar of the crowd, I noticed Frank Warren sat at ringside with a worried frown on his face. Brian also clearly felt nervous for me beforehand. I remember thinking I'll show the pair of them.

Bognar entered and I glared across at him. He appeared cool and unnerved by the tetchy reception and smiled across. That really wound me up. I so wanted to win this fight more than any before. The referee John Coyle called us together. We touched gloves and finally the bell sounded and redemption was at hand. I came flying out to nail Bognar with every punch, only to get caught by one moment of slackness and he put me down again.

I couldn't believe it! It was a half decent shot, nothing more. A flash knockdown and all that had been hurt was my pride. Being so keen to drop him, I'd lost concentration and, taking advantage, Bognar trapped me on the ropes and unloaded. It was heavy going for a while, but I held on and come the end of the first, it was fair to say all was not going to plan. Brian told me to relax but I was in no frame of mind for a tactical battle. This had to be put right my way.

The second round began and, as I charged in to throw more bombs, I was off balance, Bognar caught me and down I went once more. This was beyond embarrassing. I noticed a look of bewilderment on Warren's face and Brian shaking his head. We fought on and for the first time in the fight I hurt him with a cracking shot to the body and he hit the canvas. Bognar took the count, the noise from the crowd increased and I sensed blood. He was on the ropes and I was hitting him with everything and more. Finally the bell saved his neck, but at last I was back in the fight.

Round three and I went out determined to end it. Quickly I got Bognar trapped on the ropes again and I let fly. All the hurt and pain of the last fight and what had happened since came out in a devastating barrage of punches. He was reeling, three more left uppercuts in a row floored him and that was it. The referee gave Bognar the decency of a count, but his night and short reign with my crown was over. I'd taken this man's heart and body. He wouldn't be donning a sombrero that night. I leapt in the air as the Velodrome exploded in noise. I had my title back and far as I was concerned, all would now be made well in the world.

Happy as I was to shut up the many doubters, the night itself was slightly tarnished when Anthony Farnell was unbelievably stopped in the first round by the unfancied Takaloo. A twenty-six fight unbeaten run ended in a sickening manner that left everyone connected with Collyhurst and Moston in utter shock. None more than Arnie. I had taken my seat at ringside reserved by the Warren camp. Nobody told me to move this time around and as I got ready to watch Farnell put away the Iranian-born fighter with ease. I'd seen this guy fight in our gym twelve months before and I had no doubt he was there for the taking.

Yet to my disbelief Takaloo caught Arnie on the jaw early on with a ferocious uppercut that dropped him to the canvas. A collective gasp could be heard across the Velodrome as he staggered back to his feet. Arnie was hurt badly and Takaloo immediately launched a savage barrage that proved too much and as his legs almost crumpled beneath him, the referee showed mercy and stepped in to end the contest. Pandemonium then broke out as Brian rushed to grab Arnie and Takaloo celebrated wildly, unable to believe what he'd just done. The atmosphere suddenly turned nasty as fighting broke out at ringside. Nobody saw that result coming and whoever said they did were liars.

Finally the security guards calmed matters down and after the doctor had checked out Arnie, he was ushered away in the protective arms of Pat Barrett back to the dressing room. His face was a mixture of anger, tears and utter shock. I joined him in there and apart from a consoling arm around the shoulders and meaningless words you just felt helpless.

'You'll be back mate.'

There really wasn't much else to say.

For this was the business we'd chosen. One minute you're up, you're the champ, you're the best in the world, you're the man and you feel nothing could bring you down.

The next boxing can destroy and leave you reeling.

And it can break your fuckin' heart.

19: HAUNTED

'Everytime I stepped into the ring somebody wanted to kill me.'

ROBERTO DURAN

NOTHING LASTS FOREVER in this life and nobody knows that more than me. People, friends, lovers and enemies come and go. Whether good or bad, sometimes you're glad to see the back of them, others, it cuts you up. Wondering was it me, was I always fair? And what about them? Were they in the wrong? Was it an act of mercy or selfishness? Either through caring too much or fear of reputation? Brian was a friend. No, he was a second father and one who gave me more chances than I deserved. I was nothing before him and no doubt I fell again from grace years later, although in between I had that magical night under the Edinburgh stars.

But Brian continues to be in my thoughts and prayers. At the time I did and said things I now regret, although I stand by the reasons for doing so. But I'm a fighter and I saw in my opponent's eyes that he was all but spent. No matter what Brian or anybody else thought, I almost had him and it still leaves me haunted.

Nothing lasts forever in this life…

Amidst the celebrations following the Bognar rematch, and there were many, I found myself already half pissed on a plane to Belfast, a guest of the Royal Irish Fusiliers. I'd been invited over to their barracks for an army boxing competition, courtesy of a mate, Jimmy, a Regiment PT instructor. On landing, direct from the airport,

I was taken by helicopter to the barracks. There, I was treated like a king. The army lads couldn't have been more obliging and that included the use of a free bar in the officer's mess. Oh how little they knew! Well, it would've been impolite not to make full use of it and along with a couple of senior NCOs and Jimmy, I joined them in a marathon session.

This culminated towards the end of the night with me throwing up in spectacular manner all over the mess floor. Now afraid the tap would be switched off on the booze, I staggered back up to the bar for a last fling off the top shelf. I pointed up because I had lost the power to speak. The words came out but not necessarily in the right order. The serving soldier looked at me, shook his head, and then called across to one of the NCOs back on our table. 'Sarge, surely Gomez has had enough?'

The Sergeant in question stood to his feet, rather wearily and simply growled. 'Leave that man alone! He can do or drink whatever he wants!' Before falling back into his chair. A memorable night they tell me. Not that I can remember much about it.

I stayed at Jimmy's house and flew home the next day. To say I was rough on that journey back to Manchester wouldn't do the word justice. On reaching the top of the aeroplane steps I turned and threw up down onto the runway tarmac. Not a nice way to say goodbye to Belfast and some wonderful welcoming people. A concerned air hostess came to my aid and I told her it was down to my fear of flying. The small matter of me smelling like a whiskey distillery probably made this kind lady think something else was the cause. Suffice to say I slept all the way home and I'm still waiting for an invitation to return but I'm not holding my breath. Word was I caused more grief to the British army that night with the free bar than any enemy with a rocket launcher could ever claim to have done.

Life, at least in scattered moments, felt like it was coming together. Money was rolling in. I owned five bedroom houses in Moston that

I was renting to family and friends and even thought about selling our home in Crumpsall and moving out towards Rossendale way; far from temptation. Away from the old faces, the gangsters, (real and wannabe). Put distance between me and the drugs and the drink and the trouble and strife on every corner. A new start, plenty of fresh air and one that could only be good for the kids. Everything was coming up roses and so long as I kept fighting and winning maybe a happy-ever-after ending was within reach.

But something wasn't right with Brian. Although we'd mended some fences, I still felt there was a coldness that hadn't been there before. It wasn't the same. I just don't think he trusted me anymore and the boxing ring was the only place I could hope to win that back.

27-10-2001: Craig Docherty: I was set to defend my British super featherweight title against this up and coming undefeated Scottish fighter from Glasgow with a record of twelve wins and a draw. Twenty-one year-old Craig Docherty. Of all the boxers I've fought Docherty was the only one who took me on from the opening press conference until the first bell. He traded insult for insult with me. Every push, shove and head butt I tried to wind him up with was given back. I tried everything but Docherty was always more than game. At the weigh-in it almost exploded into a riot! We both had to be dragged apart. I had to admire his guts. 'I'm from fuckin' Glasgow, Gomez. You don't scare me!'

In the dressing room, pre-fight, Sky were interviewing Brian and I was having my hands bandaged. I pretended not to be listening when in reality I heard every word. Thinking Docherty might have the television on in his dressing room, I walked up to lean on Brian's shoulders and looked deep into the camera before whispering in the most sinister way possible. 'And still,' before moving away. Only for him to come flying back with another trick by coming into the ring, through the ropes wearing a tee shirt with the words: 'New British champion' emblazoned upon it. Now I could hardly read or write, but I understood this and remember thinking, oh this kid, he's going down!

Finally we got to fight and after I'd had a good look I pummelled Docherty quickly into submission. I took care of business in the second round. This was a brave lad. A street fighter who'd come to have a tear up and stand with me toe to toe but he was getting murdered. I hit Docherty with everything, body and then head shots cutting him badly beneath the left eye. His face bloodied and taking far too much punishment, the referee Terry O'Connor stepped in to stop the fight. It'd taken me just four minutes and forty-two seconds to retain my title. I went across to check on Docherty and we embraced. From that day we became good friends and have shared some crazy times in Carl's home city. Once with him having to lend me the money to get back to Manchester after one particular late night adventure.

Enough said.

At the post-fight ringside interview with Sky, I thanked both Brian and Frank Warren for sorting my life out. I was wise enough to play the game. Warren came across and poked his head through the ropes.

'We're going to give Mike two more fights then look at a world title shot.'

Praise the Lord!

I was sat at home one night trying to be good when the phone rang...

'Mike, it's Lumby, I'm in big trouble mate.'

He'd been having a beer in the Thatched House pub on Moston Lane when a large gang of drunken Manchester United supporters entered. They were off to see their team play in Amsterdam the next morning and were busy getting in the mood. One knew Lumby was a serious blue and pulled him.

'Would you believe it! Lumby the bitter fuckin' blue without his tinker mates.'

An argument started and Lumby was told if he got on his knees and begged then he wouldn't get a kicking. That'd never happen.

The next minute myself, Bones and Val's boyfriend Steve came charging through the door. Suddenly the atmosphere changed and Lumby looked extremely pleased to see us. We must have cut a strange sight. I was in my slippers clutching a pickaxe, Bones had only one sock on and was carrying a hammer, whilst Steve was soaking wet from jumping out of a bath and was holding a wrench.

I walked over to the lads.

'What's going on?'

One look at Bones, Steve and recognising me in particular and they swiftly sobered up. It finished rather amicably for a change with one of them having to go outside and have a straightener with Lumby. In the end the kid bottled it and apologised.

'Your mates are different than other gangs.'

'In what way?' asked Lumby.

'Well it's loyalty innit.' He pointed back to the pub. 'They obviously just dropped everything when you needed them. It's like fuckin' Goodfellas with you lot.'

He was right. It was a family thing... And it got us out of the house!

Alison was heavily pregnant. Me? I was the same old. I'd slipped again and was boozing and back on the coke. Fighting in a ring was the last thing on my mind. I'd gone AWOL from the gym but this time around there were no phone calls from Brian. Everything was going crazy around me. It was like living in a minefield. I had four drink driving charges, a road rage charge and a community service order to serve. I'd also damaged my shoulder in an argument at some traffic lights with some guy who was screaming abuse, but never recognised me until we both got out of the car. He probably still regrets doing that.

It needed something huge to save me from myself and Alison giving birth to our third child, a beautiful little lady we christened Louise after my late sister, was what did it. If I wasn't going to rob a bank then I had no choice. To support my family I needed to get back in the ring. Frank Warren's promise of two more fights then a world title shot and the lure of a huge payday was the bait that saw me walking back up the steps of Collyhurst and Moston gym.

I remember it was a freezing cold, rain-lashed Mancunian Monday morning. I entered and was greeted warmly by the lads but eyed with obvious suspicion by Brian.

'My office,' he said. In there Brian read me the riot act.

'I think you should be thinking of retiring and not taking another fight.'

I didn't agree. 'Let me prove I'm worth a last shot Brian. This isn't about me, it's about my family now. I've grown up. I really need this.'

He said nothing, just sat back in the chair, stroked his chin and stared at me. I felt he was looking inside my soul. It was weird. I knew he genuinely feared for me and my lifestyle but had simply grown too weary. The lads said that every time a story got back to him of my escapades, his face was a mask of indifference. And then here I was! A stone overweight, twice as loud with a huge smile and full of the same old fuckin' excuses.

Finally he spoke. 'My prodigal pain in the backside, that's what you are Michael.' I smiled and could feel the ice slowly melting. 'I'm getting old son and my time now is too valuable to waste on hopeless causes. No more. This is the last one for you. Okay?'

I nodded and was back in. He also must have been under pressure from Frank Warren, because nobody sold tickets like me in Manchester. I was a licence to print money. I heard later Warren had spoken to

Brian about my state of mind and fitness and they'd both agreed I was in decent enough shape to go back to work. Warren had lined me up a twenty-five year-old undefeated Londoner named Kevin Lear to fight for the vacant WBU World Featherweight title at the *MEN* arena. I finally had my fight but instead of knuckling down and throwing myself even more into training, I instead went the other way.

It was a curse. I just couldn't help myself.

The trouble was, I wasn't worried about Kevin Lear and so I was never truly focused and found myself drifting again. Nobody was pushing me in the gym. Brian especially. I got the feeling he believed I was all washed up. I'd taken an awful lot of fights in a short time and I think he thought 'just let him get it over with'. I'd heard rumours, second-hand gossip that word was going round of me being 'shot'. Oh he said this and he said that.

'He's gone, Gomez is finished.'

'Gomez has fucked it all up.'

'Fuckin' tinker boy has thrown it all away.'

People would add sugar and twist it just that little bit more. This stuff hurt but a part of me started to believe it. And so I partied even harder and fuck the consequences to get these thoughts out of my mind. Deep down I told myself I'd enough left in the tank to take care of Lear. But I'd badly under-estimated him. This kid was coming to Manchester intent on taking my head off and all I was worried about was where the next drink or line of coke was coming from. I was out of control, everybody knew it but nobody spoke up.

Why should they?

How many bullets had I to take before I shot myself in the foot again? Had the first Bognar fiasco not taught me anything? As the fight grew near I panicked. I was training and sleeping in a sweat suit simply to make the weight. It was Deja fuckin'vu. Torture, but I'd left myself with little choice.

1-6-2002: Kevin Lear: That night at the *MEN* was torturous. Lear's jab was fast, accurate, painful and cut me early, again over the left eye. Opening a war wound from the MacLeod fight. This riled me but as I lunged forward he countered with some good punches that rocked me back. Only then did I realise Lear was a serious opponent and I had a real fight on my hands. The second saw little change as I tried to nail him but every time he'd catch me with a host of good shots. This went on. Round three and I felt increasingly helpless as I was picked off with ease like a kid flicking peanuts at a blind man.

I could feel the taste of blood trickling from my nose and mouth. I was lashing out but the punches weren't hurting and Lear was walking through them. Finally in round four and after what felt like an eternity, I got inside and started unloading, yet still he managed to dance his way out of trouble. Back I went, like a bull in a bad mood, but to no affect. Lear was catching me at will and it was beyond frustrating.

Round five and six and although I was all over him, he was scoring with the more accurate punching. Lear jabbed and moved and continually landed some powerful shots. The blood was now falling in my eyes. Round seven saw me find energy to hit back and from somewhere deep within deliver a barrage to leave him reeling. For the first time that evening my supporters roared loud, at last I'd shown them something. To my relief I sensed Lear was easing off, he was getting tired. If I could hang on in, then there remained a possibility that I'd still be able to take him out.

By round eight, I couldn't stem his attacks. Lear was finding my face at will. I was shattered, going nowhere. Punch after punch rained in on me. I was taking everything Lear had, sure in the knowledge he was going to tire himself out. The man was slowing down, I just knew and could feel it. The eyes couldn't lie. He was blowing up and breathing heavily. The bell goes to end round eight and I was a bloodied staggering fighter, but still standing. I was convinced I was still in the fight. Nothing was surer. It wasn't over.

I all but collapsed on my stool and looking up was stunned to see Brian call the referee Ian John-Lewis across to our corner.

'I'm stopping it,' he said to him

I couldn't believe what I'd just heard. 'Don't stop it Brian!'

'No, no, no, Michael. You're getting hurt. I'm stopping it.'

'No Brian please, fuck, fuckin' no, please!'

'No Michael. No more.'

All I wanted to do was get away and out of the ring, but as I tried to stand Brian grabbed hold and embraced me. There were tears falling down my face.

He was insistent. 'It was too much Michael. It was just too much.'

The dressing room was quiet afterwards. I was seething, but for once kept my own counsel. I was convinced, despite taking a lot of punishment, that I'd have caught up with Lear. Brian tried talking to me. 'Michael you were gone. It was like an old man in there. You're battered, your face was a mask. You had three cuts and a nosebleed. There was nothing left. It was an act of mercy pulling you out.'

I never replied. I took off home saying nothing to nobody. As far I was concerned my time with Brian Hughes and the Collyhurst and Moston gym was over.

My world was falling apart and I dealt with it the only way I knew how. After the Lear defeat the new me proved only an illusion and in no time at all the promises I'd made to Alison disappeared in a booze and drug-fuelled haze. Even for me this was a new low. One night I ran out of cocaine and ended up smoking crack in a rat-infested drug den in Hulme. I was being recognised but I couldn't care less. Nothing mattered again apart from getting wasted. I remember one of my sisters seeing me in a pub and having to look twice because she couldn't believe her eyes. I was wrecked and not caring about anybody or anything. 'Jesus Christ Mike,' she said, almost in tears. 'You look haunted'.

I was blowing fortunes in the casinos around Manchester. The Circus on Oxford Road was a particular favourite; six grand in there alone one night. Easy come, easy go. I was knocking back champagne like lemonade. The cocaine was like sugar in my tea and I was taking lap dancers outside the clubs to strip for my own private audience. I partied harder than ever before because I wanted everybody to think I didn't care, when deep down it was killing me. I'd thrown everything away. I'd fucked up. In just twelve months, I'd been stabbed, died and come back, my boxing career had hit skid row, I'd left Brian and now for the cherry on the cake, two other women amongst many I'd been seeing behind Alison's back got in touch with me at the same time to say they were pregnant. Is it any wonder my mental state was in meltdown?

However the lowest point was still to occur when, against Alison's wishes, I sold our dream house in Crumpsall so I'd have money in my pocket to party on. Nobody could talk or reason with me. I hated myself, so why should I care what anybody else thought? All I was bothered about was drinking and whoring myself silly. The coke stayed on tap and I was dead to the world and everybody in it who tried telling me otherwise. I was pressing the self-destruct; it usually started after three pints, that gave me the urge for cocaine and then I was gone for three days. A fuckin' helter-skelter ride with no seat belt and seemingly no end...

Once the house was gone we moved back to Moston with my cousins. One night I came home late and found Alison up and she just went wild. Her heart broke in front of me. The tears flowed. I was called everything from a drunken bastard to no good scum. It was a build-up and I deserved every single word. No matter how cruel or savage. I stood and watched this girl who I'd put through so much lay bare her soul. And suddenly, call it whatever you want, I realised everything she said was right.

Alison was within her rights to dump me like a bad smell and I couldn't say a word in protest. My one salvation to try and make something for this girl and our family existed in one place. Brian Hughes and Collyhurst and Moston gym was history, thanks for the memories, but I'd try elsewhere.

I'd heard the preacher man may have been willing to talk and save my fucked up soul. It was worth a phone call.

20: THE PREACHER MAN

*'Sometimes you look in a field and you see a cow and you think it's a
better cow than the one you've got in your own field. It's a fact. Right?
And it never really works out that way.'*

SIR ALEX FERGUSON

M Y LAST MEETING WITH BRIAN was when I called
into the gym to pick up a couple of grand he was keeping
for me in a pension fund. 'I had to pull you out Michael,'
he claimed. 'It was for your own good son.'

I snapped back. 'No chance Brian. If there was one fight you
should've pulled me out of, it was the Bognar fight. You should've
made the decision.'

'No you're wrong,' he said. 'You're your own biggest enemy
Michael. And one day you'll regret it.'

The fallout from me quitting the Collyhurst and Moston gym
was poisonous for a while. I did and said a lot of things I now regret,
but at the time I raged about Brian stopping me against Kevin Lear.
In my mind I believed that happened because of what went on in the
first Bognar clash and the merciless stick he received from all parts of
the boxing world, from experts and fans alike.

The shadow of Paul Ingle's head injury hanging over him, Brian,
in my opinion, acted wrongly. Stuff did happen that was way out of
order. I started having a go one day outside the gym to wind him up

and he threw me against a wall. Brian had tears in his eyes and was clearly upset.

'Everything that happened was done to save you from yourself. You were finished in there.'

Feeling hard done to, bitter and twisted, call it what you like. I phoned the police and told them he'd assaulted me. Brian was pulled in and forced to explain his actions. Fallen pride can mess with your head sometimes. The reason I've always remained adamant Brian was wrong is that the cut man, Mick Williamson, who was in the corner against Bognar had always insisted to me that Lear was gone on his feet. I'd have taken him out in the next round or two. People who watch the fight today are free to make their own decisions. I must admit I looked fit to drop and it looked like I'd just staggered out of a plane crash, but when you're in that ring, you see things. You sense it if your opponent is in trouble. Whether it's a look in the eye, a missed punch, you just know. And I knew with Lear.

I could understand Brian was hurting. Me leaving after Anthony Farnell also must have left him reeling. Arnie blamed his training for the first round stoppage against Takaloo. Whereas Brian claimed he never wanted him to take the fight in the first place. Many people will say that we were both selfish and bit the hand that fed us but in the end myself and Arnie were the fighters, it was our lives at stake in the ring and our decisions to make.

When Arnie bailed from Collyhurst and Moston he joined Billy Graham's Phoenix gym in Denton. The brothers Ricky and Matthew Hatton were already there. It had a great reputation with some fantastic talent. I felt at the time that if anyone could save my career it was Billy. But would he be willing to have me? Everybody knew the stories, I could only hope he didn't think as so many others did that I was a lost cause. I got his telephone number off Arnie and called him.

'Give us a chance Billy?'

'Hi Mike, I half expected this call.'

Billy was receptive and invited me to his house in Mossley and the next day we met and talked. He said that before any decisions were made, the lads at his gym would need to be on board. We left it at that. I spent a restless night thinking the worst, but the following morning Billy rang and said they were more than happy to have me. Then he laid down some ground rules.

'I hate bad eggs, Michael. You're more than welcome to come to the gym but you need to cut the partying down between fights. When you're training with me pal, you don't mess about or you're out. We have a laugh at the right time but no fuckin' around when it's business. Agreed?'

We shook hands and I was in. It was a buzz and I couldn't wait to get started. I was determined to impress among the new faces. I quickly loved everything about Billy's gym. The new fighters I trained with and Kerry Kayes, the best conditioning coach on the planet. Kerry was equally well known in the world of body building. He had helped the original Incredible Hulk, Lou Ferringo. Kerry was a real gentleman. Bobby Rimmer was an absolute top class trainer and padman and a great guy around the gym and out of it. And then, of course, there was Billy. If you could merge Brian Hughes' defensive knowledge with Billy's streetwise style and offensive philosophy you'd have the perfect boxing coach. Billy watched me like a hawk and assessed me carefully. I adored doing the pads with him and Bobby also.

I sparred hard and I behaved. Billy told me it would be a long way back but when I was ready there would be some gold at the end of the rainbow. 'We'll make you some cash, Mike. Just keep on going as you are.'

The Preacher man had spoken. That was good enough for me.

The Denton gym was an awkward place to reach from Moston, so even though I was still banned from driving, I bought myself a

50cc moped... or at least got hold of one. One day, early on, I'm training and feeling a little tired and I couldn't seem to shake it off. Billy noticed and came across.

'Mike what's your diet?'

'Well I get up in the morning, I go training then I come home and have a tin of tuna and some boiled rice.'

'And what else do you have?'

'That's it.'

Billy looked incredulous. 'You have just one meal a day to make the weight?'

I nod.

'Come with me son,' said Billy.

And so I got to meet the great Kerry Kayes. When it came to the human body this man was a genius. 'You get up in the morning you have your porridge. You have your three boiled eggs. You finish training and then you have the Pro Recover. Then the Pro MR. Then you have tuna, fish or chicken with rice. You have to eat five or six times a day Michael. The more you eat regular small meals, the more you'll burn the weight.'

'Kerry, I can't even make nine stone four eating once a day!'

He smiled. 'Just try it.'

What did I have to lose? Everyone thought I was finished anyway. I did as Kerry said and it worked. Shortly after finishing at the gym one day I visited him on his beloved Denton allotment. He was generously giving me a pile of stuff to help with my training, a huge tub of Pro vital, a big box of Pro MR, Pro vitamin. Kerry ensured I had everything that I needed. I put it all in the sports bag which already had the gym stuff in and tied it onto my back, before getting off on the Moped.

This bag was so heavy, remember I was only a small kid, nine stone something and the bike was wobbling from side to side. And it just had to happen. Going up a hill in Cheetham Hill, the sound of sirens behind me and I got pulled over by the police. Now I knew with being already banned they were going to throw the book at me. I looked around and suddenly an idea flashed through my head.

'What's your name son?' Asked the copper.

'Michael Joyce.'

Luckily he wasn't a boxing fan and so off I flew. I threw away the bag on my back to distract him and raced across the road, over the wall, down an embankment, waded through a canal and across the field on the other side, jumped over another fence, down an entry before stopping for breath. Drenched and exhausted I watched and listened out for the police following me. But nothing, I was in the clear. Finally I got home. My next problem, I'd have to ring Billy and tell him what's happened.

'Hi Billy, it's Gomez.'

'What's up Mike.'

'Billy, do you think Kerry could get me some more of that stuff?'

'What do you mean? They're not for your mates. He isn't a bloody dealer!'

'No Billy it's not that, I've had a little problem.'

I told him the God's honest truth. How I'd dropped the bag, left the moped and embarked on my dramatic escape. Like a rampaging Mancunian Rambo racing through rivers and jumping over walls. Billy cracked up laughing.

'Come in tomorrow you lunatic and we'll go and see Kerry.'

When I told Kerry Kayes he just found the whole thing hysterical and kitted me out again with everything I'd lost. I got told a story that in an interview not so long ago Kerry was being asked about some hassle he was having with another athlete. At the time it was a big deal, but not for Kerry.

'Listen, I've worked with Michael Gomez. After Mike, nothing is a problem!'

I loved that man.

Now the moped was out of the picture Alison drove me to Denton but petrol money was expensive. Plus subs for the gym, it all added up and cash was tight. Trying to stay on the straight and narrow I needed another avenue. A real good mate of mine Craig Blanchard, who has sadly passed away now, had an idea.

'I'll get you a sponsor mate.'

Craig drove me to Salford to see friends of his. Two brothers Anthony and Mark Mullen owned a firm called Bridgewater Security. 'They're good lads,' said Craig. 'Salt of the earth and will help you out.' We got there and caught Anthony as he was leaving. Craig swiftly introduced me.

'Pleased to meet you Mike,' said Anthony. 'I'm a big fan of yours. Look, I've got to go out now, a bit of business has come up on a site. Somebody is robbing but come back tomorrow when I've a little more time and we'll talk.'

The next day the sun was shining so I decided to walk from Moston. I set off, down Rochdale Road, into Salford, past the casino and the Cronwell Roundabout until I came to the Bridgewater Security offices. I entered into a reception area and could hear raised voices coming from behind Anthony's and Mark's office door.

'Who do you think you are, robbing off our fuckin' site?'

Then somebody got a crack and I heard a scream. 'Aaagh!'

A different voice. 'We've warned you before and still you take the piss.' Smack! Whack! 'Aaagh! I'm sorry lads, it won't happen again!'

'Dead right it won't. You're fuckin' sacked! Now get the fuck out!' Shouted the first voice. The door opened and a young man appeared wearing a Bridgewater Security jacket and holding his bloodied nose. He looked very sorry for himself, but then recognised me and smiled.

'Alright Gomez, top fight against Thornhill mate!'

That said he walked swiftly away. 'What the?'...

My legs froze and before I'd had chance to move the door reopened and Anthony Mullen appeared; calm, smiling and looking me straight in the eyes.

'Mike, great to see you again. Come in.'

In I went, not knowing what to expect. Mark stood from behind his desk and shook my hand. I noticed blood on the shirt sleeve. I'm sure it wasn't his.

'Sit down Mike. Now what can we do for you?'

I told them about needing sponsoring as they stood above me like the Salford Kray twins with arms folded and listening to my every word.

'No problem at all,' said Anthony. 'We'll sponsor you for £280 a month. Is that enough?'

'That's great lads,' I replied. 'More than generous.'

We all shook hands, I thanked them and said my goodbyes. As I reached the office door I heard Mark's voice. 'Oh and Mike.'

I turned around.

'You ever have any problems, just give us a buzz?'

'Cheers Mark,' I said. 'Very much appreciated.'

…Welcome to Salford.

21: OH BROTHER!

'Me and our Bones would fight and argue over a game of tiddlywinks.
It's that Irish pride.'

MICHAEL GOMEZ

I WENT OUT FOR A QUIET DRINK with Thomas McDonagh from the Collyhurst and Moston gym. It was good to see him; I'd hardly seen any of the lads since quitting and felt I needed to clear the air. I'd been with Thomas since the start. His first time in the ring as a pro was against me in the gym. I remember Brian pulled me aside, 'I know you and Tom are good friends but you'll be doing your mate a favour and showing him now just what the pro game is all about.' I did as I was told and for the spell we were in the ring I used every dirty, low-down trick I knew on Thomas. Come the end I felt guilty but we shook hands, smiled and it was swiftly forgotten. Reality had dawned for him, it was a different game with no head gear and vests. A different world.

'Brian wanted me to retire, Tommy. I'm only twenty-four for fuck's sake?'

'No mate,' he replied. 'He just wanted you to do it properly so you didn't get hurt. One thing though Mike,' he went on, 'I don't understand. Why change your attitude now and decide to buckle down for Billy Graham when you could have done that at our gym?'

Thomas was right, except so much bad blood had been spilt now. The deed was done and too many words had passed between myself and Brian. It was over. Deep down it broke my heart but I'd gone too far to expect an olive branch. Not that I'd ask for one. Looking back, most claim the best times of their lives were at school. Mine was in Collyhurst and Moston gym. Even though there were days you'd stand outside and think, oh God, here we go again, because once we got inside we used to try and kill each other! Brian would stand and shake his head at the ferocity of some of our battles. 'Come on lads, calm it down.'

Yes, you'd find yourself fighting for your life against your mates in that special place above the Co-op on Lightbowne Road but it was that 'all for one and one for all' spirit that overrode everything. We were close and I knew I'd badly miss the craic. So many memories, there always seemed to be police sirens howling loudly outside and without hesitation Brian would stop whatever he was doing and shout out so all could hear. 'Good news lads. Sounds like Pat Barrett is on his way in!'

But now it was time for pastures new. I shared a few more beers with Thomas, agreed to disagree on certain matters, Kevin Lear mostly, shook hands and said goodbye. Different gyms, but we were still mates forever and we fought on.

One morning in the gym I'd just finished sparring when Billy Graham shouted me from outside his office door. 'Mike, five minutes in here.'

I was thinking, 'oh Christ, here we go'. Then the crazy thought hit me that I hadn't actually done anything wrong! The clean living played havoc with my mind. Billy's office was his inner sanctum. You'd only be invited in there if you were in trouble or it was big news. He owned a fish tank full of lizards and turtles. Sometimes I used to think Billy liked them more than some of the people he was forced to deal with in boxing. I'd seen promoters, managers, reporters and boxers go through that door smiling, relaxed and whistling, only to come out looking like they'd been mugged.

But what did he want with me?

'It's time, Mike,' said Billy, 'We've got you a fight.'

He'd lined me up against a twenty-seven year-old, hard-hitting Brummie called Jimmy Beech. Only three weeks before in Liverpool, Beech had flattened the previously undefeated and highly rated Ricky Ecclestone. At that time money was obviously important and the four and half grand would be like water to a dying man's lips, but for me, more importantly it was a chance to prove to people in boxing that I was still a force to be reckoned with. Billy realised this. 'This is a hard one to come back with Mike, but I need to see if you're worth the time and effort being put into you. And we need to see what you've got left in the tank. You up for it?'

He knew a question like that didn't need answering. My training and attitude had been spot on but until you have seen a fighter back in the heat of battle taking real punches, then you can never really be sure. But I was never better than when fighting through blind panic. When a home for my wife and kids and a whole future was dependent on me knocking holes out of an opponent. Jimmy Beech may have thought he was flavour of the month after hammering Ecclestone, but Beech couldn't know what lay in store for him when facing the born again Irish-Mexican.

A few weeks later, I was in the gym staring at a poster on the wall advertising the coming bill at the MEN arena. Ricky Hatton's name was emblazoned on the top. Anthony Farnell had second billing. I put my fingers on it and ran them down. Mine was almost out of sight. It had been an almighty fall from the stars. When I shut my eyes I could recall the nights like that against Gary Thornhill; the sombreros flying high, the Mexican music playing, the crowd roaring my name. I missed those times and it hurt to be back at rock bottom again.

Two days before the fight I was at Bones' house playing *FIFA* on the computer. We were fiercely competitive and hated losing and there was never any such thing as just a friendly contest with us. The game we were playing was tight and it was getting tense. Bones' kids had already left the room. They knew when Dad and Uncle Mike went up against each other it was best just to leave them to it. Anyway I paused the game because I needed to use the toilet. When I came back down Bones had restarted it and scored. Well I went nuts!

'You can't do that, it's fuckin' cheating!'

'I can do what I want,' he said. 'It's my fuckin' house!'

'Fuck you, Bones!'

'No! Fuck you, Midge!'

'You're out of order, Bones, fuck off!'

I turned around, picked my coat up and went to leave. The next moment he'd cracked me on the back of the head with an iron bar. I staggered and faced him, then put my hand over where he'd smacked me. It was covered in blood.

'You mad bastard. I'm fighting in two days' time and you do this?'

'You started it,' replied Bones. To that there was no answer.

Oh brother.

That night I washed the cut on my head the best I could. There was no option of stitches or staples because then I'd never pass the pre-fight medical. I could only pray that the bleeding would stop in time and the scar would heal over. Next morning there was blood all over my pillow but thankfully it seemed to have stemmed. No way was I coming clean at the gym. It would simply be a case of staying quiet and praying it doesn't get picked up by the authorities. God knows what Billy would've made of it?

28-9-2002: Jimmy Beech: I was back at the *MEN* arena – fifth on the bill behind Ricky Hatton's defence of his WBU super Lightweight title. I kept the entrance low key. My supporters were still there to see me in force but it was clearly a Ricky Hatton crowd. Shouts of 'Gomez' echoed loud as I entered the ring but they were echoes of better days. Beech was looking super confident, shadow boxing and waving to the crowd. You'd have thought he'd already won. Here was another who had no doubt been told by his trainer and everybody around him that Michael Gomez was washed up; nothing but a coke head and a lousy drunk. I went into his face and Beech just laughed. Billy had told me to channel my aggression. Keep it for when the bell sounded but old habits died hard. Besides, that night I'd enough boiling over inside to take care of business. The referee Phil Kane called us together. We eyeballed, oh Beech really fancied this…

Round one and I schooled him. I was fast, accurate and catching him with good combinations. I'd listened to Billy, 'use your brain, not your brawn'. Power was important but unless you got in position to unload it was useless. As I returned to the stool Mick Williamson noticed blood seeping from the back of my head. He looked confused before patching it up. Mick glared at me in utter disbelief. The second round played out similarly. Beech was looking to land bombs constantly. No doubt after his demolition on Ecclestone, he thought it came naturally.

In round three Beech opened up a cut on my forehead, accidental or not it riled me and I dropped him just before the bell saved his ass like a fuckin' lifejacket in a sea storm. Nothing could stop me in the fourth; a furious assault and then two minutes and fifteen seconds in, I caught Beech with a right uppercut that knocked him off his feet. He wasn't smiling anymore. Fight over and it was a punch that caused gasps at ringside. Ricky Hatton's dad, Ray, looked incredulous. It was a perfect way to show Gomez time was not yet over.

After the result was announced, I grabbed the Master of Ceremonies microphone and shouted into it, 'I'm back for good!' The cheers went up but the response wasn't overwhelming. It didn't exactly have them roaring from the back seats, 'Three cheers for Gomez!' It was met with indifference. I'd let them all down so many times before I could hear what they were thinking, 'Yeah right, mate…

another line, another beer and you'll be back on your arse again.'

In the Sky interview I called out Kevin Lear for a rematch, but ultimately never got near him. He got injured around that time and a little later on had to retire.

Later our dressing room was a crazy, happy place. The music was blaring, there were high fives, everyone was laughing and joking. The Phoenix was on fire! Ricky had retained his crown with a second round knockout and Arnie had won the WBU Middleweight title on a points decision. The atmosphere was rocking. It reminded me of better days. I was unusually quiet, content to watch what was going on. This wasn't my time. Hopefully the best was still to come. Mick Williamson came over. 'Mike, can I ask you something?'

'Course you can mate,' I replied. He looked puzzled.

Mick sat down beside me. 'I've seen a lot in all my twenty years working as a cut man. But I've never, ever seen anybody get a cut on the back of the head. Something you want to tell me son?'

By now Billy and Kerry Kayes had joined him. I was surrounded and all eyes were on me – it was time to come clean.

'Well the truth is Mick, I got into an argument with my brother two days ago and he hit me with a fuckin' iron bar. A dangerous man is our Bones. We're okay now though, he just got carried away. One of those things. I didn't say anything to anybody because I thought they might not let me fight.'

For a moment the three of them stared at me open mouthed. Then Billy just smiled and shook his head. 'Jesus Mike, you mad Paddy bastard!'

At that moment I'm sure they all knew the old Gomez was truly back!

If this incident proved anything to them, it was that the fires still burned fierce within me. I wasn't going away. Incredibly, in whacking me Bones had ultimately done me a favour, though I didn't want him to make a habit of it.

OH BROTHER!

'Welcome to the Phoenix Gomez,' said Billy. He put an arm around my shoulders. 'Let's see where we go from here.'

18-1-2003: Rakhim Minhalieyev: The lads at the Phoenix gym loved a night out but it was always at the right time and just booze and the ladies. No drugs. Following the Beech fight I was away from the gym for only three weeks. I went on the lash, but it never got out of control, I returned a little overweight and soon got back to business. I continued to train hard and live right. Alison drove me in and would sit and watch the training, then we'd go home. I was focused, I was a professional fighter and I listened to every word Billy Graham told me.

Billy was true to his word and four months later I was back in the ring, this time at the Preston Guildhall against a thirty-six year-old Russian journeyman called Rakhim Minhalieyev. I felt sharp and put Minhalieyev away in the fourth of an eight round bout. The power had returned. My left seemed to be cast from diamonds, my right of stone. I was back and I was confident. I felt like I could take on Lennox Lewis and knock him flat out. I wanted the world, and especially those in boxing, to know I was ready to tear heads off once more. I needed that house for Alison and the kids and I craved respect. Billy was happy. He knew I was almost ready but needed to be one hundred percent sure.

'Another fight to wash away any last cobwebs Mike.'

He'd obviously been talking to Frank Warren.

'Just one more then you get a shot at the title.'

5-4-2003: Wladimir Borov: At the *MEN* arena against the twenty-seven year-old tough and durable Bulgarian, I showed that I'd stopped the slide and re-established myself as a championship contender. I wasn't fantastic against Borov, I rushed my shots. Being back on home ground I tried far too hard to impress. In the end I nailed him in the third round. A left hand jab that sliced apart a cut above his eye and he was pulled out.

In an interview for Sky at ringside I was asked who I preferred for my next fight. Alex Arthur or Kevin Lear? Arthur was the up and coming golden boy of British boxing. Scottish and proud of it and being groomed for great deeds by Frank Warren. He was seen as a prodigy by Warren's *Sports Network*. The experts were saying he had the tools to go all the way.

As for Lear? Well, for reasons past I wanted to knock his head right off. 'I'll fight either of them,' I told the reporter. 'And I'll beat them too.'

But it was now the thought of taking on Alex Arthur that kept me awake at night. He was the one. If I could nail him, a house and a return to the big time would be the prize. There's an old gypsy proverb.

'We are all wanderers on this earth. Our hearts are full of wonder and our souls are deep with dreams.'

I was always on the outside listening in through doors. 'He's bad news this kid'. 'No manners and no class'. 'A couple of shots, he got lucky'. Well you could stick your insults where the sun never shone. We all dream and mine was set to come true. Alex Arthur, Edinburgh and a place in British boxing history was calling; my world, my time and my fuckin' rainbow's end.

22: AGREED

'Now set em up Joe. One for my baby and one for the road.'

FRANK SINATRA

AMAZING: It was to prove as equally, exciting and brutal a contest than anything ever seen in a British ring. Twenty-six-year-old Alex Arthur was a son of Edinburgh and the city's great pride. Taken under his wing by Frank Warren, Arthur was being groomed for great things. A world title shot was swiftly coming into sight. This was an impressive boxer. He was clever, at times dazzling, dangerous and with a fighter's heart the size of the magnificent castle that sits atop Scotland's capital city. Sports Network was throwing everything but a kilt and haggis at promoting this young Scotsman as the next big thing. Already a British champion he took a sixteen-straight-win career record into the fight against the supposed, washed-up gypsy boy from Longford. Now an adopted Mancunian adorning a Mexican sombrero who went by the name of Gomez.

If Arthur had an Achilles heel it was a huge and deadly over-confidence. Bordering dangerous towards arrogance. He knew of his opponent's wayward ways. Lurid stories reached him from Manchester that made Arthur think Gomez would enter the ring clutching a bottle of whiskey in one hand and a line of coke on a tray in the other. He believed victory was a given right in a round of his choosing against this so-called 'Mexican Manc.'

In time what happened in that Edinburgh ring on an unforgettable night would come to be regarded as one of the finest ever British domestic tear-ups. Nobody suspected what was set to occur. It was to shock all in

boxing and none more than 'Amazing' Alex Arthur...
Michael Armstrong Gomez was about to rock his world.

ON SATURDAY 12TH JULY 2003, I travelled to the Braehead Arena in Glasgow with Billy Graham to watch Alex Arthur defend his British Super Featherweight title against fellow countryman Willie Limond. Frank Warren had assured me that so long as Arthur came through against Limond, a fight in his hometown city of Edinburgh was set in stone. The contract was ready to be signed. My fee would be twenty-five grand. But I can honestly say I would've fought Arthur for nothing. For one of the few times I could ever remember, money was irrelevant. I was fighting for my life.

The phoney war had already begun. I didn't like Arthur and I knew the feeling was more than mutual. I thought he was an arrogant bastard, forever coming out with all kind of snide comments about me in the press. Then there were the second hand rumours. 'I was just a small-time wannabe gangster from Manchester,' apparently. What was the man going on about? I'd be fighting him with gloves not in a fuckin' balaclava armed with a pickaxe handle and sawn-off.

He looked down his nose at me and thought I was finished and believed I didn't deserve to be in the same ring as him. I'd dealt with people like this all my life. I got the impression if Arthur was a donut, he'd eat himself. Mind you, I wasn't behind the door in firing my mouth off either. Any chance I got, I slagged him. I told anyone who'd listen that I'd knock Arthur out when we fought and I truly believed that. I felt different. I was still my old cocky self but not full of crap with it. I was treating this sport as my job now. I wasn't messing around, I couldn't afford to. The penny hadn't just dropped, it had hit me on the head like a fuckin' brick.

The prize for beating Arthur was huge, but the penalty for defeat was as severe. If he beat me then it really was all over. Maybe I could carve out a career as a journeyman fighting once a month and living off the Gomez name to open a few pubs. Perhaps I would go back to the prize fighting. But I knew it'd only be a matter of time before I got banged up. Maybe I'd get lured into doing a bank job? Moston was home to bank robbers, it bred them. Or more likely I'd be killed in a club one night by upsetting a wrong'un gangster type or some streetwise waster with a knife or gun. There were two roads to travel. One was full of hope, the other not worth thinking about. I wasn't invincible, far from it, but at that moment in time, if needed, I was confident of putting away a fuckin' grizzly bear with my left hook. Never mind some sneering jock.

There were only five people on this planet who believed I was going to beat Alex Arthur: myself, Billy Graham, Kerry Kayes, Bobby Rimmer and Alison. She'd seen it in my eyes. She knew. The rest of the boxing fraternity were predicting that my time had gone and Arthur, in his own backyard, with an arena full of howling locals behind him, would wipe the floor with me. Frank Warren, boxing magazines, internet forums, Sky Sports pundits – they were all convinced it was a mismatch and I'd simply be a good name on their boy's win record as he went on to conquer the world. None of them, even contemplated the notion that I was preparing for the fight of my life.

Sat in front of myself and Billy at the arena was Alex Arthur's gorgeous girlfriend, Debbie. I was more interested in her than the fight. I wasn't one for studying my opponents, but Billy insisted that I concentrated and watched Arthur. 'He's a dangerous character, Mike. And if you're not careful and on top of your game he'll hurt you.' I had to give it Arthur in the way he finished off Limond impressively in the eighth round to retain his title. The kid could bang, but so could I. Willie Limond was a really decent fighter but he wasn't Michael Gomez.

On leaving the ring Arthur came across to see Debbie. I leaned forward as they spoke and couldn't resist it. 'Hello Alex. I'm gonna fuckin' spark you. You do know that don't you?'

An exasperated Billy grabbed hold and pulled me back into my seat. 'Mike, for fuck's sake not now mate. It isn't the time.'

At first Arthur just stared and then he shook his head and smiled.

'I'm gonna knock you out Gomez and when I do you'll be like your Dad.'

Then he mimicked a blind man struggling to find something with his hands. I went mad and lunged for him but Billy again restrained me.

'Easy Mike! Easy fella!' he said as I fumed.

I eyeballed him. 'Let me tell you something, Alex. My old man is ten of you. Out of respect to Billy here, I'm gonna save it for the ring. When you're in there you won't be able to hide and shout your fuckin' mouth off anymore. Because there'll come a time when the crowd steps back and we move forward. My old man maybe blind, but Mickey can see the future and you know what? He said you're fucked!'

Still smiling Arthur walked off with Debbie.

'We'll see,' he shouted back without turning around.

What Arthur said had cut me deeply. I was no angel, I was a wind up merchant, I would start a war at press conferences and weigh-ins but even I possessed some kind of fuckin moral scale. Some things were out of bounds. I think they call it scruples. Dad might have been a piece of work at times. He may never have won any fathering contests. But he was my Dad, my flesh and blood, and nobody except me and mine had the right to call him.

Alex Arthur would pay for those words.

Alex later apologised for the comment and it was forgiven and forgotten. But at the time it lit a bonfire in my head. Back at the hotel I told Billy I wanted to start training first thing Monday morning. No delays, I couldn't wait to get back in the gym. A smiling Billy led me by the arm in into the bar.

'Come with me Michael.'

He ordered two double Jack Daniel's. Firewater. Billy passed one to me and raised his glass in a toast. 'Now we're gonna set 'em up. A couple of drinks tonight and then that's it until after the Arthur Fight. You'll do and listen to everything I tell you and I promise we'll knock that bastard out. Agreed?'

I clinked Billy's glass and we drank it in one.

'Agreed.'

Come the Monday I was first in at the Phoenix gym and straight down to business. The looks on people's faces as they arrived were priceless.

'Bloody hell, Michael,' smiled Ricky Hatton. 'Has Alison thrown you out again?' Billy came across to see me before heading into the office. He placed his hands on the punch bag to steady it.

'What's up with you Gomez, can't sleep?'

'I'm gonna listen to you, Billy. I'm gonna do exactly as you, Bobby and Kerry say and then I'm gonna knock Alex Arthur's fuckin' head off.'

'Fair enough,' he said, before walking off whistling. The message was clear, I was in the zone.

I had to get out of Manchester. There were too many distractions, so to ensure my mind stayed fully focused on the fight, I left where we were staying and moved in with Lumby's Mum and Dad at their farm in Rossendale, near the ski slope. I'd sprint up and down the steps of that bloody thing every day. His Dad, Derek, was my first-ever sponsor and a lovely man. There I ate my fresh chicken and broccoli prepared by Lumby's Mum, Beverley, and I drank, trained and dreamt Alex Arthur. I lived like a monk. In the mornings I'd go to the gym and then on my return I'd go for a seven mile run in the surrounding hills. Lumby had two mates who were with One Para; Lee and Dave. They were tough, super-fit lads, they ran with me. At first I struggled to keep up but it wasn't long before I was leaving them trailing. I was in the shape of my life and getting better and better. All the time I had one face on my mind; a Scotsman who in insulting my old man had unwittingly made the biggest mistake of his life.

One night myself, Lumby, his Mum and Dad were sat chilling out watching the television in their living room. The family had a ginger cat called Jack. A scrawny little thing. Or at least I thought it was. Suddenly Jack walked past us across the floor and I couldn't believe my eyes. It glared at us as if to say, what are you lot staring at?

'Jesus Christ!' I exclaimed. Pointing to it. 'What have you been feeding that? Look at the size of him!' Jack had magically transformed into a small leopard like creature with muscles leaping out of it and a body toning that defied belief.

'Oh my god,' uttered Beverley. 'I think I know what's happened.'

She rushed into the kitchen and returned with a chewed up box of my Pro MR from Kerry Kayes. Jack had discovered this and been eating it for the last four weeks. Around ten thousand calories a day! I've still got the image of this ginger leopard leaping through the fields of Rossendale. Nobody messed with Jack!

Something strange happened in the gym one day. Stephen Bell pulled me aside and said he'd been offered good money to go and spar with Alex Arthur, up in Edinburgh. Stephen was a good mate but this was our livelihood and we shook hands with no hard feelings. Billy called myself and Kerry into the office to discuss this. None of us could understand it. It didn't make sense. Stephen in no way resembled me as a fighter. He was totally opposite and had a stand up style that was much more Arthur's than mine, which is why he was my sparring partner in the first place.

Could it have been Arthur simply trying to sabotage my training? To this day we never got to the bottom of it. A footnote to this. On returning Stephen told me that before working with Arthur, he was convinced I never had a chance. But after experiencing both mine and his punches in the ring and comparing the power… 'Mike you hit harder,' he said, 'I think you're gonna knock him out.'

Billy Graham got twenty-eight-year-old Gary Hibbert from Oldham to replace Stephen. Gary was a good lad and another who before going in with me was convinced Arthur was all but certain to win the fight. However, after experiencing what was in my armoury he changed his mind. 'I feel sorry for Alex Arthur mate,' said Gary, 'He has no fuckin' idea what's coming his way.'

23: A TRAVELLER'S SOUL

'I don't try to intimidate anybody before a fight. That's nonsense. I intimidate people by hitting them.'

MIKE TYSON

I WAS SO CONFIDENT that I started to worry. I heard a line once about the great boxing journalist Hugh McIlvaney talking about how to beat George Foreman.

'There seems only one way to take down Foreman. Shell him for three days and then send the infantry in.'

That's how I felt!

Thinking back, I'm convinced now we had Alex Arthur beaten at our first press conference. I wanted to mess him up mentally. He'd always had everything his way up there and I had to change that. I put the head on him, stared and threatened him like he'd never seen before. Arthur wasn't scared but he was startled and didn't know how to react. I was firing off like a maniac and being told by Frank Warren to calm down. 'Michael, for God's sake, cool it! This isn't Braveheart the sequel!'

But I was gone. 'Let's make it winner takes all?' I said. 'Come on Alex, Mr fuckin' amazing.' Arthur kept on smiling and tried to ignore me. I needed to rattle and knock him off his perch. I could tell by his eyes he was uncomfortable. It was working.

Also, for some mad reason, Arthur kept calling me Michael Armstrong, as if this could possibly get under my skin. In truth it never bothered me but it did give me an idea for the fight. For the first time I'd fight with the family name on the back of my shorts. That way, when I knocked him out, he could claim in years to come of officially being beaten up by Michael Armstrong Gomez. Sometimes it's just best to keep your mouth shut.

In the following day's newspapers, Arthur spoke a lot more bravely than he had in my company. They couldn't shut him up. 'A war of words,' the papers called it, but when did anything written down ever punch you in the face?

'Gomez gets involved in wars and when I looked into his eyes at the press conference, I'm not sure even he believes he can win. It'll probably take me eight or nine rounds. But if his resistance has gone, as people are saying, it could be a lot sooner. I promise everyone I'm going to outclass him on 25th October. To be honest, I was more worried about Willie Limond, who was a tricky fighter to break down. But when I look at Michael, I see about twenty ways to win and I'm so just looking forward to shutting him up.'

Fuck me he could talk when I wasn't around.

I got a phone call off Thomas McDonagh to wish me luck. I asked after Brian and Thomas said he sent his regards. 'He said to tell you Mike. If you're fit, you win.'

That was music to my ears!

The night before the weigh-in, I was an absolute wreck. Overweight by five pounds, I was thinking crazy stuff. I was utterly paranoid. I was blaming the training, the supplements, the weather, Scottish sabotage; basically everybody and anything. My head was all over the place. My mood wasn't helped by Kerry Kayes not being able to attend the fight because of a previous obligation he couldn't get out of; a Mr Olympia weightlifting competition in Las Vegas. I missed not having Kerry around, not just because he was a genius at his job, but we'd also become close friends. I wanted him there.

There was a surprise when Kerry rang in my hotel room from Las Vegas and said he'd someone with him who wanted to talk to me.

'Hi Mike, it's Lou Ferringo. I'd just like to wish you all the best for your fight.'

I came off the phone in shock.

'Who was that ?' Asked Lumby.

'The Incredible Hulk,' I replied.

'Fuck me Mike' he said. 'I thought you was off the drugs!'

Also, for other reasons, Bobby Rimmer couldn't be in Edinburgh. He was another great guy who'd played a huge part in training me for the Arthur fight. I was certain though that when I entered that ring both men would be with me in spirit.

I was drinking nothing but water – I was starving and had stomach cramps. At just after nine o'clock in the evening I got on the scales and I was nine-nine and had to be nine-four by the following morning. It looked bad. I got off panicking and immediately text Kerry in Vegas:

'*Kerry, I'm nine-nine. You've got me wrong here mate.*'

Kerry texted back: '*Go to bed, you'll be okay and stop drinking the water*'.

I dozed off. The cramps were kicking in again. I was in agony. A couple of hours went by and I got up for the toilet then back on the scales, before jumping into bed. It just wasn't happening.

I text Kerry: '*Fuckin' ell mate, nine-seven and a half*'.

He replied straight away: '*Go back to fuckin' bed*'.

I'm half in and out of sleep. My mind was playing tricks. I'd almost convinced myself Kerry was working for Arthur. That was how messed up my head was. Time went on and I got up again. It was now twenty to five. Toilet and scales.

I text Kerry: '*Nine-six and a half.*'

Within a minute my phone beeped: '*Go back to bed*'.

An hour passed. I got up and back to the toilet and scales. Nine-five and a half. It was coming off and suddenly I thought it's not the end of the world because I could lose that in a sauna. Finally something was happening so I text him again: '*Nine-five and a half.*'

Kerry replied: '*Go back to bed*'.

I remember thinking if he text me that again I'm going to lose the fuckin' plot! I got back in the sheets and stared at the ceiling before dozing off for a short while. Then, on waking up, I was back to the toilet and scales once more.

I text Kerry: '*Kerry, nine-four and half.*'

He text back: '*Go back to bed.*'

By now I was really buzzing. Just half a pound over. Shortly after toilet, scales…Nine stone-four!…I'd made it!

I text Kerry with the words: '*You're the daddy!*'

He got right back: '*I know!*'

Kerry Kayes. The man! No words. Apart from go back to bed.

The weigh-in: Billy Graham pulled me aside just before we entered the room. 'What you're gonna do now Mike is fuckin' throw it on him. Get in his face and see how he reacts.' Billy was cute, he wanted to see if this guy really was as confident as he mouthed off in the press.

'The challenger to the scales!'

To a crescendo of Scottish boos I stripped off and stepped up. Absolutely spot on! There I was. Nine stone four, perfectly cut and in the best shape of my life. Frank Warren's face was a picture. He was sweating and pulling on his shirt collar. Warren, like the rest of the boxing world, had totally underestimated me. Only at that moment when I looked at him did I truly realise just how much I was there simply to be rolled over.

Warren turned to my manager Tom Jones. 'I've made a mistake here haven't I, Tom?'

'Oh yes,' he replied. Trying hard not to smile.

'And now the champion!'

With Flower of Scotland blasting out in the background and around three hundred mad Scotsmen joining in, Alex Arthur entered stage right. I started up. 'You're getting it boy! You're getting it big style! I'm like a caged lion, I'm possessed. Fuckin' champion? You're not gonna be the champion for much longer. I'm gonna knock you the fuck out!'

Arthur stepped off the scales and was called overweight. He was told to go away for an hour and was trying desperately to ignore me. First blood to me. He obviously hadn't been one hundred percent in training. Finally Arthur came back and made the weight. He stared across with a stupid smirk on his face.

'Too much haggis,' he said before winking at me.

They called for the head to head and this was music to my ears, everyone knew I was going to try and attack him. I went for it and started acting like a demented lunatic.

'Come on Alex! Come on, I'm gonna fuckin' spark ya!'

A rattled Arthur refused to take part. 'Michael can see my head tomorrow,' he said, before walking off. And then I knew it, I had him! I'd got under his skin. Billy Graham always claimed more fights are won and lost at the weigh-in than in the ring. Round One to Gomez. Billy and Kerry Kayes had done their jobs to perfection and now it was down to me. I wasn't in a mood to let anybody down.

The fight would take place at the Meadowbank Sports Centre. It held three thousand spectators whilst my ticket allocation was a measly fifty. It was made known to me early on that any supporters that wished to come and watch the fight live wouldn't be made welcome. It was going to be hostile. Alex Arthur was Edinburgh's Prince and everyone who lived there would be in his corner. I was hearing rumours of Hibernian and Hearts hooligans facing off and whoever won got to take them on. Not that the thought of trouble would be enough to put off any of my family or close friends. The sombreros were being passed around and they would be on full show in Edinburgh.

The Armstrongs and a small band of Mancs may have been

massively outnumbered and in fear of being lynched if I defied all odds and beat the local golden boy. But they were coming. Mad, loud and proud. Two minibus loads roared into the Scottish capital, but couldn't get a drink or a bite to eat anywhere, except MacDonald's. With music blaring, beer flowing and the well-known aroma of sweet smelling roll-ups drifting through the Edinburgh air, a small part of Manchester with an Irish heart and a traveller's soul had come to support one of their own. It promised to be a special night.

24: A MAN YOU DON'T MEET EVERY DAY

'My punches are just as hard in Chicago as in New York.'

SONNY LISTON

I JUST KEPT WALKING. He was 16-0; the pride of Scotland, the Prince of Edinburgh. In front of his people. His clan. I was supposed to be a stepping stone. A sacrificial lamb on the altar of an entire city who wanted me beaten up. I entered the arena and the hatred smacked me right in the face. I could smell the venom and taste the bile. The taunts and the insults flew like bullets and cut like daggers. But I kept on walking. 'Gypsy scum!' 'English bastard!' Didn't these Jocks know, I'm an Irish-Mexican! Alison was there with my sisters, my brother and a few friends. A small band of travellers and Mancs ringed by security and surrounded by a howling mob throwing pound coins. You can guarantee Bones never threw any back. I just kept walking. I reached the ring and they were spitting blood, their faces contorted, a raging mob trying with all their might to get under my skin. I just kept walking because this lot have obviously not heard. I'm a man you don't meet every day.

The hotel room was freezing cold, there was no room service. Nobody ever answered the phone. Yet it would ring and when I answered there was never anybody there. The sheets were dirty, the showers had no hot water. Call me paranoid but I was convinced Scotland was out to get me! I couldn't sleep, my mind was racing. Come the morning of the fight and after a restless night, I awoke to Lumby glaring at me like I had two heads.

'What are you looking at?'

'Jesus, Mike, the size of you? You're massive!'

I got up, rubbed my eyes, gazed in the mirror and couldn't believe what was staring back at me. Normally after the weigh-in I'd just stuff myself but this time I'd carried on with everything Kerry advised me to do. I was having cereal with Pro MR on it right up until going to bed. I was going to see this through. The result with sticking to the fitness plan was that my body on the day of the fight was, as they say in the body building game, complete. All the carbs and proteins had processed into what was looking back in the mirror. It was like I'd been pumped up. Kerry Kayes had built this warrior before me.

It was chemical warfare!

25-10-2003: Alex Arthur: I was never one for hanging around and so we arrived at the Meadowbank Sports Centre early and settled down in our dressing room. There was myself, Billy, Ricky Hatton, who would be in my corner, and Lumby. I was pacing up and down, repeating and screaming the same line.

'This kid's going bo-bos. Bo-bos!'

The others just left me to it. As I was getting my hands taped up Matthew Macklin and his younger brother Seamus entered. At the time Matthew was very pally with Arthur. Soon we'd also become good friends. He'd come in to wish me luck but my frame of mind was such I just erupted at him.

'Luck? I don't need luck, he's getting fucked!' Seeing I was almost demonic and best left alone, Matthew shook hands with Billy and Ricky and made a swift exit. Outside he came across Frank Warren in the corridor. Already fretting after seeing me at the weigh-in, Warren's mood was hardly helped when Matthew pulled him aside.

'I've just seen Gomez, Frank. I don't want to worry you, but he's

---

like a man possessed!'

Elsewhere, outside the arena, mayhem erupted when my supporters arrived and were made to take off their sombreros to have them searched. Alison, Val, Bones, they were all there to cheer me on. What on earth the police expected to find in them I'd no idea. Maybe they wanted them for souvenirs? We'd been around a little, we weren't that stupid. There were better places than under a hat to hide your stash! Finally, after an hour with v-signs and 'fuck you's' a plenty handed out, they were allowed in. Only to be greeted by a howling mob intent on making sure their short stay in the Scottish capital uncomfortable. My brother Bones led them in. My Bones. A thin line of security guards gathered to form a protective ring. The air grew thick with pound coins, it was poisonous. They walked through, had a look and thought, nothing special. Bring it on! Welcome to Edinburgh! Alex Arthur, you are going down...

Twenty minutes before the fight I'd switched off and for me that was strange. It wasn't normal. At this time I'd usually be head-butting lockers and roaring out what I was going to do to my opponent. I looked around the dressing room and it was almost serene. Billy and Ricky were equally quiet as they prepared their corner gear. I couldn't help thinking of the people who'd come to support me. Alison and my sisters in particular.

And then I realised the problem.

The noise from the Scots was already hammering through the dressing room walls. They were going absolutely mental and it was obvious to all that defeat was something Edinburgh would find hard to accept. If I dropped their hero, things could very easily get a little crazy in that crowd. The truth was I feared for my family.

Lumby noticed something was up and came over.

'Are you alright mate?'

'Yeah.'

'Are you sure?'

'Yeah, yeah I'm sure…Lumby, if I lose this fight, am I fucked?'

'What?'

'Be honest, if I lose this fight is it over?'

'Well… yeah.'

'Right then, do me a favour?'

'Anything mate.'

'Don't sit at ringside. Go and be with Alison and my sisters because it could get a little hairy'

'Why what do you mean?'

Suddenly even before I said the words, I could feel the mask come down and I knew Alex Arthur was in big trouble.

'Because I'm gonna knock him the fuck out.'

Lumby smiled and understood at that moment what was about to happen. He left to make his way towards Val, Alison and the rest through a screaming crowd hurling abuse at him.

I was told later how the conversation went.

It was Val who saw him first. 'What are you doing here?'

'Your Mike has asked me to come and stand with you lot.'

Something suddenly clicked with Alison. 'Lumby, is this what I think it is?'

She knew there was no way I was going to lose that night.

Lumby smiled wide. 'Hold on to your sombreros, ladies. Michael is gonna cause a riot and knock this fucker out!'

Billy Graham clapped his hands together. 'Right come on it's time Mike.'

'Good luck mate,' said Ricky. He gave me a hug and with the three of us donning our sombreros, we headed out the door straight into a tartan inferno. What awaited us was carnage! The noise as we headed towards the tunnel entrance was deafening. I took off my hat and threw it on the floor. This wasn't the time for fun and games. I was going to war.

Lighting the spark to fuel the fire, the master of ceremonies announced into his mic, 'Please enter into the arena. Michael Gomez!'

My music started up. As the Mexican dance tune skipped into life the Scots raised the decibel level even higher to drown it out. We appeared in full view, my eyes looking ahead, but in all honesty everything going on around me; the jeering, swearing, insults and screaming, it all blurred out. Around the arena a huge chorus started up with every Scot present seemingly joining in.

'Who the fucking hell are you?!'

A hail of abuse and a barrage of pound coins were landing on my supporters as they cheered me towards the ring. I'd have picked them up myself if I didn't have gloves on. The faces around us as we closed into the ropes were creased in fury and spitting venom. I was called everything and more! Hundreds of cameras and mobile phones clicked and flashed. It was blinding, deafening and utterly fuckin' outrageous. I loved it! A sea of Scottish hate and bile parting as we made our way through.

'Fuckin' ell,' said Ricky. 'This is worse than Old Trafford!'

As I prepared to kick-start World War Three, two of the people responsible for getting me to this peak level of fitness were working together to ensure they both kept in touch with the fight. Bobby Rimmer was sat with beer in hand, watching the fight at home, when suddenly his mobile phone rang. It was Kerry Kayes on from Las Vegas.

'Bobby, I need your help mate. I can't get the fight anywhere over here. Could you do the commentary over the phone for me?'

'No problem Kerry,' replied Bobby. 'Let's see if the mad bastard can pull it off! Right, well, he's just got in the ring and they hate him!'...

And so with Bobby relaying events to Kerry down the line, I got ready to climb through the ropes and see just what I'd be up against.

I wasn't disappointed. 'Who the fuckin' hell are you' came roaring out again from the Scottish crowd! Their fingers pointing towards me but did I care?

'I don't think they are very keen on you, Michael,' said Billy, with probably the understatement of the twenty-first century. I was pumped up like never before. My concentration at one hundred percent. I went to every corner and stared out at the crowd. I shadow-boxed. Billy was smiling and watching as I walked towards him. 'You show them,' he said.

'Ladies and gentleman we present the champion from the nation's capital, Edinburgh. The amazing Alex Arthur!'

Everything just went crazy! It was absolute bedlam! Suddenly I heard this really decent tune that snapped me back to reality. I remember turning to Billy

'Fuckin' ell that's a sweet song!'

There's me with my Mexican diddly-di music and Alex Arthur enters to Gospel Truth featuring Latasha Spencer. I did everything but join in.

On first seeing Arthur, the crowd ceased giving me grief for a while and turned their attention to welcoming in their hero. He was given a fantastic reception. The roof almost came off the arena. I had to hand it to the Scots, when it came to looking out for one of their own, they'd turned out in both force and fury. The next phase of the plan was to disrupt Arthur from his normal pre-fight ritual. I blocked him whilst entering the ring so he couldn't do his now customary forward roll. The experienced referee John Coyle, in his last fight, dragged me away, it was mission complete. I'd broken his rhythm. All these small things added up. Outwardly he appeared okay, but I knew that I'd shaken him.

Into full sight came Arthur, smiling wide and waving to the crowd, the golden boy in the golden robe with an eighty-seven per cent knockout ratio. The incredible noise increased. I spotted the odd sombrero scattered amid the ferocious home support. I knew for a fact some of Manchester's dark knights had come down off their own back and it would've been an extremely brave jock, or at least a very pissed one, who tried picking a fight with any of them.

A little bird told me that the previous evening Alex Arthur had bad mouthed me to Sky Commentator Ian Darke. 'The only thing that's worrying me about this fight is I'm not worried.' The lack of respect and utter contempt this man held me in only gave me more encouragement. I would make him pay a heavy price. And no better place to do it than here in front of his own people.

Coyle brought us together. 'Ok guys I'll ask you to do three things. Obey the rules, listen to my instructions and let's see good sportsmanship. Shake hands and good luck.' We touched gloves.

Just before the bell sounded Billy grabbed me. 'This is your time to make your name, Michael. You're gonna upset him and show them all!'...

On this winter's night in Edinburgh when the clocks went back, I threw off the weight of the bad years. The garbage, the drugs and the drink and then I caught Arthur with a left hook after just thirty seconds.

And I knew. I just knew!

A right hand shook him up and off I went. Punches rained in. He was upright and not moving his head. It was strange because it all felt too easy. I was catching him with ease. I looked in his eyes. He'd never expected this power. Arthur started to jab, trying desperately to keep me off balance, but I kept coming. 'I know twenty ways to beat Gomez,' he'd said beforehand. Well as I nailed him in the corner with another left hook landing on his chin, he must already have been regretting those words.

Finally Arthur came alive and he caught me with a right to the head. However two more of my left hooks to his body saw out the round and neither of us heard the bell through an explosion of sound!

They told me it was a classic start to the fight. I couldn't care less at the time, my only thoughts were to destroy him. Arthur was smiling on returning to his corner. He was trying to send a message to the crowd and all at ringside that everything was under control. But he couldn't hide it from me. His was a joker's smile. Beneath it Arthur was hurting and clearly thinking this man can dig and I've got a real fight on here.

Billy's instructions were simple. 'Don't let him settle. Get after him.'

Round Two. He came out firing his jab whilst I was trying to bob and weave, trying to get close and rough him up. Arthur's punches were sharp, accurate and at times painful. I had to admit this kid was good. He smiled at Barry McGuigan, who was working for Sky and again I thought, who the fuck does Alex think he's in the ring with? I'd make him pay for that.

A couple of my shots reached their target, but I was being easily out-boxed. The bell sounded and I'd struggled to get near. It was a masterclass of its kind, though one borne out of fear, because he knew to switch off for one moment could be fatal and goodnight. I wasn't going away.

Round Three began with fast, sharp, combination punching from Arthur. The left hook to the body was his trademark and only two men had ever lasted the distance with him. But I knew he was vulnerable and that in time he would leave his chin hanging out. I just had to make sure I was close enough to hit it when the opportunity arose. Arthur's precision shots were finding their mark and I got cut about the eye. This irked and served only to fire me onwards. I went left hook happy, I found a way in close and hurt him again. I couldn't believe how many times I was getting through. Hadn't he trained for this? Michael Gomez was noted for a left hook bomb and I was catching him with it at will.

Showing guts, he opened up. We were trading shot for shot and I caught him with another left hook that knocked his head right back. Arthur was shaken, the crowd suddenly panic stricken. I went in blasting. Four straight lefts. He got one back, but I was right in his face and up close. And then I cut him!

He was suffering and had a look on his face as if to say, 'God no!' This isn't supposed to be happening!' I just went swinging, left hooks crashing and every single one did him damage. He was hanging on. Jesus, I had him! I kept letting fly and he stood there. Reeling in pain, but refusing to yield. Go down you bastard, I thought. Just go down!

An ailing Arthur threw a flurry of right hands that almost screamed out in desperation for me to fuck off back to Manchester and leave him alone. There remained a minute of the round and I had to make my superiority count. I couldn't give him room to breathe, so in I went. A left hook over the top really hurt and he fell flailing against the ropes. I followed in and every punch was making him squirm. Arthur fought back, though it was instinct. His eyes looked past me. He was brave, but was getting the beating of his life. Ten seconds left and two monster left hooks almost finished him. He was hanging on by a thread. Almost down and out. I had him on the ropes. Another left hook, then another. He was ready to fall. Arthur was out on his feet, only to be saved by the bell.

I saw Frank Warren's face and he looked like he was watching his fuckin' house burn down. Never bet against a traveller's son who would only ever stop fighting when the good Lord wished it so. Warren was learning a bitter lesson that night in that bear pit of an Edinburgh ring.

It was carnage in Alex Arthur's corner. There was blood pouring from above his eye and around the mouth and a feeling of disbelief in the air. This Irish–Mexican, adopted Manc, born in a car crash, was wrecking their world.

Round Four. I came out determined to end it and let fly a flurry of left hooks that immediately had Arthur on the back foot and struggling badly again. I was all over him, left and rights. In close and then whack! From where I'll never know, but he found the strength and caught me with a big left hook that for a second put me in trouble. I was back in Dublin looking out at the sea. I heard the roar of the waves and then back to the crowd. It was savage. I was against the ropes and he unleashed everything in his armoury to see me off. Fair do's, but I survived.

Okay then, he wanted a fight so we went to war.

His right glove permanently low it was now a case of who got caught first. We were in the centre of the ring, going at it punch after punch. I was shattered, although I was prepared to fight all night. Every time I landed, he winced. I hit him and hit him and… this man had balls, but he was in big trouble. His left eye was badly cut and again my left hooks were almost knocking him off his feet. Arthur simply refused to go down. I was all over him, his worst nightmare, but he wouldn't go away. There may have been differences and upsets before the fight, but Alex Arthur was a warrior. I respected him for that.

Round Five. I was blowing heavily. 'Suck up now,' said Billy. 'Bide a bit of time.' I knew I daren't risk giving him a second wind. It was now or never. From the start we went at it from the centre of the ring. Arthur was fighting through a fog. His eyes were almost gone. Every shot I threw landed but he kept in there and then one of his body shots caught me and I was forced back onto the ropes! It hit so hard that I almost followed through! I pictured myself on *A Question of Sport* in years to come on the *What Happened Next* section? Luckily a right hook got me out of there and I grabbed and managed to break clear.

Back I went throwing bombs and the battle continued. Again it was a free for all, as we stood there swapping punches and every time I hit him he rocked and swayed like a fuckin' tree in the wind. Finally, after what felt like an eternity, yet another left hook sent him crashing to the canvas! He was human after all! Arthur got back up, smiling, talking to the camera. Trying to convince himself all was well. The referee's count reached three and signalled to fight on. Here on his own patch this man was being taken apart. All he had left was blind courage and a fighter's heart.

Two right hooks later Arthur went over once more. I remember thinking, don't you fuckin' dare get up Alex! But he did and took the nine count. With the referee seemingly content to give him a last lash we fought on. Two more left hooks followed by a right and this time around Alex Arthur went down and he wasn't getting back up.

It was all over!

Immediately I noticed a sombrero come flying into the ring! Billy came over and hugged me. He was smiling wide. 'I told you!'

I was beyond exhaustion. I thought of Alison and the kids, of Sam Parr, forever on my mind. I thought of my family. And then I thought 'I've done it!' My whole life had come down to this one fight and I'd pulled it off. I'd arrived at the pinnacle and I knew this was my heaven! I couldn't get any higher, no matter what happened in the future. No amount of drugs or drink could ever match this feeling.

Johnny Reed came into my mind. 'Never take a backward step Michael.' I hadn't and this had been the result. Alex Arthur never stood a chance.

For I am a man you don't meet every day…

In Las Vegas, at that moment Kerry Kayes was charging around screaming loud, 'Gomez has done it! He's only gone and fuckin' done it!'

Whilst Bobby Rimmer was dancing around his living room!

I owed both those boys.

Mayhem reigned in the ring. I wasn't keen on celebrating too much because Arthur appeared to still be in a bad condition on the canvas. Despite any bad mouthing and hostility that might have gone on, no way did I wish any further harm on him. It was a relief when he got up and came across. We embraced.

'A great fight,' said Alex. 'Congratulations.' Today, like so many other boxers I've met in the ring, we're good friends. But Alex Arthur will admit himself, although he'd go on to win belts and impress once more, both of us were never the same fighters. We left something more than blood and sweat in the ring that night.

Brutal and ferocious, that fight drained our souls.

'Ladies and gentlemen, after two minutes and fifty-eight seconds of round five, your referee John Coyle has dispensed with the count. The winner, by way of a technical count out. He is the new Super Featherweight champion of Great Britain. From Manchester, Michael Gomez!'

Boos and jeers rang out from everyone apart from my supporters who remained defiant and sang loud.

'And a round of applause please for a superb ex-champion, who I'm sure will come back from this defeat. Alex Arthur!'

Cue wild cheers and mass applause. I suppose the decision to keep my crowning short and sweet was understandable. I don't think anyone wished to inflame the crowd any further. Their shock at that moment would shortly turn to looking for someone to vent their wrath on. The sombrero-wearing Mancs, still dancing and singing, were a likely target. Our entourage soon found themselves being swiftly escorted out as the mood in the arena changed from utter bewilderment to raging fury! Once presented with the belt I went over to the ropes near to where my supporters stood. All were cheering in their seats. I spotted Alison. She was in tears and I mouthed the words over to her.

'I love you.'

And so I'd finally climbed to the top of the mountain. Not knowing then I'd reached my rainbow's end. What happened from that moment onwards would be a drop into an abyss so deep, it's hard to believe I'm still here to tell the story. The night Michael Gomez scaled the heights and brought down not just Alex Arthur, but an entire city.

I wish I could end it here but sadly life doesn't work like that.

25: DIRTY OLD TOWN

'I never cease to amaze myself. And I say this humbly"

DON KING

THE AMOUNT OF HUMBLE PIE being eaten in the Meadowbank Sports Arena that evening could have fed all of Edinburgh. None more than amongst the Sky Sports pundits. Jim Watt, for one admitted he'd been too hard on me throughout the years and cut across Barry McGuigan in a post-fight interview to praise me. 'Barry, can I stop you for a minute. This young man is totally incredible. Don't let us talk now about the mistakes Alex Arthur made, Michael Gomez was fantastic and I apologise that all through his career I've never given him the full credit he deserved. Gomez will get it [the credit] from now on. That was out of this world!'

I really appreciated that. I'd always been my own worst critic and could never really disagree with the points raised. I was also grateful that certain issues were skirted over and never brought into the wider public eye. They knew I was out of control between fights and not living the life I should have been but they'd always talk of 'other issues'. The feeling was now that I'd seen the light.

How little they knew!

In the lead up to Alex Arthur I'd lived the life and fought the good fight and now, in my eyes, I was free to reap the dividends. I was Michael Gomez! I was a champion and The Man again and I'm back!

Clubs, pubs, booze, cocaine and women. Here I come! The party truly began in the changing room. My mate Austin from Manchester had managed to talk his way past security and turned up to congratulate me. He came over. 'Put your gloves up Mike.' I did so and Austin sprinkled a long line of cocaine down on the top of them. I snorted it up in one go. Now I was ready to celebrate! Lumby came charging through the door. He told me there'd been hell to pay with the Scottish fans but the riot police had come charging in through a fire exit door and escorted our lot to safety. 'I've got a present for you Mike.'

Suddenly he produced a sign with *Champion* on that he'd ripped off Arthur's dressing room door. 'Congratulations mate!' For safe keeping his Mum and Dad have still got it in their barn at home with my signature on. Lumby made it back in one piece only with the aid of Ian McLeod, one of my former opponents. Surrounded by a load of Arthur supporters keen to tear him apart, McLeod put an arm around Lumby's shoulders saying 'Fuck off, he's with me!' Not willing to tackle one of their own, they did as they were told. Lumby passed a message onto me from McLeod. 'Tell Mike, fuckin' brilliant! It was wonderful chaos!' Suddenly a song broke out. 'There's only one *Racing Post*!'

The reason being this was the only newspaper that tipped me to win at 6/1. I asked Lumby about Alison and after being told Roger was looking after her, I relaxed and got ready to hit the town. She couldn't have been in better hands. Only then to be told I had to go to the post-fight press conference.

I wasn't interested so I turned up for it in my boxer shorts. Much to Sky and Frank Warren's dismay. I looked around and it was clear nobody was happy! But did I care? I mumbled a few words and was off. I knew when I wasn't wanted. One journalist did tell me that Arthur had been rushed to hospital and that shocked me. 'I came to win a boxing match not to hurt anybody.' But that apart I couldn't get away quick enough. There'd been no congratulatory handshake, not even a well done off Frankie boy. I seemed to be in his bad books by winning - so much for treating me like cannon fodder and trying to do a number on me! My heart fuckin' bled for him! I'd also found out my cut for the fight had been dropped from twenty five grand to seventeen and a half. If there was a reason for this, I never found out but at that time I just wanted to get out of there and start partying.

Finally, after Billy and Ricky had cleared off, it was just me and Lumby left. Warren's *Sports Network* had laid on a Chrysler car with blacked out windows to take us back to the hotel but I had other ideas. I was sore but the sheer adrenaline and of course the cocaine soon spruced me up and I felt ready to drink and snort Edinburgh dry. With the Lonsdale belt in one hand and my face bruised to hell, I tapped the driver on the shoulder.

'Take us to the nearest strip club mate.' We were driving down Princes Street and the pavements on both side were filled with hundreds of gutted Alex Arthur fans, who had just seen their night ruined by a loud-mouth Manc. I couldn't resist it. I wound down the window, stuck my head out, waved the belt in the air and started to sing.

'Gomez he's from Manchester!'

Lumby and the driver were not impressed and neither were dozens of irate Scots who chased us up the road throwing bottles.

We arrived at the strip club and got out of the car. Immediately the doormen recognised me and came over. There I was, looking like I'd done twelve rounds with Mike Tyson. Grinning wide with belt in hand and desperate for a beer and more. One of them walked up to me and pointed to the car. 'Gomez, you mad bastard. Get the fuck back in the car for your own safety.' By this time others had noticed who I was. They were shouting over and it was growing a little nasty. Realising things could get quickly out of control, the doormen threw me and the belt back in the Chrysler and we headed off to the hotel.

Once I got back in the room I was manic and running around

like a lunatic.

'I told them I could do it. Nobody fuckin' believed me. I fuckin' told them!' Lumby asked who I wanted back at the hotel. We'd a private bar to ourselves and had to keep it quiet because I was public enemy number one in Edinburgh that evening. The local pitchfork and burning torches brigades were out in force. Val, her husband Steve, Bones, the Bridgewater Security lads, Anthony and Mark and the Para boys who helped me with my training up in Rossendale, Lee and Dave. We quickly clocked that the Polish barman wasn't the brightest so we signed every drinks chit to Frank Warren and put it onto Billy Graham's room.

Around two in the morning, with the party in full flow, I slipped off back to the room. There Sky Sports were re-showing the fight and for the first time I sat down and watched it. The emotions were weird. I still felt every punch from Alex Arthur and wondered what he was thinking at that moment? When the fighting was done and you were left with nothing but your thoughts. I prayed for him in hospital and asked God that he let Alex come through okay.

I got a call off Austin. He was in a nearby hotel with some friends and said for me to come over. He'd just bought a load of Moet champagne that had my name on it! A black cab was called and soon we were having a drink with my mate from Heywood. He had two soldier lads with him. One was a pain in the backside who insulted Val and for his troubles got a clip off Lumby. Austin swiftly broke it up and told his mate to go to bed. 'That's Mike's sister and his best mate you've upset. So make sure your bedroom door is fuckin' locked before you go to sleep.'

The more I drank, the more sober I got; the cocaine, the adrenaline. I didn't really need the booze or drugs because I was still so hyped up from the fight. The craziness went on. It was a night I never wanted to end but sadly everything does and come morning it was time to mend sore heads, a few fences and pay up what was owed.

On checking out we were handed a bar bill of £1500!

Running out of the main doors being chased by the reception staff was no longer an option, seeing as I was now, once more, the British Super Featherweight champion and on the back of all the Sunday newspapers and Sky Sports News every hour. No, more thought was needed and so we resorted to type. Myself and Lumby did a tactical retreat before escaping with our bags down a fire escape at the side of the hotel. Sadly, there was no happy ending as the bill was passed on to *Sports Network* and Frank Warren deducted it from my fee.

On the journey home we stopped off at a service station and I was mobbed by a coachload of football fans on their way to a match against Hibs in Edinburgh. The shout went up. 'It's him! It's Michael Gomez!' Over they came, everybody wanting a picture or an autograph. I was signing porno mags, newspapers, tee shirts, arms and legs. It was madness and I loved it! The cocaine, the booze, the adulation, a constant high…

'Gomez we love you man.'

'You nailed him Mike.'

'Well done Mike.'

'Gomez, you're the fuckin' man!'…

Ten weeks of carnage began. On arriving in Manchester it was straight to the Kestrel where I wasn't allowed to buy a drink.

'What are you having Mike?'

'I'm buying Mike.'

They sat me down and they gathered around and I told them about how I smashed Alex Arthur in his home town and shocked the fuckin' world.

I was back to the traveller. Back to the rum bastard I am. I'm drinking and snorting and I'm talking. And all they are talking about is my fight. The best conversation we could have! We are talking about me. It's all about me. We're talking about how good I am. I'm the man! I'm the man! And I'm drinking double Jack Daniels and lemonade...

And it was all about me!

'Set em up Roger. It's gonna be a long night... keep 'em coming!'

Zulu Dawn: There was no end to it; myself and Lumby arranged to meet Matthew Macklin in Birmingham. What began as a supposed catch up after the Arthur fight rapidly turned into a three-day bender where most of what happened is a blur, apart, that is, from its so-nearly explosive finale. With Birmingham City's top boys from their hooligan firm The *Zulus* in tow we ended up at a house party in an area called Hollywood on the outskirts of the city. At first all was good. They were friends of Matthew's so we appeared to have a pass with our hosts. That was until one of them turned to Lumby. 'Hey Manc muppet, get me a beer out of the fridge.' Lumby tried to laugh it off but this guy was serious. He said it again. 'Are you fuckin' deaf Manc muppet? Get me a beer.'

That was it - up I sprung. 'Who the fuck do you think you're talking to? Outside now! Two of us against any two of you.'

They must have thought I was mental considering the odds but I was deadly serious. Nobody moved until Matthew stood up. 'Right lads, enough. 'Mike is my guest, this isn't happening.' Still they stared and then I totally lost it.

I picked out their main man who was giving me daggers. 'If you're thinking of doing anything ya better fuckin' kill us because if you don't, next weekend, you'll wake up and there'll be so many fuckin' travellers outside this door you're gonna think it's Saint Patrick's day.'

For a moment it remained up in the air and then I heard a voice speak up.

'Somebody get this Manc a drink. I think he needs one.'

That broke the ice and suddenly everybody laughed and we

were all friends again. But it was close. I just couldn't help it, I never back down. Never.

You can blame Johnny Reed for that.

Speedboat: I was bored and had a hangover. Needing a day off to dry out a little, I rang Lumby. 'I've got an idea that doesn't involve getting hammered. Are you in?'

I've always loved model boats, trains and planes. Now with money in my pocket it was time to play around. We drove to Ashton and visited a model shop. Browsing around I saw a speedboat that looked mint.

'How much mate?'

'Two thousand pounds, sir.'

'Go on, I'll take it.'

Lumby stared at me like I was mad. 'Mike are you sure? That's a lot of money for a toy.'

But I was determined and couldn't wait to test it. So off we went and found a suitably sized lake in Boggart Hole Clough. Going off the picture on the box I unpacked it and put the batteries in the remote control. I was like a big kid and couldn't wait to put my new speedboat on the water. Lumby was staring at the instructions with a worried look on his face. 'Hang on a minute Mike. This isn't as straightforward as you think.'

But I wasn't listening. Oh no. Captain Fuckin' Gomez was away. In it went and at the start all was plain sailing. I scattered the ducks, annoyed the swans. Then, after going around in a circle and another it took off in a different direction to what I wanted. At first I thought it was the remote but then it just stopped and to my horror slowly started to sink. I panicked and jumped in; I was up to my waist as I waded out and ducked down to pick it up. The motor had completely burnt out. It was ruined. I felt like the Captain of the Titanic and at that moment wished I'd gone down with it.

'You should have let me read these first, idiot,' called out Lumby holding up the instructions. I struggled out of the water dripping, drenched and depressed.

I could tell Lumby was dying to laugh but seeing how fed up I looked thought best of it. 'So what do we do now shipmate?' he asked

No way was I giving up. 'I'm gonna buy another one.'

Off I walked with my boat in hand. Devastated.

'More money than fuckin' sense, Gomez,' I heard Lumby shout. Then again, that wouldn't be hard. Once back at the shop something else caught my eye. A remote control helicopter. Suddenly I was buzzing again. The carnage and fun I could have with one of those was endless. Sadly you needed a licence so instead I bought another speedboat.

And sank it.

The Press Club: Founded 1870. As drinking haunts in late night Manchester went, this place was legendary. Once the pubs and clubs called last orders and you fancied a proper all-nighter then you'd head there. It never seemed to shut and for me it was heaven on earth. Sat minding its own business on Queen Street near the Opera House off Deansgate, the Press Club was home to a chosen few. You wouldn't know it was there apart from two plaques fixed to an outside wall. The clientele were hand-picked. Not any Tom, Dick or Gomez was allowed through the door. You needed to be somebody to enter and to ensure this rule was strictly adhered to was a doorman known as H. This was not a man to cross. H's word went. No arguing otherwise you'd get it. He was a gentleman until pushed.

'Not tonight, lads.'

'Be good now and go somewhere else, eh. Like bed.'

'Never heard of you mate. Now fuck off before I lose my rag!'

That was H.

Many times in days following a good win I'd head there thinking, 'well I've been on the television and in the newspapers. Surely H will let me in?' But oh no, it never happened.

'Sorry Michael we're full mate. Come back when you've knocked out Naseem fuckin' Hamed.'

And then the keys to the kingdom showed themselves after beating Alex Arthur. I was out with Lumby one night and I decided now or never, more in hope than anything else. We set off down Quay Street and past the Grapes pub. Around the corner from the Opera House and there he stood. Breaking hearts and heads; H.

I approached him and felt his eyes fall upon me. Here we go again, I thought. Another knock back. And then to my shock H smiled wide.

'Gomez, what a fuckin' win! We're proud of you son. In you go.'

He opened the door, patted me on the back and we was in. Little did H know what he'd let himself in for. Once inside, my eyes lit up. It wasn't much to look at but the Press Club was *the* place; a drinking den with real class and atmosphere. Everybody mixed. There were no airs or graces, just drinking and drinking...

Away in the darkened corners I spotted celebrities; soap stars, footballers, journalists, policemen, powerful businessmen, gangsters, lawyers, judges and local politicians. This was where the wheels of the city were oiled and greased; deals were done on a wink, a line and a handshake.

'We'll sort it. Your problem is now ours. He won't fuckin' bother you no more.' It could be a crooked councillor or the local mobster... this was a world away from the light, forever in the shade. Once H let you past, there were few rules except whatever happened in the Press Club, stayed in the Press Club.

I had some memorable nights in there and more than my fair share of scrapes. One night I remember trying to get the ex-Manchester United player Paul McGrath on the cocaine but he wasn't having it. I didn't care because it just meant more for me. We did have a good booze with him though and ended up driving all the way to his huge house in Hale where the plan was to continue the party, only to see through the gated doors that his wife had thrown all of Paul's clothes out on the lawn and she wasn't letting him in.

Another night it so nearly went off with the Donnelly brothers, Christopher and Anthony. Again it was drunken madness. We got into a daft game. They bought one bottle of champagne so I got two. Then three and so it went on. Words were said until calmer heads prevailed and matters calmed. I was never one to back down but those boys were equally serious. Before the *Gio-Goi* days everybody knew they were not known to fuck around with rumoured links to the *Quality Street mob*. Me, I'd be too far gone on the booze and cocaine to care.

I was gathering a reputation as a huge pain in the arse. There were times a gang of us would walk into nightclubs and just take over. I'd be on the dance floor ballooning on. I'd grab some girl who was out with her boyfriend and it would just explode; glasses flying, there would be blood spilt and we'd be scrapping. Friends of mine would get a kicking, one almost lost an ear but I just couldn't help it. An adrenaline rush. I got bored and just wanted a fight. That was me back then. Come the morning I'd remember nothing. If I needed to apologise, half the time I wasn't even sure what I was apologising for.

Word got back to the Mullens at Bridgewater Security who happened to run most of the doors in Manchester where I'd been playing up. Anthony called me. 'We're hearing crazy things. Just fuckin' calm it, Mike. Nobody needs the hassle.'

I took their friendly advice on board but only to a point.

I got invited to the Prestwich and Whitefield Manchester City Supporters Club branch to sign autographs and present the prizes in a raffle. As ever Lumby was alongside me and I took my Lonsdale Belt to show people. They are a welcoming bunch at Prestwich and it turned into quite a session. By closing time I'd had more than a skinful and as a bonus to the free hospitality, got lucky in the raffle and won a bottle of House of Commons whiskey signed by Tony Blair. We said our goodbyes and headed home in a taxi back to Moston. Talking away we settled in the front room and I couldn't resist.

'Get the fuckin' Blair open!'

Hours later Lumby glanced around the room and with a look of sheer horror on his face.

'Mike where's the Belt?'

'You had it?'

'No I fuckin' didn't! You did!'

For a second I panicked. We ran outside and there it was. Still leaning against the window in the front garden where I'd left it after getting out of the taxi. For five hours the twenty thousand pound Lonsdale Belt had sat there in the middle of Moston and not been stolen. I was starting to think it had a charmed life.

'You lucky bastard,' smiled Lumby. 'Somebody is looking after you Michael.'

If so then it was definitely a full-time job.

On the home front events were crazier than ever. Either somebody hit the wrong person or someone's door was going in. It never ended. Every weekend was mayhem with one or more of the family either causing or getting grief. Even when I stayed home I'd be dragged in to help sort matters out.

I swear to God trouble lived alongside me.

And never more than one particular night when a whole load of family and friends were involved in a bar brawl in a Harpurhey pub. It began when one of my sisters was insulted and her boyfriend went mad and attacked the guy, to the extent that he bit his ear off and the man ran screaming in pain through the fire door, leaving his ear behind on the floor. Knowing he had to come back for it they put the ear in a glass with lemons and water and left it on the bar. Twenty minutes later the man returned waving a kitchen knife and screaming like a banshee. Sadly for him he was quickly disarmed by a flying chair and given a good hiding. On leaving this time around the man was given his ear to take with him. Whoever said the Armstrongs weren't generous?

Thinking all was now over they settled down, only for the sound of the pub doors bursting open later in the evening as the Noonan clan arrived tooled up with guns and axes and ready for war. It turned out the man in question was close to one of the brothers. Now I knew the late Damien Noonan quite well, when he noticed my family was involved I immediately got the phone call.

'Michael we've got a serious problem mate and it needs sorting.'

A few times Damien had saved my neck; once he stepped in to avoid me being shot in the leg in a revenge attack. One word from him and the trouble ended. This man was the real deal.

The next day I met Damien in a Harpurhey car park with Mr one ear and the lad who bit it off. It was agreed there'd be no bad blood. The two shook hands and peace was declared. But it'd been close to all-out war on the streets of North Manchester over one stupid insult. Happily it all ended well for once. Like I said, trouble lived with me every waking hour in this dirty old town. It really was time to get back in the ring.

26: BUTTERFLY

*'Live everyday as if it were your last
because someday you're gonna be right.'*

MUHAMMAD ALI

3-4-2004: Ben Odamattey: I got the call off Billy Graham that I was
to fight Welshman Gavin Rees for the vacant WBU World Super
Featherweight title at the Nynex. I refused offers to go back and train
up in Rossendale because I simply didn't think I needed it. In my
own mind, if I could destroy Alex Arthur like I had what chance did
this man have against me? Then Rees was forced to pull out through
injury and in came Eric Odumese from Ghana, only then for an
injury to affect him.

Finally a third opponent was named, another Ghanaian, Ben
Odamattey. At the press conference I told Odamattey straight. 'I'm
gonna knock ya the fuck out.' Not surprisingly he didn't take kindly
to this and all hell let loose. His trainer pulled him away and glared
across at me with a real look of disdain.

'Who do you think you are? You don't just knock out African
fighters Michael. This will go twelve rounds.'

But I wasn't having it. 'I'm gonna fuckin' spark him. And then
you!'

He simply shook his head. 'We shall see in the ring young man.'

The head to head saw me attempt to head butt Odamattey but
this time around he stayed cool and simply laughed it off. A grinning
Frank Warren pulled us apart. 'Take it easy Michael. Two have already

pulled out, I don't want another one.' At least Warren was smiling again.

I'd been firing in the gym and tore holes out of a light welterweight who I was sparring with. He pulled up, forcing Billy to end the session early.

'Ease off a little Mike. Don't burn it. This Odamattey is a strong kid.'

I was lean, mean and happy to be back in the day job. My last shot at this title ended when Brian stopped me against Kevin Lear and I'd no intention of losing out again. As the fight closed in I moved into a flat with Matthew Macklin, just around the corner from the Phoenix gym. The idea was that there I would behave and get a good night's sleep. At home it'd been hard to concentrate on Odamattey when the kids were at my feet all the time, or watching the Teletubbies on the television. Whereas all I had in mind there was ripping somebody's head off. Well I'd love to say that's what happened but it was a case of if I could, I would and Matthew was staggered at my behaviour. I went easy on the booze and cocaine but the ladies? Oh the ladies! Now that I was away from home, I simply couldn't help myself.

'Gomez,' asked Matthew. 'Where do you get the fuckin' energy?'

I had to win this fight because if I came through it then I was after a real name, one that would catapult me onto the world stage. Superstars such as Eric Morales and Diego Corales were in my sights. I knew it really was now or never and I couldn't afford a slip-up. As to whether I'd ever be offered such a contest was the only doubt in my mind. I knew my beating up of Alex Arthur had put a lot of noses out of joint but if I kept winning they'd be left with no option but to give me a shot at the big boys.

Or so I thought.

It was a three round slaughter against Ben Odamattey. I was fast and on him from the first bell. I didn't give him room to breathe. I let fly with everything in my armoury. Left and right hooks, upper cuts, body shots and right crosses. Odamattey was caught in a whirlwind and couldn't hold me off. It was vicious and brutal but I had to make a point and nail this guy fast.

I hit him with everything I had. The shots rocked Odamattey badly and I put him down in the second for a standing eight count. From that moment on it was a matter of when, not if. Come the third I battered him into submission and in the end he all but surrendered. It'd been a blast and proved that the win over Arthur was not a one-off but actually the rebirth of Michael Gomez. After the fight, sat at ringside, I spoke to Adam Smith of Sky Sports. Adam asked me if I fancied a rematch with Alex Arthur? Although I'd prefer Corales or Morales there was big money on that contest but I doubted Arthur would ever want to tangle with me again.

'Adam, you want it. Sky TV wants it. The public wants it. Frank Warren wants it.'

I look around the arena.

'But where's Alex? Anyone seen Alex?'

Sadly it never happened.

25-2-2004: Justin Juuko: I was told many times in the lead up to this fight that the thirty-one-year-old Ugandan was a dangerous opponent. Well, I was the one defending the WBU Super Featherweight title, last time I looked it was my name on the belt and far be it for me to boast but I could be pretty fuckin' dangerous if the mood arose. Juuko had an impressive cv, he'd taken part in some fantastic battles against some of the world's great fighters and had defeated a number of our top domestic names including Charles Shepherd and Gary Thornhill. On a higher level he'd been in with the very best but lost to Floyd Mayweather Jr, Diego Corrales, Miguel Cotto and Carlos Hernandez.

I assured everyone that what happened to Thornhill and Shephard wouldn't be happening to me. In years past Juuko was an opponent many boxers might have avoided. He was rough, tough and could bang. The rumours were he was on the slide but I wasn't taking any chances. I trained like mad, I did everything right. I'd worked hard to improve my footwork and moving my head. Also, with there being only a short spell between this and the Odamattey fight, there was little chance of me going too far off the rails. I was back in the flat near the gym with good intentions. Just fighting and knocking Juuko back to Uganda on my mind. Well almost! Again Matthew looked on with a mixture of shock and admiration as he walked into the kitchen every morning and there'd be a different girl sat having a tea or coffee. Or in more dodgy cases going through the drawers looking for money!

As far as I was concerned, from that point on in my career, with time running out, I only wanted wars in the ring. No easy nights. I appreciated the paychecks off Uncle Frank, but there was a part of me, the gypsy heart I suppose, that loved a tear up. Outside the ropes this got me in endless scrapes but inside I was given free rein to wreak mayhem.

I'd already proved myself at British, and European level. It was time for the world to see that the kid born in a car crash, who'd robbed, loved, risen, died, shocked the world and partied like it would end in the next half hour, was the real deal. Ranked number five in the WBO and WBA, I could make a real statement by doing a job on Juuko; after all it'd taken Mayweather ten rounds and Corales nine to overcome him. But Morales remained my main target. If I could drop Juuko double quick and somehow make myself a mandatory challenger, then no amount of politics could ultimately prevent my shot against 'El Terrible.' It was all about getting close enough, so close that you could rattle, intimidate and dent their pride. Infuriate them and then ultimately get them in the ring.

I was good at that!

Fighting in my second home (Widnes) I put Juuko down after

just eleven seconds with a left hook. It was a mismatch and the more I caught him the more wound up I became. I wanted a war not a slaughter. I went after him with everything I had. It wasn't a boxing match, more a mugging. A beating. Juuko was a washed-up fighter, but that wasn't my problem. A single mistake and he could still flash one and catch me out. So I was relentless with no mercy.

The bell sounded and Billy was happy enough.

'You're doing great Mike. The only way he's gonna beat you is if you're not aware of what's coming back. Now go and get him!'

There was nothing coming back at all from a man who once created havoc at this weight. Juuko couldn't lay a glove on me. The second round was no different. I saw no lack of courage in his eyes, just desperation and a hopelessness that he couldn't keep me off. I almost felt sorry for him. Almost. When the end came it was swift and painful and achieved without breaking sweat. As the referee Mickey Vann stepped in, I thought job done, but was left also feeling a little empty. This hadn't been why I trained so hard. I'd got myself in shape for a proper battle and felt cheated. Then again, don't forget this man had been in with the best and what I'd done to him felt, even to me, cruel.

In the interview for Sky Sports, post-fight, I couldn't hold back and let fly.

'I was the one who said to Billy I didn't want to fight Juuko because I thought he was a fighter on his way down. I want to be in wars! I want to get in there and get hurt. I want to take risks, maybe get knocked out. I want real fights for these supporters. I want the top names.'

Of course all this was out of my hands. All I could do was keep winning and keep up the pressure. Sometimes faces just don't fit. Maybe it was payback time for when I refused to play by the rules but I doubted my dream fight against Eric Morales would ever come about. It was simply a case of keeping my fingers crossed and knocking over whoever they put in my path.

1-10-2004: Levan Kirakosyan: Four months after I took apart Justin Juuko, I was back in the ring at the *MEN* Arena against this tough, durable and hard-punching, thirty-one year-old Armenian. During the weigh-in I was being watched closely by officials who had warned me beforehand to behave. 'That's enough now Michael. Any trouble and you'll be fined.'

But something always just snapped with me at this pre-fight stage. I was coiled like a spring. When I got close to Kirakosyan I couldn't help myself and just went for him. Fuck the consequences. I needed to do this; it was a state of mind verging on madness that said I was ready to fight the whole world if need be. I was a snarling, wild-eyed lunatic who walked that thin line between sanity and madness. 'Possessed' I've heard it called. I wouldn't argue with that. I looked at Kirakosyan afterwards and I'd rattled him, his poker face startled and he stared at me like I was nuts. Mission complete...

I appeared to be edging closer to a breakthrough in the ratings. I was placed number five by both the WBA and WBO, whilst the IBF had me at ten. To get near a shot at the big boys this was where I had to be. But one mishap and I was sure they'd dump me so fast, I'd be back in the abattoir punching slabs of meat and selling shit cakes again. Against this opponent I had to take care of business and look good doing it. Kirokysan came with a reputation of being a banger. Billy Graham warned me he'd put away Giuseppe Laurio in three rounds, that was a lot faster than Ricky Hatton could, I was ready. I was primed. I'd claimed after the Juuko fight that I wanted to be involved in wars and for six exhausting rounds I got one off the hard hitting Kirakosyan.

I finally finished it in the sixth when his corner retired him with eye damage, but he'd given me all kinds of trouble. At times such was his power that I found myself back pedalling, not through choice, just his sheer power rocked me. I started well and dominated for the first three rounds. I was catching him and he was bleeding from both eyes by then. However, as I looked to open up, Kirakosyan threw caution to the wind and had a right go. At the end of round five Billy was starting to sound a little worried. 'Claim him, Mike. Claim him!'

I looked at Billy quizzically. With the crowd noise and the punches slamming into my face I was confused. I respected Billy immensely but I really didn't think it was the right time to put a claim in? Kirakosyan delivered a couple of bombs that hit home and come the finish it was with a huge relief that I finally got him out of there. Whether I'd shown enough for the sanctioning bodies to warrant a big title shot was another matter. Did I have the necessary backing? I remained doubtful.

At ringside I listened on to Frank Warren talking to Ian Darke, after interviewing me. 'Frank, Michael is rated in the top ten of the WBA, the WBO and the IBF. At twenty seven is it time to strike?'

'It certainly is and that's what we'll be working on now and in the New Year hopefully Mike will get his chance.'

I listened on and watched Warren's eyes. I could always tell.

'Which avenue will you be exploring?'

Warren appeared a little rattled. 'Like I said, we'll look at the best one and make a decision next year?'

Darke turned back to me. 'Who do you want?'

'I want to fight one of the top guys because I've been around ten years now. I want the best in the business. I love a fight. You've seen what I gave the crowd tonight. I want to fight Eric Morales. I want to be in a top-class war. I've made my mark on British boxing when I beat Alex Arthur. Now I want to make it on the world scene with Morales.'

I wasn't holding my breath. Meanwhile as the future was seemingly being sorted, I thought fuck it, I'll take a break. Time to chill...

I was off to Thailand!

Fool's Paradise: With thirty-five grand in my pocket from the Kirakosyan fight I had money to burn. Plus I'd never stopped dabbling in selling the cocaine, weed and whizz so it was a case of bring it on! I'd heard so many good things about Thailand. Together with two mates, Steve and Paul, we embarked on the eleven hour flight for a week's sampler. The plan undoubtedly involved booze and bar girls, not so much the drugs because we'd heard the police didn't mess around over there. Also we had the idea of seeing the country. Take in the sights. Three lads from Moston expanding their horizons. Oh we did that alright, although mostly it was done from the comfort of a bar stool and a girl on each arm!

I wasn't too sure at first because I loved going out and being recognised. I adored the attention. In Manchester it helped with getting in the clubs and with the ladies. But who'd know me over there? Boy was I wrong! We landed at Bangkok airport and the first thing that hit you was the stifling heat when disembarking from the plane. It was a furnace till you got used to it. After gathering our suitcases we hunted down a taxi limo and drove to Phuket.

There, I thought I'd died (again) and gone to gypsy heaven!

The hotel was stunning. After dumping our stuff in the bedrooms we headed off to the roof where there was a bar and swimming pool. With the sun beating down from a crystal blue sky I was living the dream. As darkness fell and a few liveners had been put away the time came to see what all the fuss was about. In we went to put on our best clobber and aftershave.

I'd bought myself a whole heap of stuff whilst on a bender in Birmingham. Including a £280 Armani shirt that was so bright and garish you needed shades to look in the mirror. Alison hated it, she thought it was horrible.

'You look like a pimp!'

BUTTERFLY

We needn't have bothered, as I soon discovered. Here in Thailand you could walk about in a thong with skid marks and so long as you had money, nobody would care. Soon it would just be vests, shorts and flip flops for us, but not that night! We were dolled up, looking sharp and loaded!

Then we heard it.

On walking out of the hotel a massive scream broke out from all the bar and street girls. Hundreds of them! 'Sexy men!'

'You come see me Sexy men!' I'm sure at that moment I waved. I do remember turning to Paul and Steve and with a glint in my eye declaring loud. 'I fuckin' love this lads!'

We didn't need to be asked twice and strode right into their midst. Just for that split second it felt like being in a boyband, albeit one with a little fuckin' Moston edge! Our big plans of seeing the real Thailand disappeared in a flash and that opening evening was spent in the first bar we entered!

Paul got off immediately with a girl called Nam whilst I got friendly with her mate, April. Before the week was out I'd also gone through May, June, July and August! It was mayhem. Happy go lucky sex, booze and utter carnage. Everything went and nothing was out of bounds. After that first night we moved around and discovered some crazy places. There were so many bars and you were allowed to put money down on a girl, around twenty quid and she'd wait for you. I was all over! I was leaving money everywhere we went! My own private fan club. This was why they called it a fool's paradise. Because everything was so cheap you'd leave huge tips and do crazy things. Gomez was feeling the love again!

One night we staggered into a place that had a boxing ring where customers could get in and chance their hand against whoever was up for it. Well for me Christmas morning had arrived! Birds, booze and boxing! Immediately I thought, I'm having this! Only when stepping up, the manager, an old Thai guy with more scars on his face than a fuckin' Harpurphey stray cat, stood in my way. I offered him the money asked, five hundred Baht, but the old man shook his head and grabbed me. He took one look at my hands, staring close at the knuckles. Then a quick glance at my flattened nose before shaking his head. 'You no fight,' he said. 'You fighter. You dangerous man.'

I was disappointed, although he did have a point and probably saved my neck (not to mention somebody else's). I was out of my head on booze and if I had got rattled in there, I could have done some serious damage to an unsuspecting opponent.

The next day, after staying in bed with a savage hangover, I finally rose and went out for some fresh air. As I left the hotel a dozen of the bar girls opposite waved across and smiled in my direction. They suddenly started shouting. 'Ah Mike Butterfly! Mike Butterfly!'

I was thinking what the hell is going on? A young Thai lad stood nearby burst out laughing on hearing the girls. I approached him. 'Do you speak English mate?'

He nodded.

'What are they saying about me?'

'They are saying you like a butterfly. That you float from girl to girl!'

I started to smile. What a fuckin' compliment! Well if it was good enough for Muhammad Ali, it was good enough for me!

On coming home we lasted a week and then I made the decision of going back to Thailand for a fortnight. All ideas of staying in shape, training and condition and indeed more importantly being a good husband and Dad vanished with the thoughts of what lay in wait in that fool's paradise.

This butterfly wanted to simply spread its wings and go float some more!

27: RAINBOW MAN

'I've found that taking short cuts will get you to the place you don't want to be much quicker than they get you to the place you want to be.'

LENNOX LEWIS

WITH ALISON AND THE KIDS away visiting relatives, I was alone in the house. It should have been the perfect opportunity to knuckle down and concentrate on getting back in shape, but oh no, that was the signal to go wild! I was free! I had money in my pocket and I just went ballistic. I erupted! I went out to the pub every evening. I was arguing, causing grief and fighting. I was snorting cocaine, I was smashing E's. I was drinking loads of beer. I was drowning in Jack Daniel's. I was seeing a different girl every night. I was out of control and piling on the weight. I was getting away with murder and being pulled by everybody telling me to calm down.

'Mike what the fuckin' hell? Wind it in.'

They were all in my ear; Billy Graham, Pat Barrett, Bobby Rimmer, Kerry Kayes and others but I wasn't listening. I was in a Moston fuckin' playground sprinkled with cocaine, birds and booze. It was my life and I was loving it. Everyone was hearing stories that made them think I'd gone too far.

'Fuckin' Gomez is out of order!'

In Manchester I was knocking out doormen left, right and centre. I was being barred or thrown out of bars and clubs for openly doing a line and not bothering who saw it. I was off my head. I never slept. I was a rollercoaster spinning to fuck knows where. Night followed day. Morning came but I'd still be around; another glass, another snort. Crack open the whiskey and see in the day. It never ended. When everybody had gone home and the music stopped and the lights had gone out, I went on.

Like a storm on a sunny day and you look up and see colours in the sky. I was still around.

I was the rainbow man.

Reality bit hard when Billy came around to the house and told me that a title defence of the WBU belt had been arranged and I was boxing again in just five weeks' time. I'd be up against another tough character in the shape of twenty-seven-year-old Argentinian Javier Osvaldo Alvarez. A street kid who loved a scrap and rumours were he was coming to Manchester in the form of his life. Then there was me; a thirteen and a half stone, dishevelled cokehead and ragged drunk. I was panic stricken and in two minds whether to take the fight. In the end I decided there really wasn't much choice. I had to go ahead with it, otherwise I was finished. No more big pay days and I could definitely kiss goodbye to any dreams of a shot at Erik Morales.

After watching me closely on returning to the gym Billy decided he'd seen enough and I was called into his office for a chat with him and Kerry.

'You need to sort your head out Michael, I warned you on first coming here. I won't tolerate this crap.'

'You're destroying all your good work, mate,' added Kerry. 'The stuff you're shoving up your nose and the amount of drink you're putting away is enough to kill you, never mind just mess you up as a boxer.'

I listened and did try to lose the excess weight, but for the first time in my life, I knew it was a losing battle. I'd struggled like hell before by living on nothing but water and babyfood; starving myself to make the scales. Somehow I'd always got away with it, but on this occasion I had to lose almost four stone in five weeks. I was also suffering nose bleeds from taking too much cocaine but I kept that quiet. My body was saying no more. The years of abuse had finally caught up with me.

Despite all this I threw myself into it. I started doing ten-mile runs in a sweat suit and was almost living in the gym. It came off but I was being left weak as a baby, to the point that I was regularly getting put down in sparring. My punch resistance was on the wane. Inside I knew this and it scared me to death. I'd also cut out the carbs and that affected my speech. I was mumbling all the time and nobody could understand what I was saying.

Come the day of the weigh-in I still had five pounds to lose in the sauna. If you check out Bobby Rimmer's nose back then it was bright red! Not because of boozing but the fact he was with me all the time. Billy never left my side and I know it hurt him to watch me struggle. Even at the head to head where I'm convinced I'd psychologically won so many fight previous, I was quiet. There was no energy to spare. I was a shell and needed every ounce for the actual fight.

What made all this ever more harder to take was, due to Joe Calzaghe pulling out, I'd be topping the bill at the *MEN* Arena for the first time. It's always easy to blame other people but nobody poured the whiskey down my throat or put the cocaine up my nose. Nobody made me cheat on Alison so many times that it hardly seemed wrong anymore. Nobody made me fuck it all up. The man responsible is the man I still see every day when I look in the mirror.

It wasn't Brian Hughes or Frank Warren. It wasn't any drug dealer or bar man. It was me. And whatever happened against Alvarez, I was sure I had it coming.

The *Manchester Evening News* pulled me and asked for a few

words. I tried so hard to look and sound my usual cocky self.

'This is the first time I've headlined at the *MEN* Arena and I'm going to make it a special night for the fans. The old Gomez is back. I'm an exciting fighter in my own right and I give the fans what they want. Excitement, drama and knockouts.'

Now just who I was trying to convince? The public or myself?

11-2-2005: Javier Osvaldo Alvarez: They announced my arrival. The lights went out and the music started up. Sky Sports commentator Adam Smith gave a wonderful piece that could stand forever as an epitaph.

'One of the most engaging, erratic, entertaining and thoroughly watchable British fighters of the last decade. The frightening, ferocious, amusingly appealing and complex character that is Manchester's Michael Gomez.'

I stood there at the entrance to the arena. My sombrero on with a serious look that sent out the message Gomez is ready for business. Well this was a night I wasn't necessarily out to win, just survive. I knew I was in trouble even before I walked to the ring.

Watching those scenes now there's a look in my eye that I'd never seen before. It wasn't fear, more uncertainty of the unknown. As against Lazslo Bognar in our first fight and Kevin Lear, I knew I had to get Alvarez out of there early before I ran out of steam. It wasn't so much 'where do I go from here' but more 'how the fuck did it come to this?' Ten years playing Russian roulette between fights and now I was playing with a fully loaded gun.

I began okay in the opening two rounds but come the third and fourth Alvarez's right hand was smashing into my face like a hammer. This kid was good; clever, sharp and fast, whereas I had one plan. Go forward and nail him but I wasn't moving my head, I was taking full blooded shorts and I couldn't (didn't?) want to get out of the way. I'd been cut twice, I was a mess. I was predictable and I was in big fuckin' trouble. Normally I loved these kinds of fights, I lived for a tear-up but I couldn't get near him and I was getting hit by shot after shot. A right hand shook me and then I was caught on the ropes. Punch after punch, left hooks, right upper cuts, Alvarez let the lot fly and I was throwing nothing back. I survived just by clinging on.

I wasn't running away; Johnny Reed's words were forever ingrained in my head. 'Never take a step back Michael.' But I was getting killed in there.

Back in the corner my face was a mess. Mick Williamson went to work but a quick glance around at Billy, Bobby and Kerry confirmed what I felt, these were faces etched with real fear. After being battered around the ring, even though I felt lousy, I still tried to have a sense of humour.

'Did I win that round Billy?'

He looked at me as if I should have been committed right there and then.

'No.'

Round five and as I tried like hell to gain some kind of rhythm, I could feel the blood spilling down my face. The crowd tried to urge me on and I finally caught Alvarez with a fierce left hook and he didn't even breathe heavily. I was again being backed up against the ropes, not really by the power, more the sheer amount of punches. The shots rained in. I was stood trying desperately to fend him off. I could hear Billy and Bobby screaming advice but it was all just a distant blur. A dreamlike noise. All was hazy. Echoing. Breathing hard, my head was moving a spilt second too late and nothing was missing. Punch after punch, it couldn't go on. The mind was giving instructions but the body had given up listening. It'd had enough.

Fuck you Gomez, no more.

The bell to end the fifth round sounded and Billy gave a small speech that said to me it wasn't long before he pulled me out.

'Don't be too honest Mike. Get out of the fuckin' way, jab and move. No fuckin' going out on your shield, lad. I'm not allowing that.'

I was groggy on my feet as round six began. Shouts of 'Gomez' rang out from my supporters. Amongst them many were crying I was told later. I was trying so hard to get my jab going, but I couldn't make a dent on him. Alvarez just kept coming and hitting. I knew the clock was ticking and then a right hook and a left hand caught me and down I went, more through tiredness than the strength of the shot. I was a rag fuckin' doll. Up I got to be met by a blitz of punches. Alvarez again let fly everything and in stepped the referee Mickey Vann to end it. All I remember of that moment was the total silence outside the ring and the screaming and shouting in Spanish inside it.

I was in another place. I was back in Ireland running alongside Bones with the stolen goat. I was at our Louise's funeral. I was holding my first-born Mikey in my arms after he'd just been born. Only then to be shocked back to reality and an explosion of sound as voices and faces crowded around me.

Billy, Bobby, Kerry, Mick and the doctor were making sure I was okay.

Of course I was okay. I'd survived the storm right? I was still around. If you looked up to the sky you'd see my colours. Because I was the fuckin' rainbow man...

And I'd thrown everything away.

28: IF I SHOULD FALL FROM GRACE WITH GOD

'They never drank water but whiskey by pints. And the shanty towns rang with their songs and their fights.'

THE POGUES

FOLLOWING THE ALVAREZ FIGHT I fell back into the boozing and drugs with the greatest of ease. I was dealing and robbing. I was fighting in pubs, on pavements or in family feuds. All the time I was wrecked, going from day to day in a cocaine haze. As far as I was concerned, boxing could do one. It was over. Finished. Besides, there were many other things going on to pass the time.

One of my sisters was out in a club in Newton Heath sat with her friend just talking, she got caught up in a gang fight and was slashed by a flying glass. The man responsible was a known idiot, lived locally and thought it was hilarious. And so we set to work. When anything happened like this, it was a call to arms; the word went out and it would always be a meet up at my Dad's for a war council. He never said much but when he did we listened. Although now totally blind, Dad never failed to surprise us. One night Lumby's car was robbed and he found it by following local events on his CB radio before the police. He rang Lumby with the news.

'I found your car Steven, it's in Blackley.'

A shocked Lumby couldn't believe it. 'Micky, how the fuck?'

At Dad's a decision was made - we'd get tooled up; this one called for balaclavas, hammers and pickaxe handles. If needed there

217

could be thirty lads willing to fight our corner: family, mates and travellers, it was a tough crowd. We had a name and address so a van load; myself, Lumby, Bones and one of the sister's boyfriends at the time, went to deal with it. For a night and a day we hid in the bushes outside his house on a Moston estate. Nothing. Not a curtain twitch. No sign of life.

We were there that long we needed matchsticks in our eyes to stay awake until finally the front door opened and the man in question appeared. Looked left and right and seemed confident that everything had died down and there would be no retribution, he set off whistling with a bag of empties to put in his wheelie bin. But the man never made it and got the beating of his life. A month later he was able to walk again, he left Manchester and never came back.

These incidents were commonplace. There was always a war at our doorstep. It just went on, and on...

Another time, shortly before Christmas, a family relative was dragged out of a car on Lightbowne Road, near the Collyhurst and Moston gym and given a beating for something that wasn't even his doing. He simply had the misfortune to be related to my family. This was a harmless man who'd been in the worst place possible at the wrong time and got a bad kicking for it. We couldn't let this stand.

Again the phone calls gathered the clan and we met at Dad's flat. The questions were asked. Who done him? Where do they live? What the fuck are we going to do about it? Unluckily for one of them we already had an address. This time two vans set off. One blocked the entrance to the road, the other, full of lads, pulled up outside the house and we went tearing into his garden. Bones was good enough to knock on the door.

Somebody asked me in a pub once if my Bones was a joiner?

'No, why's that?' I asked

'No reason,' he said. 'It's just that everytime I see him he's got a hammer up his sleeve.'

An old man answered with two small kids by his side. Neither was older than seven or eight. The house was kitted out in festive decorations. I remember The Pogues *Fairytale of New York* was playing on the radio.

Bones stood there grinning.

'Is Anthony in?'

'He's in his room upstairs,' answered the clearly anxious old man.

'Thank you,' smiled Bones. Up he went and as the screams and shouts echoed loudly I passed over a hundred quid to the old man and pointed to the kids.

'Get them something nice for Christmas. This has nothing to with you or them.'

Back down came Bones, clearly satisfied family honour had been restored.

'Merry fuckin' Christmas,' he said on passing us and heading back to the van.

That was how we lived. We existed outside the law with our own rules. You injure one of ours, we'll hurt you more.

And me? Well this was now my full-time job. The night I smashed Alex Arthur was now just a distant memory, a far-off echo in the wind. And the ring glory didn't look like returning anytime soon.

Brass, gaffs and whiskey in a jar: It came as little surprise that Frank Warren dumped me like a bad smell and I couldn't really blame him. Maybe I hadn't always been the best paid when I was under his wing but when I think back to how I'd carried on at times… Warren always wanted his fighters to live their lives properly, be ultra-professional and if they were good enough the money and fights would come. Well Coronation Street, a glass of warm milk and then bed was never going to be me. That was no life for a traveller's son. I'd had a go and ultimately messed up.

But would I do the same thing all over again?

What do you think?

I lost contact for a while with the Phoenix gym. Embarrassed and in no need of lectures, no matter how well meaning, instead I went along on my trail of self-styled destruction. Nobody could talk to me because I simply wasn't interested enough to listen. I fooled myself into thinking this was me all along; the boxing, the discipline, the pride in battle and honour in defeat, the magic of the ring, the roar of the crowd, the shouts of 'Gomez' roaring out in an arena and the sombreros being hurled into the air were all just illusions.

Even the love of a good lady seemed like surreal. Nothing mattered but me. It was all about me, the booze and the cocaine.

I was still at home with Alison and the kids, although I knew I was on less than thin ice with her. The booze, drugs and all that came with it, Alison despised, but could just about stand. The fooling around was something else. I'd always been a little cute not to do it in Alison's face, but by this time I couldn't have cared less who I upset. Her included. I was going to brothels in Ancoats and others so close to home you could throw stones at our back windows. I was taking out girls in local pubs and acting up like Billy Big Time. I was knocking people out and causing trouble because I could. I was alienating so many but did I care?

My response when pulled was always just another line and session on the booze. I was freefalling into oblivion; kids, family – nothing, it seemed, could prevent me hitting the floor and breaking into a thousand rotten pieces. I'd fallen from grace not just with God, but myself and anybody else who ever really cared about me. Redemption felt so far beyond my fucked up, cocaine-stained self, that it wrecked me. There would be no more last chances…

Or so I thought.

Billy Graham rang to say negotiations to fight Scottish boxer Willie Limond had fallen through, but something else had shown itself. An unexpected shot at the Irish Lightweight title against a journeyman fighter called Peter McDonagh. Even that, in my messed up state, was enough to shake me sober.

The opportunity to fight in Ireland appealed to my gypsy soul. It would feel like I was going home. We had an old saying:

'Bury me on my feet, for I've spent an entire life on my knees.'

If it was fate that I should go out on my shield then at least let it be in Dublin's fair city. Let this traveller's son go home and fight one last time.

29: A ROCKY ROAD TO DUBLIN

*'From nothing to everything is a long way,
from everything to nothing is one stop.'*

WLADIMIR KLITSCHKO

IT WAS TIME TO GO BACK across the water. This Irishman was heading home. It only felt like five minutes ago that we were all getting off that boat at Holyhead and our time in England was just beginning. Now, twenty years later, here I was heading for Dublin to take a fight against an opponent that if I had looked after myself properly, would never have been allowed in the same arena as Michael Gomez, never mind the ring. Billy Graham had shown faith that I didn't deserve. He could easily have washed his hands of me and nobody could have blamed him. More likely, many would have applauded.

So I owed this man for standing by my side and giving me a last chance to prove that the fighter who rocked the boxing world by beating Alex Arthur still existed. In my head he'd never gone away, even if my body was wishing I'd never put on a pair of boxing gloves. And so I trained like a demon but again making the weight proved an ordeal. I suffered and tortured myself. It was all hot baths and creams to make me sweat. The move up from Super featherweight to light-welterweight had still proved a battle to make. But I'd been focused, I was hungry again. I'd missed the limelight, the ring and knew if I switched off then the alternative was back to the gutter.

At the first press conference I could feel the old fires burning. I told Peter McDonagh he'd never met anybody with my power and that he'd last no longer than five or six rounds before I knocked him out. He brought up Kevin Lear, claiming I was washed up. That I couldn't go ten rounds.

'I won't need to go the distance to beat you,' I said. 'And fuck Lear! I was sniffing cocaine and drinking booze for weeks before I fought him.'

A lot of the Irish journalists laughed and I wasn't sure whether they thought I was joking. McDonagh was actually a good lad and we had a lot in common. Born in Galway, Connemara, his family came over on a boat and like us, McDonagh's mother left when he was just a small kid, leaving his Dad to bring him up. Similar to me, he found the best way to communicate in a new country was with your fists in a gym. In his early twenties McDonagh was put behind bars on a charge of attempted murder, which led to him crossing paths with former Conservative MP Jeffrey Archer. He got friendly with Archer who helped him to learn how to read and write. Never one not to duck a scrape outside the ring, we were in so many ways kindred spirits! I'd later learn that a month before we fought, his pregnant wife Shannon was diagnosed with cancer. Luckily it was treated in time and the baby was also fine. This was the stuff that really mattered in life.

Back at the press conference we faced off as I threatened to start the fight early and he stood up equally keen to do so. I liked this kid! But at the time he was in the way and my only thoughts were to drop him soon as possible on the night.

McDonagh had an unlikely ally in his corner. One who I'd seen on the television, but never in my wildest dreams did I think I'd be up against. The spoon-bending psychic Uri Geller. I'd been told Geller was channelling positive energy into McDonagh. That he was acting as his mind coach.

'What does that mean Billy?'

'It means he's shoving a spoon up his arse Mike. Don't worry about it,' the Preacher replied.

A journalist pulled me in the gym. 'Mike, are you worried that Geller's magical powers could get inside your head?' That just made me laugh.

'Uri should just stick to bending spoons,' I said, 'and I'll concentrate on bending McDonagh's ribs.'

Mother's Ruin: If Uri fuckin' Geller telling the world he was playing with my mind wasn't bad enough, things turned infinitely worse with the return of a woman I'd thought was out of my life forever. In England I'd come out with a throwaway comment about my Mother to the newspapers saying how she taught us to shoplift as kids back in Ireland. It was the God's honest truth, any of the family would admit that and I thought nothing more of it. Until one day I'd gone home after training just relaxing on the sofa when my phone rang. It was Val.

'Midge, I need a word, can you come round to ours?'

She sounded worried and immediately I thought the worst.

'Val what's up, is everyone okay?'

'Yes love, everyone is fine. I just need you here now.'

Off I went and sat there in total shock as Val told me she'd had a call off Mam's solicitor to say I was being sued for the comments I made regarding the shoplifting. I couldn't believe it. She was insisting that we'd had a perfectly normal upbringing and always gone to school. It was total crap and obviously just a scam to try and make some money out of her own son!

It turned out she was living in Blackpool. Not that we cared anymore.

As I arrived in Dublin for the fight this news was burnt into my mind. It was all I could think about. I'd earn between seven and ten grand for fighting Peter McDonagh. If, by some mad scenario, she succeeded then it could easily all go to her. This woman who had wiped the blood off my head when I was born, who had kissed and wished me luck for the life that lay in front, this rocky road that had now come full circle and ended up back in Dublin.

Well there was no chance of Mary 'Bertie' Armstrong ever getting a penny off me!

They could Hail Mary and tell her that.

Never.

28-1-2006: Peter McDonagh: The National Stadium in Dublin rocked with the noise of my supporters. I had fans from across Ireland who'd come in their swarms from Longford, Inchicore and Ballymun as crazed Mancunians danced and sung among them. I had family and friends there. It was a special occasion for the Armstrong clan and they were all roaring out my name. Listening to this beforehand, my heart was breaking because I knew something wasn't right. There was still enough in the tank to beat McDonagh, of that I was sure but other demons were in the National Stadium that night. The type you can't fight that exist only in your head.

Say it ain't so Gomez?

Before the fight I was my normal, crazy self; pacing up and down the corridor, screaming loud to McDonagh in his dressing room that I was going to kill him. He was game and came out, only for it to end with security guards separating us and me being led away back to my camp. What followed is something that still haunts me to this day.

Now I'd been a fighter all my life. I'd had to fight for my breakfast. I'd had to fight for the clothes. And if you weren't up first you didn't get them. Therefore the slightest notion I'd ever even considering throwing a fight was sheer madness. Commentating for *RTE* that night was Steve Collins. He talked about smelling a rat when I turned my back and walked away in the fifth round and slid under the ropes. There was no rat, at least not in the arena.

GOMEZ

It just came into my head. I saw her face and thought what am I doing in here? No way is she getting this money.

McDonagh kept punching away. He came after me swinging, but I wasn't there anymore. I went down, but felt nothing. Mentally I was shot. I hadn't been training to beat McDonagh, I was slaving to try and rid the stuff in my head about that woman. He was celebrating and jumped onto the ropes with arms raised high. McDonagh sank to his knees and burst into tears as he was hugged in the ring by his corner and family members. But no offence, Peter McDonagh was never in my class. The person he'd beaten that night wasn't Michael Gomez. It was a broken man who had suddenly decided in the midst of battle, inside the ropes, that the price for victory wasn't worth it and that it was best just to walk away and never return.

Immediately following the fight all hell let loose. Despite the insistence of boxing officials, I refused to attend the post-fight press conference. This only incited even more controversy. What was Gomez hiding? Did he throw the fight? Television, radio and newspaper journalists were encamped outside my dressing room door. Inside, nobody spoke, the lads knew I was hurting. There was a question in the air but none daren't ask it.

Why Mike? Why?

They'd never understand.

Later that night, two members of the Irish Boxing Union came to my hotel room and told me both our purses were being withheld for twenty-one days, whilst an investigation took place regarding my quitting in such strange circumstances. I felt sorry for McDonagh because I'd heard they'd started lighting huge bonfires in Connemara to celebrate his winning. It was a great honour in Ireland to win a national belt and not taken lightly. He was adamant in a television interview afterwards that everything had been above board and the fight was clean. 'Look at my face,' said an angry McDonagh. 'Do I look like I've been in a fixed fight? Do you think I like looking like this? I've heard the allegations but I watched it on TV. That was a perfect punch. I broke his heart.'

It was broken alright…But not by him.

I was on the front page of the Irish newspapers for a week. Rumours were ablaze in Dublin that I was part of a possible betting scam. I was hearing all kind of weird and wild tales regarding me but for once there wasn't a hint of truth in any of them. The original controversy arose because *Boylesports* had earlier suspended the betting on the fight because of what they said were 'unusual' betting trends. Following heavy betting on McDonagh to win the bout in the fifth, sixth, seventh and eighth rounds at 125/1 and later 25/1, *Boylesports* closed their book. Their spokesman came out to calm boxing fans, some of whom were baying for my blood.

'We are not saying anything untoward was going on, but there were unusual betting trends on a certain outsider to win in certain rounds. You don't have to have a lot on to take thousands out with those odds. There were 20 Euro bets and minutes later 50 Euro bets. We then cut the odds to 25/1 and there were still more inquiries from people wanting to put hundreds on. That's an awful lot of money to have on a round. And so we suspended all betting earlier this afternoon.'

I've pulled some scams in my time. I'd been a villain, a crook and a thief, but I swear to God, none of this was my doing.

As for Uri Geller? McDonagh was quick to praise him. But if he really thought that spook had rattled me he needed locking up. McDonagh had lost eleven in eighteen before we met. He'd won two of his last seven. This guy was a journeyman and without *her* coming on the scene, I'd have taken him apart.

There was no magic and no hypnosis. I was a ghost, a shadow of the fighter I once was. My heart was no longer in it and my spirit was so fucked as to be beyond repair. That was it. My boxing career was in tatters. My warrior's sword and shield had been tarnished. My colours lowered.

It was finally over and that would be hard to live with.

Billy Graham scoffed at suggestions that I'd thrown the fight. Billy found it all embarrassing and couldn't really get his head around what went on. 'It'd be tragic if Michael ended his career under a cloud. The whole thing is laughable. If he was going to throw a fight why put himself through all that again? Michael has worked so hard and shown real guts and ambition to get back to the top. He's gone to the well many times and shown indomitable courage. There's no quitter in Michael but it was really all over some time ago.'

No action was eventually taken against myself or Peter McDonagh. The *BUI* (Boxing Union of Ireland) announced that we were both to be awarded our purses after a union investigation found no evidence of any wrongdoing.

McDonagh walked away with the vacant Irish Lightweight title whilst I retired.

The investigation heard evidence from the referee, the ringside doctor, the British Boxing Board of Control and bookmakers before returning a verdict. *Cashmans, Eastwoods,* and *Paddy Power* all submitted their evidence. Boylesports, however, who suspended betting on the fight a few hours before it was due to take place, didn't submit any evidence despite requests from the *BUI.* Why? I have no idea. I knew no matter what I claimed and despite being cleared of all wrongdoing, it really was the end. This kind of mud sticks to your reputation and with my background, people would always think the worst. I may have come back from the dead but now I found myself in a living hell.

Where did I go from here?

30: DOWN IN THE GROUND WHERE THE DEAD MEN GO

'Too young to die: Too drunk to live.'

RENEE MCCALL

IT WAS A SERIOUS QUESTION but I think my mates thought I was joking. We were pissed and it was probably just put down as crazy talk.

'What happens when you overdose?'

No alarm bells went off.

'Why you mad bastard?'

'Just curious,' I replied.

I listened to every word as they told me. An idea was forming in the back of my head. One that'd solve everything.

The pain of my mother trying to sue me.

The hurt I'd caused Alison.

Sam Parr dying.

The shame of Dublin.

The loss of my boxing career.

This being the one thing that gave my life true meaning.

As for *that* woman, it was Dad and Val who brought us up. Last time I saw her she was fuckin' off in a taxi with her girlfriend. She was no Mother.

Alison. Every girl I've been with, none could hold a candle, but still I did it.

Why? Because I could. She'd be better off without me.

RIP Sam, soon I'll be able to say sorry to your face, mate.

Dublin. Uri Geller never put a fuckin' spell on me. It was no body shot, it was her. I beat myself. 125/1. Steve Collins smelling a rat. Well for what it's worth. Not fuckin' guilty. The rumours, the sly comments. It happens. Robero Duran against Sugar Ray Leonard. 'No Mas.'

I never turned my back, I kept taking the punches. Like Duran I just didn't want to fight no more. No fuckin' Mas!

And so I made my plans. Another beer, a line and then I'd ask around. It'd soon be over. Just one hit that's all it takes.

Just one...

Carnival of Sorts: To keep the money coming in I was earning a nice few quid selling cocaine to a group of out of town lads. It was a decent number that saw me clear about £400 a week. After Dublin I'd just gone mental. Now retired from boxing there was nothing to stop me and I was sleeping around, snorting and drinking like a man determined to cram as much into his life because he knew it would all soon be over. I blew fifty grand in two months. I couldn't even be bothered talking women into bed anymore, I just went to prostitutes instead. Why? Because I could and had the money to afford it.

A last carnival of sorts.

As for the cocaine? I couldn't get enough and was always looking to buy more. When the money ran low, my credit never lasted long. Too many bridges burned. All the fights, straighteners, arguments and bust ups over the years. The kicked in doors and smashed windows. The pickaxes, knives, hammers and balaclavas. The gang wars. My lot running riot. Me causing mayhem and out of control. It was payback time and many people were loving it

'Last time Gomez, from now on you pay up front.'

'No worries, you know I'm good for it.'

'Yeah maybe once,' they'd mock. And I couldn't do fuck all about it. I was desperate. Nothing mattered but cocaine, cocaine, cocaine...

I started to owe a lot of money to many dangerous people. But secretly I thought, fuck it. Where I was going you can't follow, so take a fuckin' running jump.

I was running low and got a call from my out of town friends.

'Mike can you sort us out?'

'No problem,' I said. 'The same service station car park. Twelve o'clock tomorrow.'

'Cheers mate you're a star.'

Yeah once maybe, I thought. But not now. My star had well and truly crashed and fuckin' burned. Not anymore.

I needed cash urgently and I had a plan. If it went wrong, fuck it. Nothing to lose these days. I went to Tesco's and I bought some flour and also picked up some of the clear bags that they pack the fruit and vegetables in.

I poured the flour into the bags and I had my cocaine. The next day we met up, it all went well and I was away before they ever had chance to check their merchandise. As to what happened when they found out? Did I care?

The next day I got the call. 'Gomez, what the fuck?'

I switched off the phone and just started laughing.

With the money I went to see a dealer and bought a stash of heroin. Also I sorted myself enough cocaine for a last fling. That night I went home.

It was late, way past twelve and Alison was in bed.

I pulled out the heroin whilst sat on the sofa and with tears falling down my face, I started to eat it. I was throwing it in my mouth. I was forcing it down.

At first nothing happened but then I started feeling sick and getting weird pins and needles. Next thing I'd collapsed on the floor having a fit.

It was Alison who found me. She rang an ambulance and I was rushed to hospital where they immediately pumped my stomach clean and ruined the best made fuckin' plan.

I wished it to be over.

Just over…

I wanted nothing more than to be down in the ground where the dead men go.

After a short stay in the hospital, where they insisted I saw a psychologist, I ignored all medical advice, discharged myself and headed home. I got a taxi and Alison was waiting for me at the door. Suddenly I got that image in my head of the first time I ever saw her. Walking down Lightbowne Road. The one true love of my life and the mother of my kids. Alison looked me straight in the eyes.

'So is that it then?

'Have you learned your lesson?'

I stood for a moment, just staring, before turning around and heading off to the pub. I never looked back.

Caravan. A short cut through Moston cemetery with balaclavas and pickaxes in hand. A friend of ours was being picked on and despite it being only minor, the mixture of booze and boredom meant it was decided we'd do something about it. Monumentally pissed, we strode past the Irish Martyrs Memorial and jumped over the wall onto Moston Lane.

The plan was agreed. Leave him alone and smash up his caravan.

Anybody walking past and seeing three hooded men tooled up would have got the shock of their lives. We arrived outside the house and went to work on his pride and joy. A ten thousand pound caravan that by the time we'd finished with it wasn't worth a tenner. The sound of police sirens saw us finish up and we raced off into nearby Boggart Hole Clough. There we headed down onto Rochdale Road and the long but safer way home.

Walking down a side street I noticed one of the lads was blowing a bit. He was a large size, seventeen stone and obviously wasn't really cut out for this type of midnight excursion. As we approached a corner shop I put my hand on his shoulder.

'Are you okay mate? You look knackered.'

'Are you surprised?' He said. 'Look at me, I'm not fuckin' built for this!'

Next minute I went across to a wheelie bin and hurled it through the shop window. The sound of smashing glass and alarms started to blare and off we sped once more. My mate suddenly finding another gear and going off like Usain fuckin' Bolt.

He'd thank me in the end.

Great exercise…

Up on the Roof: In an effort to stay out of trouble and jail, I got myself a job working for a local demolition firm. The guy who owned it was called Frank. He was a good bloke, a huge boxing fan and a friend of mine.

'Gomez, I'm gonna give you a chance. I'll pick you up tomorrow morning at seven o'clock in the Jag.'

Now Frank also tended to spread his wings and dabble in other stuff. The type of 'stuff' that could see you banged up in Strangeways faster than a judge could bang down his fuckin' gavel. But to try and get myself in decent shape again I was up for a bit of hard graft and muscle. The cocaine was killing me both mentally and physically. I needed something to take up my time, otherwise I was on a reunion night out with the Grim Reaper. We'd already met once and I wasn't keen on seeing that bastard again for many years yet.

Frank was paying £350 a week and I'd the mortgage, a rack of bills and the kids to think of. Anything I'd made from boxing I'd blown.

All those fights, all the blows I'd taken and I was skint…

The next day I'm sat waiting and hear a horn bibbing. It's Frank. I get in the back with another local guy, a friend of mine called Mick.

'Where's the job Frank?' I ask.

'Newcastle,' he replied. 'Treat it as a fuckin' holiday lads. Away from the wife and all the strife!'

He went on to say that we'd be working on a roof ripping off the slates on two derelict houses in the middle of a Geordie council estate. Strange, I thought.

A long way to go for that? We arrived there and waiting for us were two more lads. Plus a truck, a forklift and pallets. The area was cordoned off and we started work. It all looked very professional. Frank obviously knew his stuff. Myself and Mick went up on a ladder to the roof and got stuck in. I'm enjoying myself. It was honest graft and it felt good. We were stripping the slates, carrying them down then stacking them in the truck.

After a while Frank was looking at his watch and appearing edgy.

'Hurry up lads eh,' he shouts up. 'I'm fuckin' going on holiday in six month.'

Mick smelt a rat. He'd been around in this game for years and knew the score. 'Frank is up to something Mike.'

Now I was curious because I also knew about roof work. Bones and my brother-in-law Steve had both worked in this game and they'd often spoken about the strict health and safety rules and how you couldn't breathe on sites like this anymore without a harness and hi-viz jackets. We had nothing. Plus these days they had machines for taking down the type of slates myself and Mick were working on. Finally it was all finished and with everything stacked nicely and ready to be moved, we called it a day and headed back over to the Jag.

I watched through the window as the now packed truck sped away and the site was cleared like we'd never even been there.

Suddenly a smiling Frank popped his head around from the front seat.

'Congratulation boys, how does it feel to have robbed those

slates?'

I knew it!

'Frank you mad fucker!' I exclaimed.

Mick just shook his head. 'You better make this worth our while.'

Frank was grinning like a Cheshire cat. 'Don't worry there'll be a nice little bonus in both your pay packets.'

But I wasn't really bothered because nothing shocked me in this life anymore. If they ever wrote a book nobody would believe it…

31: LOVE YOU TILL THE END

'Notice who is in the locker room after you lose, not after you win.'

ANGELO DUNDEE

I KEPT HAVING NIGHTMARES and it was always the same one. Back in that fuckin' Dublin ring but I couldn't lift my arms. Every time I cornered McDonagh he'd just laugh in my face. I'd look out over the ropes and there were rows of smirking faces. This was payback time for the grief and shit I'd brought on people over the years. They were all there and loving it. An arena full; Frank Warren, Brian Hughes. I saw Sam Parr way at the back, but I couldn't tell whether he was smiling or crying. But there was one other who would forever catch my eye. Mary Beatrice Armstrong. She was sat there with arms folded giving me the cold stare. One I knew so well. I'd wake up with a rush, jump out of bed and keep walking around the bedroom until it went away. Alison would sit up and watch as I paced up and down until the images faded. But next night I'd be back there and the crowd remained the same.

The libel claims got nowhere as the family gathered around me and told all who'd listen and those who wouldn't that what I'd told the newspaper was true. When she realised the odds were against her, Mam disappeared off the radar again. A sad state of affairs, but over the years we all hardened to it. It was her loss; sons, daughters, grandchildren and now great-grandchildren. The Armstrongs never went anywhere.

Retirement was turning out to be the early death of me. I was depressed and in a very bad place. Haunted by my suicide attempt and that dark night in Dublin, I just kept falling into an downward spiral. The money was gone. We were living on handouts and benefits. The faces around in the good times disappeared now the tap ran dry. I'd been my own worst enemy and close friends, proper mates, had been driven away by my behaviour and actions toward them. I'd committed the dreadful sin of believing that, because of my name and reputation I could do anything and get away with it. But you can only hurt and push people so far. No matter how much they love you, they'll walk away eventually. If you act, talk and walk like a thug and your head is so far gone with booze and cocaine that you'll say and do anything without an inch of remorse, could I really blame them for cutting ties?

I'd pulled some desperate tricks and what's worse I don't remember doing half of them.

Perhaps there was one last chink of light? One final grasp at a lifejacket to stop me sinking before I drowned in a sea of self-pity and drugs. One last chance that my body wouldn't be found at some crack house in Cheetham Hill and I'd make the front page of the *Manchester Evening News,* maybe even the leading story on Granada Reports, with a few nice words from the boxing community and flowers on my grave. Apart from family, I reasoned, who would truly mourn for me? Michael Gomez, the Mexican Manc who fucked it all up, both in and out of the ring; another traveller's son who let it all slip away. And what will they say to my kids in years to come? He was a true warrior but once the lights faded and they stopped singing his name, he just couldn't handle it.

A boxing cliché...

I was convinced it would end in a morgue at Collyhurst police station with coppers taking secret photos on the mobile phone to show their mates. Maybe they'd put a fuckin' sombrero on my head. 'Do you remember him?' They'd say... 'He used to be a boxer.'

And then there was the person who, despite everything I'd put her through, would always be my night and day. When Alison found me after the overdose she finally broke. All the heartache and pain endured during the years saw her reach an all-time low. Congratulations Gomez, you'd finally all but destroyed the only girl you ever truly loved. She'd lost so much weight and looked easier to snap than a twig. We'd known each other since we were kids and I'd never seen her like that.

Alison would scream at me, 'How could you ever treat me and the kids like this Michael!'

I'd no answers. No excuses. It was just a place I was in at the time and I had to get out of. No, I couldn't leave it like this. As long shots go it was all I had left. Probably the only job I was capable of doing that didn't involve wrapping up when you heard police sirens.

I had to get back in the ring.

One bridge I hadn't burnt was with Bobby Rimmer. Nearly fourteen stone and feeling like an old man, I reached out. Bobby had set up in his own gym and also owned a pub in Denton called the Prince of Wales. I called in there to see him and asked if he'd consider training me.

'Well can you still do it?'

'I'm gonna give it my best shot Bobby.'

He smiled wide. 'That's all I needed to hear Michael.'

With that we shook hands and I was back in a world that I'd missed so much. In the gym I threw myself back into training but instantly knew something wasn't right. I was shot; I'd known this for a while now and was constantly fighting an inner battle. There were two voices in my head both against and for.

'You can't do this Mike it's gone. It's over.'

Then another part of me would rage equally. 'No, no! You've got to do it!'

'No face it Mike, you're fucked!'

And on and on…

Now Bobby Rimmer was a decent bloke and brilliant around the gym, but he would be the first to tell people that Michael Gomez was in a different class to any he'd trained previously. Indeed at times it was me teaching him. None of this helped as I sweated and battled to rediscover my fitness and the old fire and fury of days past. If it was still in there, I needed somehow to reignite it to have any chance of making a mark and prove to Bobby I wasn't just wasting his and my time. We made a good team though and slowly I felt it coming back. The Gomez of old was gone forever, but the power and the courage wasn't going anywhere. However something came up which meant I'd have to hang up the boxing gloves for a short while and change into my suit and tie.

No it wasn't another court case.

I'd a date at the altar with the measure of my dreams.

It was at San Rocco's restaurant in Cheetham Hill that I went down on one knee and asked Alison to finally marry me. On 7 November 2007, at Saint Luke's church in Moston, Manchester, I did the right thing by Alison Davies and we became husband and wife. Bones was my best man and I purposely kept it a small family and close friends affair with very few gangsters or boxers. Countless times over the years myself and Alison had got engaged, but me being the type of character I was, something always ruined it. I'd use it as a peace offering and never with any real intentions. Not this time. I knew she'd wanted this for so long and after all the garbage I'd dropped on her plate, I felt this was the best way to prove for both us there could be a new start. A fresh beginning after all the promises, millions of lies and a thousand broken hearts.

I so wanted to make things right.

When I first saw Alison walking down that aisle in a gorgeous dress, so prim, pretty and proper, my heart leapt. She'd never ever wear make-up and on that day she did and looked even more beautiful. I loved this woman. I never wanted to get married really, everyone I knew who'd gone down this route ended up hating each other and getting divorced. But not anymore. For one split second I lost concentration after looking at her bare shoulders. 'Where's ya bra?' I blurted out loudly, so all the congregation could hear. Quick as a flash and typical Alison I was put in my place.

'It's strapless you idiot.'

I didn't deserve this girl. Our first song was *Keep Bleeding Love* by Leona Lewis. When I think back now, I don't know whether to smile or cry.

32: THE BELL FROM THE GRAVEYARD

'You always say 'I'll quit when I start to slide'. Then one morning you wake up and realize you done slid.'

SUGAR RAY ROBINSON

I could have been a contender: If I had a tenner for every time somebody said to me my life would make a great movie, I'd be a millionaire. In 2007 it so nearly came true. I was contacted by a writer/ television presenter Andrew (Barney) McHugh who'd written the screenplay and I jumped at it. Events moved fast and a cast was gathered, backers were said to be in place and it seemed just a matter of time before they began shooting. Even to the extent that filming locations in Ireland had already been checked out. Actors such as Kelvin Fletcher, Jody Latham and even Ricky Hatton playing himself had been lined up. A trailer was made that attracted huge interest and even taken to the Cannes film festival where it went down really well. I couldn't believe it was happening and I was walking around with a *Gomez the movie* tee shirt on every day! The boxing world was ablaze with the news and I had people both excited and worried asking if they'd be in it!

'Make sure they change my fuckin' name Michael.' I heard that quite a lot.

Then disaster struck when at the last minute the financier got cold feet and pulled the plug and everything just ground to a halt. A playboy millionaire who'd promised us the earth, only to suddenly find himself up to his ears in court cases involving fraud and other stuff that unfortunately blew up when we least needed it. 'Just keep going,' he told us. 'The money is there for you.'

Only for it ultimately proved not to be and we were hung out to dry.

Devastated didn't do it justice. There had never been a great movie on a British boxer and I was convinced mine would be the first. Happily the dream never died and today the Gomez movie is alive again and my hopes of being on the big silver screen remains alive.

Gomez may yet conquer Hollywood!

6-5-2007: Daniel Thorpe: I was desperate for a rematch with Peter McDonagh to scourge memories of the Dublin nightmare, but neither him nor his people were interested. I even said he could have all the money apart from my £1,000 trainer's fee. Nothing, they didn't want to know. Instead it was Salford promoter Steve Woods of *VIP Promotions* who got me my first fight back. A late change of opponent saw twenty-seven-year-old Thorpe from Sheffield in the opposite corner. A decent enough fighter, a tricky southpaw, but if I lost to him then it really was all over. It took place at Altrincham Leisure Centre and I was nervous, but fired up. I wore my sombrero whilst entering the ring alongside Bobby. It was nice to see Ricky and Matthew Hatton sat at ringside to support me. Both lads wearing their hats also! In the first round I was like a man possessed and just tying a little too hard to impress. Thorpe did catch me with a right hook smack on the nose and I remember thinking, oh fuck he's broke it again! If this thing got any flatter I'd look like a Doctor Who villain.

The second saw an improvement and I calmed down a little to catch Thorpe with some savage left uppercuts. The power was still there, but I felt like it would have to be rationed more these days. Come the third I was all over him, I unleashed a left hook that dropped Thorpe and the referee stepped in to end it. It had been a mismatch, but still a dangerous contest, for I was walking into it unknown. He'd rocked me in the first and that wouldn't have happened in the past. It worried me but at least I knew whatever lay in store, the Mexican Manc was not yet a totally busted flush. I could still bang. I smiled as sombreros flew into the ring and picked one up. It was good to be back. I couldn't know how long this feeling would last but at that moment Michael Gomez felt alive again.

24-6-2007:Youssef Al Hamidi: One month later I was back in the ring at Wigan's Robin Park Centre. My opponent from Dewsbury, Al Hamidi, had never been stopped. This fact apart he shouldn't really have troubled me but he did and in the first round caught and cut me badly over both eyes. For this fight the nightmare returned on the scales and I'd struggled badly to make the weight. Against Thorpe I was nine-thirteen, Al Hamidi, nine-six. The lightest I'd been for nearly two years. I was bleeding badly because of the sudden weight loss and the fact my skin was so tight. The blood covered my face and I knew once more it was all or nothing. I had to get Al Hamidi out of there early, otherwise it really was the end of the road.

Again.

As I returned to the corner I heard a voice shout out from ringside that still until this day echoes in my head. But I never found out who it was?

'This is sad!'

Those words cut deep, I was no charity case, I was a fuckin' fighter. I'd never wanted or asked for sympathy. It was my life and they were my choices. Good or bad. Rattled by this I chased Al Hamidi and finally with nothing but grim determination and a huge heart I cornered and stopped him in the third to win the fight. But it was nothing to shout about. There'd been no slick boxing. No head movement or sweet combinations. I simply overpowered my opponent through a manic will to win. I ended leaving the ring in a bloodied mess and the dressing room resembling the Somme. Is this how it all ended? You simply can't stem the wounds?

In the aftermath of this tear-up Frank Warren rang Steve Woods and asked him what he thought I'd got left?

'It might not be the old Gomez, Frank,' replied Steve. 'But fuck me, he hasn't lost one bit of his heart.'

That was never going anywhere.

Since joining Bobby Rimmer I'd found myself becoming almost an elder statesman in his gym. The younger boxers were always asking advice and I was happy to pass on anything I'd learnt during a 'colourful' career. My stablemates were all good lads, but some of them were in total awe of me. They'd heard the stories and knew none were made up. In fact many were played down! I'd laugh about it but always tried to stress that inside the ring you had to look after yourself. I'd remember how Brian spoke to me and in the best way I could I'd copy him with my own words.

'Do as I say within these ropes lads. But outside them the exact fuckin' opposite!'

Maybe away from the ring I wasn't in any position to hand out Fatherly tips, but inside, if I could offer the slightest nudge towards making the lads better fighters and stop them getting hurt, then why not?

One day, when wrapping up, I got the call off Steve Woods I'd been dreaming about since embarking on this latest comeback. Even though it'd only lasted a total of six rounds so far, I was telling everybody that I felt ready to move up a class. I was in a rush. There was no use waiting around because I wasn't going to get any better.

'I've got some great news, Mike. I've just come off the phone to Frank Maloney. He's the manager of Carl Johannsen and wants to offer you a shot at his British Super Featherweight title.'

I was back in. Johannsen was a decent champion but far as I was concerned, I could beat him. I still had enough and he was only

After being pulled out of the fight with Kevin Lear and my fall out with Brian, I switched to Billy Graham's camp in Denton. The Preacher Man had a fine stable of boxers including my old mate Anthony Farnell and the Hatton brothers. Kerry Kayes (left) and Bobby Rimmer (below) were key components of Billy's set-up and gave my career fresh impetus.

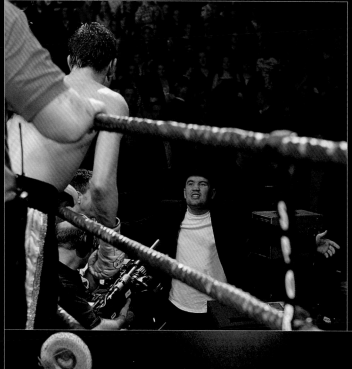

The build up to the Alex Arthur fight actually began 3 months before when I was ringside for his British title fight against Willie Limond in Glasgow. We had a war of words (left) at ringside so you could say the fight started there...

There were only about 4 people who thought I could beat Arthur - the atmosphere inside the Meadowbank Sports Centre was electric that night but slowly their cheers turned to stunned silence. With seconds left of Round 5 I floored him.

Billy Graham often said that more fights are won in the weigh-in than in the ring. Here I am eyeballing Carl Johanneson before our controversial British title fight in 2007.

A pep talk from former foe Alex Arthur before the Amir Khan fight, "don't forget that left hook, everyone thought you were finished when you fought me - you did it then you can do it again."

Gomez and Khan moments before the first bell.

When I knocked Amir Khan down in the second round I thought 'Hallelujah, praise the lord' and then he got back up and beat the fuck out of me!

I'm now the proud owner of the WBO intercontinental belt and outright winner of the Lonsdale belt

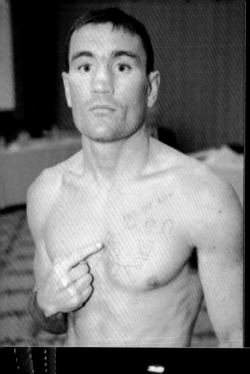

Ricky Burns had told everybody
he was going to get a tattoo done of
me knocked out on the canvas. So
before our last press conference I'd got
Kevin Maree to draw on my chest a
matchstick figure of Burns
lying sparkled. Went down well

Ricky Burns finishes off the
Mexican Manc and this time it
really was all over in the ring for me

GOMEZ: THE NEXT GENERATION

I'm really excited about Mikey's career as a boxer, he's a lot better fighter than me, more skilful and a lot more dedicated but has he got the heart I had? I don't know and neither does he, only time will tell. He's a hot head just like I was, if he can control that then he'll go far.

keeping my belt warm. This was an opportunity to reclaim a title I considered my own. We already shared a history of sorts. We had both fought Levan Kirakyson with Johannsen being stopped twice and with brutal force by the tough Russian. Whereas, after being landed a couple of bombs in the fifth, I finished him in the next round. We'd also sparred together three or four times before.

I remember after one session Carl scratching his head and looking at me like I was crazy. 'Why do you make everything a war, Mike?' Well I knew no other way. To be fair, he was a strong kid who could smash but then so could I. Also, I was stronger, I believed I hit that little bit harder and could take a better shot. I'd been in countless wars, undoubtedly too many, but I'd won more than I'd lost. Publicly the pressure would all be on him. He was the champion and I was the comeback kid with general consensus seeming to be I was nothing more than a washed up bum chasing a lost dream.

It appeared Johannsen had everything to lose. And me? Nothing.

The truth being, if I got beat then where did I go? You don't hear the bell from the graveyard. I simply couldn't afford to let it happen. But nothing was right in training. In an interview I gave six weeks before the fight I think I was kidding myself, never mind the journalist and readers... 'The weight is virtually spot on where it needs to be. The diet's working and still giving me all the energy I need to train. I've had a couple of nights off the running this week to make sure I don't burn out. I know a lot of fighters say this but I truly am going to be in one of the best shapes of my life. I'm ready to fight Johannsen tonight, never mind in six weeks. Bobby has been working hard on getting the head movement back. Also, we've been concentrating more on my feints and getting the jab working faster and better. It's all coming together great and I've no doubt my left jab will be a massive weapon come the fight'...

The reality was I was shaking with both anger and frustration at not being able to do naturally what I'd always done in the gym.

Everything was wrong. Again, it was all rushed as I buckled down too late. Once more I'd be training only to make the weight and losing it too quickly. I tried to fool myself by just going through the motions. God knows I'd been there before, but who was I kidding? It was over and I felt finished. Yet there remained a part of me that refused to admit this. Sparring was terrible, my timing was shot to pieces. If a thoroughbred racehorse had been in a similar condition it would have been less cruel to put a swan-off against its head and pull the trigger.

Nobody had a clue what was happening. Bobby Rimmer wasn't experienced enough to spot the signs. Maybe I should have said something? No blame on Bobby, it was my doing. I knew, I'd felt like this for almost two years and should have walked away. But this couldn't happen, not with me. Never. Pride before the fall and all that.

My mates in the Paras from Rossendale always told me they'd never worried about the bullets they could see, it was the one you didn't that had your name on it. A punch was the same and I'd no qualms about facing up to it when the time came. After all, I was a fighter. It was always fated to end for me getting my fuckin' lights turned out. Besides it was in the small print. Written in the stars. People like Michael Gomez could not expect a happy ending. Not that I could ever read...

If I'd still been with Brian Hughes or Billy Graham then they'd have told me straight. 'It's over Michael. Your time is up, son.' But oh no, not in Gomez world. I just continued arguing with myself, 'come on fuckin' do this!' But it was gone. Everything was just so hard.

On the speed bag and body pads my combinations were slow and disjointed. I was all over the place. Nothing flowed. What was once natural and felt good, now just took so much effort and broke my heart. Every punch was a second slower and I knew.

...I just fuckin' knew.

33: WAR OF THE ROSES

'In the ring the truth will always find you.'

JOE LOUIS

EVEN BY MY STANDARDS, the press conference with Carl Johannsen was spectacular as it spilled out into the street. Finally, we were dragged apart by Bobby Rimmer and Kevin Maree. An Irish lad, Kevin was an ex-fighter making his way in the trainer's game and we'd invited him into our corner. I'd no problems about the fight being staged in Doncaster, only a short distance from Johannsen's hometown of Leeds. Such was my need for the fifteen grand on offer, I'd have taken on a whisky-sodden gorilla with bad toothache in a cage. A contest like this would surely see a neutral referee and with Larry O'Connell officiating? No problem. Besides what was home advantage? I'd sold more tickets than him and had coach loads of sombrero waving Manc lunatics heading over the Pennines to support me. Come the night I'd no doubt it'd be a Gomez crowd.

I told all who would listen that I was coming to knock Johannsen out. I was giving it loud, I was snarling and snapping.

'Mike, what the fuck? Calm down,' said Bobby.

Johannsen hit back. 'You're finished Gomez. You're all washed up.'

This was music to my ears as I wanted a tear-up, I wanted it brutal and savage from the opening bell. 'He's got my title. I never lost it. I vacated it. Now I'm coming to take it back and regain my rightful spot as number one Super Featherweight.'

'It's mine now,' smiled Johannsen.'

Again we squared off, it was working. All would be well on fight night. This man was a warrior and I'd get my wish. More importantly, I needed it to end quick because otherwise I never had a prayer. No tactical masterclass, no wait and see.

Just instant carnage.

A war of the Roses.

19-10-2007: Carl Johannsen: At the press conference beforehand I'd been informed that the referee for the fight was to be Larry O'Connell. This pleased me no end because despite having no worries about the judges, it was always good for peace of mind not to have someone local. Then an hour before the fight, the dressing room door opened and in waltzed Mickey Vann. Like Johannsen he also hailed from Leeds.

There exists a photograph on the wall at Bobby Rimmer's gym that captured my expression as Vann entered. It's one of utter disbelief. Now straight away, I'd no reason to disbelieve Vann's integrity. I still don't but there are other ways to favour fighters without really thinking you're doing anything wrong. And that night in Doncaster I fell foul of what I still consider to have been a scandalous decision. I should know because I'm convinced he did the same for me one time as he admitted as much.

I'd wanted a war and swiftly got my wish with Carl Johannsen as we went hell for leather from the opening bell. 'A meeting of cornered rats,' I'd called it beforehand and with nowhere to run or hide inside the ropes it was brutal. Like me, Johannsen could only fight one way and forty-two knockouts between us meant few bets were placed on the contest going the distance. It was toe to toe. My kind of fight. Around the Doncaster Dome it was a sea of brightly-coloured sombreros; like a Mexican army on tour rather than a load of lads and lasses from Moston, Harpurhey and all points Manchester. Johannsen had decent backing but they were easily outshouted by my supporters who raised the roof.

I was catching Johannsen, though equally, he was letting fly some cracking shots that rocked me. Nothing could split the opening rounds but come the fourth I felt the first nagging signs of tiredness set in. Unusually, Johannsen was jabbing from afar. I knew some of my left hooks had hurt him. I could only assume he was fighting under instruction for this wasn't his normal style. Seeing this inspired me and with a new lease of energy, I went looking for a brawl. The left hooks were still firing but he was catching me on the way in and I was getting hit far too often. Round five wore on. It was truly a savage, mad contest and I couldn't complain. This was what I'd called for and Johannsen obliged me. Good for him.

Why did I love this fuckin' sport? Could it have been that apart from sex and getting high, it was the one thing that made me feel alive? I was getting hurt in there but enjoying it! With every punch Johannsen was probably putting paid to my old age but did I care? It went on. In I'd go low swinging left hooks but I was so tired. I was gasping for breath. Please God just give me that moment.

I wasn't begging for a miracle, just a drop of his guard and I'd take care of the rest. 'Gomez, Gomez' thundered out the travelling Mancs! Young and old, I owed them this one.

'A classic contest. Blood, guts and spirit aplenty,' they said on Sky Sports.

As round five ended, he cornered me and it was vicious. I was being nailed and couldn't get out. I survived, just. Come the next I'm going forward, I'm punching but could hardly lift my arms. Thirty-three seconds remained when he put me down. I clambered to my feet and Mickey Vann gave me the count.

'You okay?' Vann asked, he looked in my eyes.

Yeah, I was good; hurting, exhausted but ready to keep going. I'd been worse.

I nodded and we fought on. Another right hook from Johannsen slammed into my face and this time Vann reckoned he'd seen enough and stepped in to call it off! I went mad, I pushed him twice in the chest. This wasn't right! I was tired, shattered even, no way was I beaten. Johannsen fell into Frank Maloney's arms and Bobby came over to me, but I'd gone.

I was fuming with tears of rage. Fuck you Vann, I thought. Your mate, eh?

I didn't hang around, I climbed through the ropes and I was away. Out of sight. Disgusted and convinced I'd been the victim of a blatant home decision and I shouldn't have been stopped. After an earlier victory over the Mexican Oscar Galindo when Mickey Vann was also the referee, I'd come across him in the corridor afterwards. I'd won with an eleventh round stoppage, but that fight had been just brutal as this.

'I done you a favour there Mike,' he had said.

Had Vann helped Johannsen as he claimed to me or do the passing years and the bitter pill of defeat just distort the truth? It's a long time ago but it still hurts.

In the dressing room I could hear the chants of 'Yorkshire, Yorkshire, Yorkshire' roaring out from the victorious Johannsen supporters. Congratulations to Carl, but was it finally over?

Is it ever?

34: CALL MY NAME

'You have to know you can win. You have to think you can win. You have to feel you can win.'

SUGAR RAY LEONARD

L IKE POURING WATER ON SAND the fifteen grand was gone in seconds. Since getting married I'd stopped fooling around, but the boozing and drugs carried on unabated. One simply led to another and like a magician who made rabbits disappear in a hat, my trick came in the form of handing cash over the bar or to dealers. Hey fuckin' presto I was skint again and needed to get back in the ring.

29-3-2008: Baz Carey: This fight against a hard nut journeyman, Baz Carey from Coventry, would take place in Glasgow. Kevin Maree had some great contacts up there, including two who had kindly agreed to sponsor me; Eddie Beattie of Whiteinch Demolition and Pat Gilloly who had a plant hire business. I was adored in that city because of the carnage I'd wreaked on their great rival Edinburgh. So many Glaswegians have told me that on the night I beat Alex Arthur, the celebrations in parts of Glasgow was matched only by what was happening in Manchester. Well this lot would do for me! The feeling was mutual. I loved the place and wasn't allowed to buy a drink in any pub I ever set foot in up there. One old man said to me once in a back street boozer, as we shared the odd whiskey chaser or two, 'Boy if you'd had been around in William Wallace's Braveheart's time, the film would only have lasted an hour.'

This was six rounds of pushing, shoving, wrestling, pulling and somewhere in between a boxing match broke out. I beat Carey on points, but it was hard graft. This was one tough bastard who I couldn't rattle before the fight and in it he seemed happy enough to just try and stifle me. That I came through was more due to pure heart than anything resembling technical ability or a supposed gulf in class. I took the money and couldn't wait to get out of there because as the night called, I belonged to Glasgow.

And it belonged to me!

On returning to Manchester with Kevin Maree, all the talk in the car turned to what was happening around the Lightweight and Welterweight divisions. There was only one name on our lips. A young kid from Bolton who Frank Warren appeared to be grooming for a future shot at the world title. Twenty-two year-old Amir Khan. The kid was flash, lightning quick and box office. He'd already started gathering belts. The Commonwealth Lightweight and the WBO Intercontinental Lightweight titles. The way Warren was handling Khan reminded me so much of the way he built up Alex Arthur.

And everybody knew how that ended.

However there was trouble in *Sports Network* paradise. Khan had dumped his highly-rated Salford-based trainer, Oliver Harrison. Publicly they were all claiming it was amicable but everyone in boxing knew that Harrison was seething and only found out from the newspapers and a letter shoved under his gym door. Very classy and scant reward for guiding the unbeaten Khan through his first seventeen fights. Amir's father claimed Harrison couldn't take his boy to the next level. I'd love a shot at Khan and said as much to Kevin.

'I could nail him early, Kev. Khan is good but his chin is made of fuckin' glass. I'd smash it into a thousand pieces.'

Kevin smiled. 'Imagine if we could get Oliver in the corner to help you do it?' I laughed at that suggestion. It would've been perfect, but sadly there was no chance of that happening. I could never be that lucky. Besides, Warren would surely be mad to risk letting me loose on another of his prodigies. Once bitten…

Or so they say.

I received the call personally off Frank Warren. 'I have an offer for you, Mike. How do you fancy Amir Khan in June? A Saturday night in Birmingham and live on ITV? I'll pay you thirty-five grand. What do you say?'

Of course I accepted.

It was strange though because I felt almost insulted at the same time. Did they now think that little of me? Was I just a fuckin' stepping stone for Warren's new golden boy. I knew I was finished at the top level. I still had the power, but the timing had gone. I'd become resigned to that fact, I'd learned to live with it. So long as I could fight and make a few quid then so be it. It was a living because I knew outside the ring I could do nothing else and I was petrified of what lay in store when the boxing was finally over. And yet the offer from Warren still stuck in my throat. I'd been playing a stupid game and kidding myself thinking I was the only one who realised that the magic was no longer there. The reality was crystal clear for all to see. And it really hurt.

Thirty-five grand or not.

Oliver's army: Sometimes things happen in this life that just leave you thinking there are other forces at work. Within a month of my conversation with Kevin in the car returning from Scotland about fighting Amir Khan and the possibility of Oliver Harrison coming on board. Well, guess who got in touch?

It was a phone call that had me dancing around the gym! Oliver Harrison contacted us to say if we agreed to stay quiet and give it absolutely no publicity, then he'd help in preparation for the Khan fight.

My first meeting with Oliver was like going back to school. The man was sheer class. Bobby, Kevin and the other boys in the gym immediately made him feel like part of the family and suddenly beating Khan was no longer an impossible dream. Oliver sat me down and within moments all my self-doubts started to fade away. 'Mike you've won nine titles, you can do it! You've got the power and we'll work on your conditioning. Amir is never gonna knock you out and it's not as if you're an old man. One shot that's all you need. Hit him hard on the top of the head and he'll go. Believe me. It's not as if you haven't done it before.'

Soon I was flying in training; the sparring, the speedbag, working the pads. As the weight fell away so did the doubts and in their place came a belief that Amir Khan would be facing a Michael Gomez he really didn't expect. I listened to every word Oliver said. It was gold dust. More importantly, I felt the old swagger returning and the belief that nobody could beat me was back. Call it misplaced arrogance, stupidity or simply the desire to prove that despite what the world was saying, Gomez time was not yet over.

One of the first things Oliver changed were my sparring partners. I'd now spar with quick lightweights like a lad from Salford he recommended, Lee Gillespie, instead of bigger lads such as middleweights Brian Rose and Jack Arnfield. I chased Lee around the ring constantly until finally I caught up and though Khan would be infinitely harder to hunt down, one thing was certain; if I cornered him and he'd nowhere to run then we'd see what Frank Warren's boy wonder was made of, if the heart for battle truly existed inside because make no mistake, Amir was about to enter the fight of his young life.

As agreed with Oliver, we never went public on him helping me train, but stuff inevitably leaked out and word reached back to the Amir Khan camp who went mental. An irate Khan let fly whenever Oliver's name came up. 'He's disloyal and was unable to teach effective defensive tactics. You definitely lose respect for a coach when that happens because it is only two months since he split with me. Top coaches would never do a thing like that, so it shows what kind of person he is.' In reality Oliver was shabbily treated by Khan's crowd. In time history would show that the 82nd Airborne would have had trouble protecting that chin.

When I was pulled by journalists on the matter I just shrugged my shoulders and smiled. 'It's all rubbish mate, print what you want. Bobby Rimmer is my trainer.'

Meanwhile, Amir was not a happy lad and despite claiming that he wasn't worried in the slightest about facing me, behind the scenes I was later told they were panicking on Oliver knowing the inside track. Was there a silver bullet to put an end to their gravy train? Was Gomez truly past it or could you really teach an old dog, especially a wild one like me, new tricks?

It wasn't rocket science that myself and Oliver were working on. I'd been around long enough to know your time does come and go in this game. There was a plan, I knew where to hurt Khan, but the problem would be getting close enough to land the shots. But I was fit and firing. There was enough left in the tank for one last almighty fling – this traveller's son was set to roll back the years. Albeit if a miracle was to happen it'd better be fast!

Two weeks before the fight I decided to play with Amir Khan's head and decided not to show for the press conference at the Birmingham National Indoor Arena. Why not? He was the star and nobody had ever done that to him before. It might give Khan something to think about. Let the boy simmer. Not turning up was never anything to do with a lack of respect, it was all about the fight. For Michael Gomez the war had already begun. But Amir definitely wasn't happy!

'In the end it's what I do that matters and I'm going to win this fight handsomely. Gomez has threatened all sorts of things and I've no doubt that he will use his greater experience to make them happen. That just makes me even more determined to beat him up. The response from the Birmingham fans has been fantastic and I will be sending them home happy with what they have seen'…

Hooked; line and fuckin' sinker. I'd reeled him in. Amir Khan would be coming to fight and I'd be waiting.

The weigh-in: I was relaxed and came in at nine stone eight. I was quiet, I said nothing. All part of the masterplan. Let him come expecting a snarling maniac only to find a Michael Gomez utterly relaxed and in control.

Amir Khan stepped on and weighed in half a pound under.

In the head to head he tried to give me the eyes but I just ignored him and stared back. No words, no pushing, no head butts. No need.

Khan didn't scare me and he knew it. However, come the end, I couldn't help a wry smile appearing on my face. As if to say, 'behave yourself, lad. I've seen it all before.'

Again I was still playing games over Oliver Harrison's involvement in my training. For obvious reasons, Oliver wouldn't be in my corner, but he couldn't have helped me more. I spoke to *Setanta Sports* and carried on the charade.

'None of it's true. It's been a ruse, a wind up. It was said to get under Amir Khan's skin and we succeeded. Oliver Harrison hasn't been working with me. This was a rumour started to unsettle Khan. Besides what can Harrison teach Michael Gomez? I've been staying with my trainer Bobby Rimmer. We're the ones who've done it. They've come here today expecting me to stare him out but I didn't do that. They expect me to get in his face and do what I normally do but I didn't. I'm doing everything differently from what they expected. I've stayed in since Christmas. I've been a good lad, honest! And I'm ready to go to war. I'm ready to do this.'

I was then collared by a very pretty lady from Frank Warren TV, who asked if I really felt I had any chance of beating Khan?

'Look, I've been finished for five years. This is exactly what they said before Alex Arthur. One thing you don't do is go to a traveller at the end of his career and say there's a chance of making some big dough if you knock out Amir Khan. And that's why I'm gonna beat him'.

She went on. 'Why didn't you turn up at the press conference? Was it because you were nervous? Even worried maybe?'

This made me smile. Pretty but dense. 'Listen, I've been dead for forty-eight seconds. I've been clinically dead for forty-eight seconds. If death doesn't scare me, why should Khan?'

On my thirty-first birthday, I prepared to reap the whirlwind that was Amir Iqbal Khan. The boy was confident. Cocky even.

'I know how good I am and I know Michael Gomez is not going to beat me in a million years. It's laughable. Gomez can be as fit and prepared as he wants, but with my power, speed and skills, I'm going to break him down big-time. I'm in the best condition of my career.'

I had to give it the kid, he sounded like me!

Only hours before the fight, I was still in my hotel room with Kevin. Suddenly an advertisement for the fight came on the television. I watched spellbound and it truly felt surreal. The contest against Amir Khan was huge. Win it and I was well and truly back.

'Mike look at this,' said Kevin. He was stood at the bedroom window. Across the road was where Khan was staying in a hotel much more grand and lavish than ours. He was leaving for the arena in a huge entourage of six limousines. It was like a movie premiere. A showbiz extravaganza! Cameras flashed, photographers and journalists flittered around him like Khan was some huge visiting, Hollywood star.

Meanwhile me and my corner were going by taxi!

Ten thousand people had packed out the arena for our fight. It was Saturday night at peak time. There'd be millions watching a live execution. But why put myself through any more agony and pain? Here and now was the perfect place to go out with thirty-five grand off Uncle Frank, keep my head down and just do five or six rounds then retire on my stool. Go out with a weak surrender, a white flag and patronising accolades.

'Oh he was good once.'

'Should have looked after himself.'

'What a waste.'

'Gomez threw it all away.'

I could disappear with a whimper. Or there was another way. The path I'd always followed. I could come out banging and go after Khan and hunt him down from the opening fuckin' bell. In doing so, he could rain mayhem down upon me and end my world. Or maybe, there was just a chance I'd get close and once more ruin the party and send everybody home crying. Then through gritted teeth they'd give three cheers for the bad guy.

And be forced to call my name.

One last time I went to war.

21-6-2008: Amir Khan: It was lovely to see Alex Arthur come into my dressing room beforehand and wish me luck. Our epic tear-up in Edinburgh is still classed as one of the greatest fights in the history of British boxing.

'Do to Khan what you did to me Mike,' smiled Alex, as he shook my hand.

'Good luck pal.'

The master of ceremonies voice roared out.

'Please welcome into the ring Michael Gomez!'

I heard an eruption of noise. The smoke cleared and in I went. A last walk maybe? To a soundtrack of *Kiss my Irish Ass* by the Dropkick Murphys, I made my way. I was wearing an Irish tricolour robe with matching shorts and a blue sombrero. Once in the ring I roared across to my supporters who might have been outnumbered but were defiant, loud and still believing. Who could ask for more? The noise was already deafening.

Then they called for Amir Khan and the roof almost came off!

Nice entry, I remember thinking. Very dramatic music and Amir looked a million dollars in a white and silver robe. I almost applauded myself. But looking the part was easy, to live the dream you had to earn it. Through the ropes he came, waving to the crowd. I noticed Frank Warren smiling and admiring his latest prodigy. Hopefully he'd soon be suffering flashbacks to that night in Edinburgh five years before.

Reluctantly we edged gloves. I kissed my medallion, I crossed myself and walked towards the centre of the ring at the sound of the bell. It was a call to arms. Almost immediately I thought I was surrounded and that there was six of him in there. Christ, this kid was fast. Khan's hand speed was just devastating. It was like being up against the fuckin' Road Runner. I tried to track him, I bobbed and weaved, but his shots were crisp and clean and not one missed my face. He delivered rapier combinations that would just stop me in my tracks. I was stood taking hits; two, three, four and five punches a time and I couldn't get near him.

Khan hit with such precision and pace, but didn't necessarily hurt. It was all about speed, though he did cut me above the eye. Another flurry of six punches and a right to the head and down I went. Dropped in the first round. Later Kevin told me he was halfway through filling the water bottle, then thought it wasn't worth bothering with, such was Khan's ferocious start. But no way was I going to go out like this. No fuckin' way! The referee, John Keane, gave me the count and we fought on. Khan was simply too fast and getting off so many shots, I swear it felt like I was in slow motion and him on fast forward. Finally the bell sounded and I headed back to my corner hardly able to believe what I'd just endured.

Angry with myself, I wasn't listening to a word Kevin and Bobby was saying. I was being embarrassed in there and I couldn't let that stand. I wasn't having it. It hurt like fuck and no way on this earth was Michael Gomez going to be remembered as a stooge to Amir Khan's blistering punches. I was going to chase Khan to the end of the earth and whatever it took, I remember saying to myself, 'I'll catch this kid'.

After all these fuckin' years, it wasn't going to end like this.

No, no, no. This was nothing to do with belts or titles. It was pride.

Round Two began and I immediately went after him. Khan was jabbing and moving, but I was his shadow and then with a powerful left hook over the top, I caught him on the top of the head and down he went!

The arena went mad!

I stepped back to a neutral corner whilst Keane give him the count. I remember I got straight on the phone to the big fella and I said, please God, please! Sadly, he was engaged and Khan staggered back to his feet. Suddenly the years fell away and roared on by the chants of 'Gomez, Gomez' thundering out from my supporters, I went in to finish him off.

Khan was rocked, he'd tried telling his corner that it was a slip but I'd really hurt him and we'd see as I hunted him down, whether the hype was real or just that.

This was my fight now – a world of pain I loved and hated with equal measure. Left hooks tore into his midriff and Khan covered up, he was on the ropes and I let fly with everything I had. As I punched, I prayed and I looked to end this fight with just one shot that would land golden boy Amir Khan back in Bolton. He was in a strange land now, one where anything could happen. He was at the mercy of a traveller's son chasing a few quid and needing only to win a fight to take it!

Welcome to Gomez world!

Come the end of round two, Khan had rallied slightly and caught me with another couple of fast combinations that proved there was indeed heart along with the hype, but I still believed sooner or later I'd catch him again.

In the third I came out swinging left hooks. It was a free for all and Khan hit back with a rat-a-tat-tat blur of stinging punches and for the first time that night, I began to feel my legs. Determined not to give him any hint of this, I punched my chest as if to say, I'm all heart. If you're going to win this fight, you'd better be prepared to come with me to a place you've never been before.

I could see through Khan's eyes and they told his story. This was intuitive; the light to his soul showed he was hurting. Call it the gypsy inside me but I knew. Amir Khan was in the fight of his young life.

I noticed at ringside Frank Warren's face and it was an expression I'd seen before. In Sunshine on Leith I destroyed Warren's last action man and now I'd every intention of destroying his latest favourite toy. Still I was bobbing and weaving, looking for the one shot to end it, but Khan's response was to come roaring back with a bombardment that left me thinking he had three hands. A ghost of a glove.

I was slowing down and missing whilst Khan cut loose, forcing me to just keep walking onto punches. The round ended and I sagged on the stool. Breathless. I knew my time was running short but at least I was still in there. He may stop me but I wasn't going down. In the corner Bobby and Kevin were trying to give me advice but for the first time in my life I truly felt I was alone in there. I missed Brian and Billy. In a battle like this I needed the sort of guidance that came only from a chosen few. God bless the lads, but neither had experienced this level of boxing.

Round Four and I was still carrying the fight to Khan when I caught and knocked the breath out of him, I'd hurt his ribs! In I went throwing bombs. He covered up and I was on him like a fuckin' rash, the crowd roared; all was manic and madness. A furore.

Then Amir ignited and from seemingly reeling came flying back with a flurry of punches that knocked me from one side of the ring to the other. They just kept coming, like being caught in a fierce hailstorm. Bang! Bang! Bang! Not one on their own hurt, but when they land together you're in trouble.

I came back throwing wildly, just to stem the tide. I noticed Khan was holding his glove to protect his rib. I'd bought the ticket and had two targets. The head or rib. Toe to toe we stood in the centre of the ring. My home, too tired and weary to move. Come on Amir, I thought, let's end it and off we went throwing punches. Only to be halted in our tracks by the bell sounding. One night a best friend, another your worst enemy.

Everything Oliver Harrison had told me to do I'd tried, but so many times the punches were a split second off, or I'd move my head just not quickly enough and get caught. I came out still trying in the fifth to nail Khan but was being hit so many times in return. One body shot caught and I felt the wind whistle out of my mouth, causing me to go down on one knee and take a count. A delayed reaction. John Keane looked me in the eyes.

'You okay Mike?' I nodded, but I wasn't.

I went after Khan once more and he rocked me with a powerful right hand. Still I tried to attack but was being hammered on the rebound by his endless barrages of punches. It was unrelenting, my head was knocked left to right and back again. On and on. Shot after shot, Khan was using me for target practice. Finally Keane stepped in and stopped the fight. I could claim he shouldn't have done so but I would have stood and taken that punishment all evening. I'm sure Keane took this into consideration when ending it. Five rounds of carnage. Khan came over and embraced me. 'You're a warrior man.'

Afterwards he said that in fighting Michael Gomez he'd moved up to world class level. I appreciated those words.

I liked Amir Khan but I also feared for the kid at that time. Someone had to grab hold of him and sort out his defence because that chin was vulnerable beyond words. They needed to protect Khan. There were even punchers at domestic level who would've put him into tomorrow. Manchester's own John Murray for one. Three months on from our fight, Khan was knocked out in the first round by a little known Colombian, Breidis Prescott. I was sorry to see that. Happily in time Amir went on to become a world champion and it was great to see.

He's a tough kid. A nice kid.

I was getting a lot of praise following the fight but personally I was devastated. The loss was made infinitely worse for me by the realisation that I shouldn't even have been in that ring. It was over a long time ago. The most maddeningly and frustrating thing was the realisation that if I'd looked after myself and not careered off the rails between fights, then that night Michael Gomez wouldn't have been viewed as a washed up fighter who gave his all in a last gallant effort to reclaim the glory days…

The fuckin' glory days I ask you? I can't even remember half of them.

Maybe with just a little more respect for myself my career might have been up there. I could have been a one in a million and so much more than a supporting act. A shining fuckin' star and one so bright you'd have to wear matching shades with a sombrero. Diego Corales and Erik Morales would've needed a great night and been fully switched on to have got me off their fuckin' trail. Instead I would always be just a contender, because I lost the one fight I always needed to win. That one with the man in the fuckin' mirror.

He beat me.

It was never anybody's fault but my own. And when there's no one else to blame, where do you turn? You don't. You simply burn up inside.

I lived a lie. The Alex Arthur fight proved what I was truly capable of when fully focused. Sadly, beating Arthur and training as I did was the worst thing that ever happened because it meant a part of me always believed, well I'd done it once, I could do it again. But you can't just switch it on, it simply doesn't work like that. The human body isn't a machine. It lives and breathes. Wears and tears and if you don't look after it then eventually, especially in this business, it will hang you out to dry.

If such a thing was to happen inside the ring then all bets were off. A stretcher or a shield. It mattered not. The last bell.

Amir Khan was an exceptional fighter with exceptional vulnerabilities. I could, should and would have beaten him if I'd lived the life. Booze and cocaine never created champions and great fighters but it sure as hell fuckin' destroyed more than its fair share. And so congratulations to Amir. For me it was back to the wilderness. Put another sombrero on the fire.

Where did I go from here?

35: WISHING ON A STAR

'There's no more honest place in sport than the boxing ring. You can't tell lies in there, you can't pretend.'

RICKY HATTON

AFTER THE FIGHT I went back to the hotel and the phone rang non-stop with people telling me how well I'd done. Now I'd been on ITV, I was a star again and when out and about in pubs and clubs around Manchester everybody wanted to give me a line or buy me a beer. Being the person I was, I turned nothing down, because I knew sure as night followed day that the time would come again when the offers weren't there. So I made hay and milked this Mancunian kindness for all it was worth. But still I wanted to fight on. To try and gather up all I could from an ever -decreasing Gomez gravy train.

By now I'd split from Bobby Rimmer and gone full time with Kevin Maree. There was no bitterness or recrimination with Bobby, it was just a natural end and we're still good friend today. He's now a fantastic trainer and Brian Rose is reaping the rewards. I wish him all the best. I always loved Bobby.

28-9-2008: Chris Brophy: Whilst sat in the office gym chatting with Kevin Maree, the phone rang and it was Steve Woods. Something had come up. One of our lads, Shaun Horsfield, had been forced through injury to pull out of a fight and they were discussing a possible replacement. Without even thinking I butted in.

'I'll do it.'

At first, due to the lack of time I'd have to prepare and the fact I was hardly in great condition, both were dubious but I eventually talked them round.

'Come on lads, it's Gomez time again! You know it makes sense.'

It wasn't with any great enthusiasm that they agreed to me stepping in. I shouldn't really have been surprised at the reluctance for it was only four days before the fight and I was nearly eleven stone in weight.

'I'll be okay,' I said. 'Don't worry about me.'

It was only a fight after all.

On entering the ring with all my belts on show, I noticed Chris Brophy glaring across. Little did I know then, but this wound him up like a cuckoo clock! At the Municipal Hall in Colne, Lancashire, in front of five hundred people, I put the thirty-three year-old middleweight Brophy away in two rounds of a four round contest. I'd good support at such short notice and was determined to put on a show for the small band of loyal travelling Mancs. But it was a brief yet violent contest. Brophy shocked me and came out like a man possessed! I was getting a mauling and it was just a case of biting down on the gum shield.

I got through the first and sat back on the stool, before looking up at Kevin.

'Who's rattled his fuckin' cage?'

'You did with the belts!'

The second round saw me catch Brophy early with a peach of a body shot and down he went. Fight over, but it had been scary for a while. It was short and sweet, though hard work. Brophy said later that seeing my belts beforehand inspired him and he treated this fight like a shot at a world title! However it all ended well and I'd got away with it. To take this fight with no time for preparation and in a weight division I'd never previously fought might have been brave, perhaps foolish. Others said I was downright suicidal, a blown-up featherweight fighting at middleweight! Yet that few quid kept me ticking over, I'd fight every day if I had to find beer money and cash to keep Alison and the kids fed and clothed. I was warming to the fact this was the way of things now. Without noticing, I had become a journeyman. I was brawling but I wasn't in boxing to worry about my good looks.

You pay and I'd fight them. Just keep me in that fuckin' ring.

10-10-2008: Baz Carey: I genuinely didn't like this man and I was fired up. We'd fought the previous March and since then I'd heard he'd done nothing but bad mouth me after I beat him. So this was one contest that, even at this late stage in my career where I was winding down, I had no problem getting up for. The contest would take place at the Dalziel Park Country Club, near Motherwell. At the press conference I'd told Carey I'd not just batter him in the ring but afterwards I'd do the same thing in the car park too with no gloves or referee. He seemed up for that and it was like the good old days were back!

I'd missed them.

I went on with him just glaring at me. The old adage of 'if looks could kill' came to mind as I went into overdrive.

'I took it easy last time, I was too casual. I was dead nice to him and being friendly. And then he goes around slagging me off? What a bad mistake that was because now I'm not just gonna punch his head off. I've decided to knock him out!'

I continued to wind him up at the weigh-in when I stuck my face into his. Carey went off like a rocket! Finally we were dragged apart. Come the fight it was a rough, bruising and dirty affair. Beforehand in the ring, I did the same thing again and he erupted once more with the promoters having to come between us. I beat Carey well on points over six rounds to earn a pittance of two grand but even then at the end he was hardly in the mood to shake hands and make up. I've heard to this day that Baz Carey is still bitter. No pleasing some people.

21-12-2008: Chris Long: Again in Motherwell, just four days before Christmas, I went in against the twenty-eight-year-old Long, who was a former champion kick boxer. Top class I was told; he'd fought for not just British but European and world titles. We had a decent scrap for six rounds and I beat him on points but it was a close affair and Long was a good kid. I'd now reached forty-seven fights in my professional career and three more of similar vain for a round fifty would be some achievement. All due respect to Chris Long but with the time now drawing near when I'd have no choice but to put the gloves away, it'd be nice to have one last tear up at the top level.

But who'd give me a shot now?

Around this time I received a phone call from Dean Powell, a good friend who had matched a lot of my fights, but who was in Amir Khan's corner when we fought. That was the business. There were no hard feelings because at the end of the day it's just a job. Everybody does what they have to in order to put food on the table for families and get by in life. Dean asked if I'd consider going over to Amir Khan's camp to help with his sparring, which I happily agreed to do. It paid well so it was a no-brainer. Off I went, money for old rope. What was he going to do, knock me out?

On the first day there we were just settling in. I was joking with Amir about taking it easy on me or I'd get angry. The kid was top class and made me feel welcome from the off. That was until we got in the ring and he let fly with an uppercut that rocked me solid. I winced and pulled up slightly, but nobody mentioned it. Not the type to miss anything, in an eyeblink, Dean clocked this. He'd been around a long time and understood straight away that my time as a top class fighter was up. Not so long ago there was no way on this earth such a thing could have happened, I would've just kept on walking through Khan like the fuckin' terminator before letting loose and giving him hell. But Gomez time was truly over. Dean had an idea. He was also close to Ricky Burns, the current Commonwealth super featherweight title holder. In his role as match-maker Dean contacted Burns with an offer.

'Gomez is shot and tailor-made for you in Glasgow Ricky. It's bound to be a sell-out. The city loves you both.'

Burns wasn't so sure. At first he didn't want the fight because of my record against Scottish fighters. Over the years I'd wreaked carnage over the Jocks and he didn't fancy being added to a long list of his fallen countrymen but Dean convinced him that I was ripe for the taking. I also was up for it. A last decent pay day in a city I'd grown to love, so why not? I'd watched Ricky Burns fight and knew I could beat him but then I also thought the same about Carl Johannsen and Amir Khan. There was that constant battle inside my head between reality and fantasy; deep down I really knew my time had gone and that was the frightening thing. They say the one person you can never fool is yourself, but by God, I was giving it a good go.

Kevin Maree knew that to prepare properly for the Ricky Burns fight he had to get me out of Manchester. I stayed out at the Stirk House hotel in Gisburn near Clitheroe and trained in his leisure centre nearby. Kevin and my two sponsors Pat and Eddie ensured I'd everything I needed, the best food and accommodation. Nothing was too much trouble. I threw myself into it. I went running in the hills around Burnley. I was losing the weight to fight back at super featherweight but in the gym it was a living nightmare. During sparring I was getting caught constantly. I was forever making excuses or just trying to laugh it off.

'Heavy one last night lads.'

But my timing was a split second off. I'd move and hit, but the co-ordination was shot. I was out of sync. Nothing was right. I was dying inside, but nobody was saying anything, so I never spoke up.

Perhaps it wasn't being noticed or maybe people didn't have the balls to say anything? I do know that I so missed Brian or Billy at that time. I would've hated it and caused absolute murder and screamed the house down but they'd both have told me straight.

'It's over Michael… It's all over.'

I gave everything, I'd train like a madman, but I was doing it all to just try and revitalise myself and not for the fight. I was looking for a miracle but my body had simply given up. I kept going and playing this damn, fool, stupid game.

I was wishing on a star that had fallen from the sky many years before.

36: BAD BLOOD

'I don't want to be remembered as a beaten champion.'

ROCKY MARCIANO

WHEN ASKED ABOUT the capabilities of Ricky Burns by a journalist, I thought why mess around? Just take the pin out of the grenade and roll it in the direction of Glasgow. If by some miracle I was going to pull this off, then like against Amir Khan and Carl Johannsen, I needed to draw Burns into an early war then we'd see what he's made of.

'I think Ricky Burns is one of the weakest Commonwealth title holders at the moment. He's not very strong and he doesn't really impress. I don't mean to put him down, he's tough and no one's stopped him yet, but I've always wanted to be Commonwealth champion. I was number one contender for four years and Frank Warren never put me in for it. And now? Well, better late than never. I'll just have to knock Burns out to win it.'

Over to you Ricky.

We'd already had words four months before when I'd gone to see Burns with Kevin Maree in the first defence of his commonwealth title against Yakubu Amidu at the Kelvin Hall in Glasgow. Myself and Kevin were sat two rows from the front. After he'd stopped Amidu in the seventh I turned to Kevin. 'Fuck it mate, I'm getting in the ring.' In I went to confront him. What better place to start a war and dent his pride than in front of his own people. At the time it was done on a whim. 'Come on Ricky what do you say? Where's your bottle? You won't get anyone to fight better than me. Let's get it on.' This was before Dean Powell saw me get caught by Amir Khan in sparring. Obviously Burns thought then I was simply some punchy Manc lunatic trying to kickstart a fight against him and a watching, seething Kelvin Hall. A ferocious Glaswegian bear-pit with clientele to match that made the Meadowbank arena in Edinburgh seem like a nun's needlework class.

When the fight was made official Burns fired back. 'Gomez was a great fighter in his day but now he's just looking for one last pay day. Well, this is his chance to live up to his high opinion of himself. Nothing will give me greater pleasure than to beat him up.'

And all this was before the Press conference when it really got serious.

Press conference 1: We went head to head and it so nearly turned into all-out war two weeks before the actual fight…

'All I'm thinking about is beating Ricky Burns and I will beat him. I promise ya! I'm straightforward. If I don't like you, I come to your face and tell you.' Ricky was in the papers saying he's gonna finish my career, but then to my face is dead nice and shakes my hand. 'We'll see on the night. I'll beat Ricky Burns. I'm telling you that now.'

Then I turned to Burns. 'I'm gonna take you back to school, pal.'

'The only thing you'll be walking away with is your pay cheque,' he shot back. 'I don't really get tied up with all this. Michael is Michael and that's just the way he is. I'm in this for the love of the sport, not to bad-mouth people. He's been bad-mouthing me so I'll give him a chance and we'll see come fight night who's going to get shut up. No disrespect to Michael Gomez, he's always a danger and can punch, so I'm going into this fight 100% focused. If I go into this fight with any doubts and there is an upset, I'm back down the waiting list again for another title and I can't afford that.'

'Trust me,' I replied, 'I've nowhere to go if I lose this fight. I'm not young enough to come again so your man here is going down'

And so the circus moved outside for the photoshoot… Minders, security guards, camps and promoters stood between us. Somebody came up with the grand idea of doing a photograph on a car park roof overlooking the Glasgow landscape. Big mistake! Off we traipsed, only for myself and Burns to start the fight early and nearly send the entire crowd over the edge as they dived in between us. Wiping out camps, promoters and a host of journalists and cameramen would've been a first even for me.

'Come 27th March I'm gonna fuckin' drop you Gomez!'

'Keep dreaming, dickhead. Keep fuckin' dreaming!'

And on and on…

Get out of my face: The day before at the pre-fight press conference it almost exploded again at the finish. The atmosphere was truly poisonous. No need for hype. 'I know I'm gonna beat Ricky Burns. He's made a big mistake by being disrespectful to me: he's a little fuckin' idiot and I'm going to smash his head in. I'll take him to school.'

I turned to Burns. 'I'll write you off now, you little shit.'

He smiled. 'I believe I'm moving down a level with this bout.'

'You're a fuckin' muppet!' I shouted.

He continued. 'I won't be intimidated by his mind games and nor will I be suckered into a slugging match, which would suit him. This doesn't affect me at all. If he wants to turn this into a circus, then that's up to him. I won't be drawn into any of this nonsense. Once we're both in that ring there will be nowhere for him to go. I've trained for twelve hard rounds but I don't see him lasting past eight.'

I stood up and went for him, but was dragged back. At that moment I hated Ricky Burns and he no doubt thought similar of me. Now we'd exchanged pleasantries it was time to move on to the head to head…

I was so looking forward to this.

All of us were stood hanging around surrounded by our camps. Both ready to erupt if we got too close. Burns had made a comment in the newspapers that after beating me, he was going to get a tattoo done of Gomez knocked out on the canvas. Fuckin' hilarious. So just beforehand I'd got Kevin to draw on my chest with a pen a matchstick figure of Burns lying sparked. That went down well with Glasgow's finest when I showed it off!

I couldn't wait to get in this guy's face. But I wasn't finding it easy due to the fact I was flanked by two security bruisers who never left my side. Their eyes were constantly on me. Obviously the order had gone out to them, 'Watch Gomez like a hawk cos he's a mad bastard.'

I was wired. I got the call to finally face off against Burns and you could cut the air with a knife. This was, after all, Glasgow. Like Manchester, a fighting city. His crowd were no shrinking violets. Steeped in a tradition of great fighters and hardly known for welcoming anybody from south of the border, especially those like me who enjoyed trash talking and trying their almighty best to land the nut on one of their favourite sons.

'Fuck off ya tinker!' I heard the voice coming from his camp. It was Alex Harrison, Burns' manager. Fuckin' charming, I thought. I stared over at him and he looked really pleased with himself. One classy fucker. Not that it bothered me. It was the IRA stuff they hurled at me earlier on in the day that pissed me off. I'd no fuckin' idea where that came from.

'Oi!' shouted Kevin to Harrison. 'Cut that out. No racist talk!'

I was shepherded into Burns' face and held back so I just couldn't reach him!

Burns: 'Get out of my face.'

Gomez: 'Fuck off you prick, I'm gonna be in your face tomorrow.'

Burns: 'Good. Because tomorrow I can do something about shutting you up.'

'You're a fuckin' danger to yer self,' roared out Harrison again, who appeared more rattled than his fighter. I had to give it the bastard, he was getting into the spirit of things.

Myself and Burns continued.

Gomez: 'We'll sort this in the fuckin' ring.'

Burns: 'Yeah we will and I'll retire ya permanently.'

Harrison lets fly again. 'Go back and sleep in yer fuckin' car!'

This was verging on all-out war... bad blood.

I'd come to Glasgow looking for a proper battle and I'd got one!

I hadn't lost my touch.

37: GHOST OF A TRAVELLER'S SON

'The end of laughter and soft lies. The end of nights we tried to die. This is the end.'

JIM MORRISON (THE DOORS)

27-3-2009: Ricky Burns: Highly charged didn't do it justice. I'd a decent turn out from Manchester but as I looked around there were as many police as punters in the arena. Anybody would think Michael Gomez was in town. Sadly there was no last miracle as the final fight unfolded. At the Bellahouston Leisure centre in Glasgow, in front of a raging Scottish crowd that bayed for my blood, it all came to an inglorious end in the seventh round.

The fourteen years of chasing rainbows was over. There had been too many fuckin' storms. The referee Howard Foster called it off when Burns staggered me with a sweetly-timed left hook and then let fly with a blinding combination of around twelve punches without reply. I was almost out, my knees sagging. Ian McLeod, Craig Docherty and Alex Arthur had bitten the dust but finally a Scot had struck gold and nailed the Irish-Mexican. It'd taken them long enough and ultimately it was a washed-up Michael Gomez. They'd got me when I was gone.

The fire and furore I'd shown pre-fight proved to be just bluster as Burns celebrated wildly and I was helped back to my corner. With the noise coming from the crowd you'd have thought Scotland had won the World Cup and the Eurovision Song Contest all at once. I had to give it Burns, who'd been on me from the opening bell.

Working behind an unerringly accurate jab, he landed constantly and any attempt to crowd him out was bettered by his manoeuvring away and continuing to hit. Burns was simply younger, fitter, faster and landed consistently. I had no spark.

My best shot was always to try and work on his inside, but there was nothing doing. Everything just felt old and worn out. Burns was docked for holding, but it was just a matter of time. I was simply taking too many shots throughout. What did annoy me was him saying he'd take me out in seven and doing so. That really irked. I'd like Rocky Burns to have come face to face with the Gomez who smashed Alex Arthur, instead of this ghost of a traveller's son.

I did catch him once in the fourth; a right uppercut which threw off the years and gained speed and power by doing so. I rocked his head back, but fair do's he showed composure, took it and moved on. Burns kept his cool as I tried every trick I knew inside to rattle him. The kid just carried on busily marking up both my head and body with some classy precision shots. I got a cut in the sixth and finally the story ended in the seventh.

At the finish there was no drum roll. No trumpets sounded. There was just a weathered old boxer whose time in the ring was brought to a brutal halt.

At least I could say I was a warrior, I wouldn't have wanted it any other way.

This was how it should be. No complaints and no more doubts.

I spoke to Sky Sports at ringside and confirmed this fight would be my last. 'Ricky Burns performed well. But taking nothing away from him, he just beat an old Michael Gomez. It was stupid taking this fight on, but it's now definitely over. I'd like to thank all my supporters throughout my career. They've been superb. I'd also like to thank Brian Hughes, Billy Graham, Bobby Rimmer, my sponsors Pat and Eddie. The promoters Steve Woods, Frank Warren, Frank Maloney and these days, Kevin Maree; a manager and my friend. Also you lot at Sky Sports, maybe I'll come to you for a job?'

There was a stilted silence from the reporter. He looked worried to death!

'It's been a great ride, but the end has come now. There'll be no tears though.'

…At least not in public.

I looked around in the dressing room and there were very few people present. It felt like the funeral of a tramp few knew, but felt duty bound to show at the grave, because they'd let onto him now and again. Amazing how defeat acts like a bad smell and many you considered friends suddenly disappear from your side; there is a long list of people who don't call your mobile any more. I was sat quietly trying so hard to hold it together with young Mikey, who was crying his eyes out, when Lumby came across and showed me his phone.

'There's a message for you off Billy Graham mate. Do you want me to read it?'

I nodded.

Tell Mike he doesn't owe Manchester nothing. x

And then I just lost it. The tears fell and I sobbed. Alison entered. She stood there staring at me for a moment, not talking.

'So is that it then? She asked. 'Is it really over?'

'Yeah,' I replied. 'It's over.'

Years later, Alison said one look at me that night and it was clear something within me had died. 'It was like a light going out in your eyes, Mike.'

She sat down and put her arm around my shoulders. I didn't deserve this lady. Sky's Adam Smith came in to see how I was. Adam had followed and been with me since the early days. He'd witnessed the mad, bad, good and utterly crazy times. He knew where the bodies were buried so to speak. The real story.

'Is it over Adam?' It was like I desperately needed someone of his ilk to just say the words. End it…Just end it

'Jim Watt has always told me it isn't our job to tell fighters when to retire. I don't disagree with Jim on many things, but I do on this.' Adam came across and sat next to myself and Alison. He looked me straight in the eyes. 'Yes it is over. Get out whilst you can, son.'

We stood up and Adam shook my hand and he hugged Alison.

'Thanks for the memories Michael.'

And with that Adam and the boxing career was gone.

38: WATER IN A PINT POT

'If Newbiggin is confused about his sexuality now, he won't have a clue by the time I've finished with him.'

MICHAEL GOMEZ

I'D NEVER HIT WOMEN but I was definitely going to make an exception in the case of Rob Newbiggin (aka Mercedes). For a few quid, soon as I retired and to keep things slipping out of control with the pubs and clubs, I dipped my toes into the murky world of unlicensed boxing. I knew in doing this it would definitely throw up some weird, wonderful and sometimes really dangerous opponents, but never did I dream that Newbiggin would show his face. Or faces. A friend of mine, Danny Hornsby, who ran KO Promotions was putting on a fight show at the Ritz in Manchester called '*Who is the Man?*' A freak show? Degrading? Well I was desperate and on my arse and I needed instant walking around money to pay bills and for booze, so I thought, why not?

I heard a story once about Roberto Duran and what he'd been reduced to at one time. Duran knocked out a horse with one punch at a fiesta in his mother's home town of Guarare. Somebody bet him twenty dollars and a bottle of whiskey he couldn't do it. Well this poor mare was laid flat and Roberto got his cash and firewater. So in my mind I was in the company of boxing Gods. The sport is littered with tales of fighters forced to not just sing for their supper when they retired but carry on fighting for it too. Queensbury Rules applied in the unlicensed game but were rarely adhered to. You did whatever necessary to win. Different rules, same ring. I got paid a grand. Hardly a fortune but I wasn't in any position to turn anything down. Danny said I needn't worry about selling tickets, he'd just stick my name on the poster and immediately double his audience and fill the Ritz. I'd had some wicked adventures in there but none took place with boxing gloves on. Besides, I'd desperately missed it; the roar of a crowd, either for me or against. It'd feel good to get back between the ropes. I was nowhere near top condition. Overweight, touching nearly thirteen stone but I'd the experience and could still hit, so what'd I got to lose?

The day before the fight I was at home on the sofa nursing a lousy hangover. I'd spent almost a week in Val's pub in Cheetham Hill called the Imperial and was in a right mess. The phone rang and it was Lumby. He sounded panic stricken. 'Gomez, have you seen the Sun newspaper this morning?'

Oh Christ, here we go, I thought. What have I done now? Had some girl sold her story? It nearly happened in Long Legs nightclub a couple of times but we managed to stop it.

Gomez: 'Is it a bird?'

Lumby: 'Not in so many words, well not yet anyway?'

Gomez: 'Mate, what the fuck are you going on about?'

Lumby: 'Well it's about a man wanting to be a bird. You best go and buy a copy now!'

That said he disappeared off the line and left me with no idea? Almost straight away my mobile went again. This happened two or three more times with people only repeating the same as Lumby.

'Mike have you seen it?'

'Fuckin'ell Gomez, this is weird even for you.'

'Are you going to fight him or fuck him?'

Bones rang. 'Don't say anything, just go and buy the fuckin' Sun.'

I thought was this all a wind up? But such was the insistence and worried voices, something made me think I'd better go and check it out.

So off I went to the newsagents. I browsed through until there I was in The Sun. Bold as brass. A picture of myself stood next to another boxer covered in tattoos. It was obviously my opponent Rob Newbiggin for the following evening. I recognised the guy. He was a decent painter as well and had once done a mural of Billy Graham's reptile tank that housed his lizard (Liston) back in 2007 at the Phoenix gym. Billy was so pleased with it he'd let Newbiggin train there for a while and I remember him sparring with Matthew Hatton. I'd watched that and knew I'd nothing to worry about.

Not being able to read the article, I bought the paper and headed home. I turned to the pages and passed it over to Alison.

'Can ya tell me what this is all about?'

Her face went a funny colour and I'm sure she was trying not to laugh.

'Do you really want to know Mike?'

I exploded! 'Alison, please just tell me what it says?!'

And so she read it and I nearly had a heart attack!

Rob Newbiggin was fighting me so he could raise enough money to pay for a sex change. Then after the operation he would like to be known as Mercedes!

I remember thinking this is the day before we go in the ring and I've just come off a week's bender (if that's the right word) I'm fat as fuck, I've not trained because it's an unlicensed four round contest and suddenly I'm up against a guy who wants to be a woman! If I get beat here, my reputation as a Manchester boxing legend was gone. All those years it took me to build up a legacy and it'd be over. I'd be a laughing stock and have to go back living in that Ballymun caravan. Even then that wouldn't be far enough to hide. I wasn't worried, I was panicking! What the fuck was happening here? No way could I let it all end like this.

My mind was working overtime to find an excuse. I'd ring

WATER IN A PINT POT

Danny up and say I'd sprained an ankle and couldn't fight but then I thought, well that'd mean no money to go on the beer with. There were also bills to pay and mouths to feed. Then another idea came to mind; I'd go in there and pretend to break my hand in the first round. Just go down on one knee and retire. Again I thought, I couldn't do that because it'd feel worse than actually getting beat. No, there wasn't a choice. I had to go through with the fight and just give my all and if the worst possible scenario occurs? If Gomez gets beat, well the answer was simple.

…I'd hang myself.

Rob Newbiggin: Aka Mercedes: I climbed into the ring first and thought what the fuck is happening here? We're at the Ritz right, and I'm the star. Surely I should've been getting in second? I'm Michael Gomez, the Manchester legend! Two times British and world champion. A warrior. The master of ceremonies, or in this case more of a circus master, then stepped up to the mic and announced loudly with a wide smile on his face.

'And now please welcome into the ring Rob Newbiggin. Aka Mercedes!'

All I could hear were people laughing. A hostile crowd was there to not just watch me get beaten but laughed out of town and humiliated. I looked around and there were enemies everywhere that I'd ripped off with cocaine deals, or who I'd fallen out with and sparked over the years in various scrapes. I'd hardly any friends in the place, only bad faces and even more dangerous memories.

In my corner were two mates, Michael Barton and Darren Coyle, so at least I had some support. Also my old manager Kevin Maree was in the building. He'd come and wished me luck beforehand and looked upset. No doubt seeing what I'd been reduced to. Kevin later said he watched the fight from the back row with tears in his eyes. The first round began and I was already sweating. Not because

283

I'd warmed up but because the booze was coming out of me in buckets. I was so slow, rumbling around the ring like an elephant whilst Newbiggin was in decent shape; fast, rapid and moving like a fuckin' fly I couldn't swat. I tried like hell to get near and so desperate was I to win, I even bit him. For which I was rightly docked a point. but there went the round. I was one down.

Come the bell I fell back on the stool and neither Michael nor Darren said a word or would even meet my eyes. So I knew it must have been pretty bad. I got a drink of water from a pint pot, they sponged my head, wiped me with a towel but still nobody spoke. The silence was deafening. I couldn't blame them really. Who in their right mind would honestly want to be associated with this farce?

Round two and I simply couldn't tag him. Newbiggin was flurrying me with pesky little shots. He wasn't hurting but every time one hit I saw my career flashing before me and I was thinking, all those years. It's gone. The second round finished and I was clearly two down. Back in the corner things were getting that bad Michael had fucked off to the crowd. He didn't want anything more to do with it.

Luckily Darren had stayed but he looked embarrassed for me.

'Mike, you need to do something now mate. You're getting shown up in there to be truthful.' Insightful from Daz but nothing I didn't already know. I came thundering out like a mad man in the third. By any means I had to beat this guy. I went in hunting and I hit with a jab that made Newbiggin blink. I thought here we go, I like that. I'd finally hurt him! I charged! No educated boxing skills or technique involved. I dragged, hustled and pushed him into a corner and caught the confused Newbiggin with a fierce left uppercut. Where it came from? God knows, but down he went and happily didn't get back up.

I thought praise the Lord!

After the fight I went straight home. No beer, nothing, just bed. The next morning, it was a Sunday and I went to my local church,

Saint Luke's and prayed to God, thanking him for that uppercut. I was convinced my little sister Louise must've had a word with the big guy.

'Stick a bit of gold dust in that punch for my big brother Michael please.'

It was sheer power from above that floored Rob Newbiggin. It was ironic that after my last time in a ring I ended up going to church instead of a pub.

As for Newbiggin? I'd fought a lot worse. Good luck to him but at the time I really could've done without days like this. I was later told the fight made the *New York Daily News*. Better late than never I suppose.

39: ENLIGHTENMENT

'I am the resurrection and I am the life. I couldn't even bring myself to hate you as I'd like.'

THE STONE ROSES

THE LAST BELL: It's the oldest story in the world that when the final bell rings for many fighters, it can inevitably equally toll and signal the worst. Michael Armstrong Gomez had been fighting since he was eight years old but always against someone whom he could hit back. Now the opponent was one impossible to attack and hold off. It came in waves, mostly at nights. Demons in the head. Ably and abetted by enough cocaine and whiskey to send a sane man mad and make a mad man sane. The buzz of fighting had proved impossible to replace. Everybody around him suffered in the fall out but nobody felt the pain more than the man himself. Even today he carries with him the weight of his guilt at how it all fell apart.

As we reach the final chapter hopes of a happy-ever-after scenario remains more than possible. That Gomez is even alive to tell his extraordinary tale is for many a minor miracle. Self-destruction in a fighter is nothing new. For many of Gomez's similar background a career in the ring is the only alternative to a life outside the law that ultimately ends in and out of prison or even worse. Shot or stabbed and forgotten. That even today the mere mention of Michael's name is enough to see boxing fans smile wide and talk only of memorable nights and the great times he brought means Gomez time will never be forgotten.

ENLIGHTENMENT

Maybe not the greatest boxer or finest role model outside the ring people still care about this man who fought, laughed, drank and partied amongst them. The last bell has indeed sounded and whilst the battles in the ring are over, there remains many outside still to face. And so with the cheers of the Gomez chants echoing only now in far off memories it's almost time to say goodbye as the last chapter closes on the 'Mexican Manc.' But Michael's story is far from over...

ON THE RARE NIGHTS I went to bed sober, I'd cry myself to sleep. It felt like I was drowning without the water. That was retirement for me. I'd sit there like a zombie, utterly dead to the world. I wasn't interested in anything. Alison would try so hard to start conversations. She'd mention how the kids were doing at school or one of my sister's latest escapades. Who'd fallen out with whom? The boyfriends? Bones' adventures. 'You won't believe what your crazy brother has done now!'

But nothing ever came back. I was a blank. It was like talking to a brick wall. All I'd do as Alison would get upset and lose her rag is utter a single word. Only eight letters but one that stabbed her heart.

'Whatever.'

I couldn't give a fuckin' toss about anything or anybody but little did I know I was edging towards a nervous breakdown. It was all fucked up. I was burning the candle from both ends. I'd start the day at the gym in an attempt to stay sane. But then I'd leave and go straight to the pub. There people would give me a swerve or just leave when I walked in knowing I was a ticking time bomb when I'd had a drink. I was out of control. The respect was gone. I'd be staggering from the bar and somebody would take a pop knowing there'd be no comeback. No more rising from the floor, I stayed down. No count just the end of the road. So called friends from the glory days had long since deserted for new gravy trains.

I was invited to many funerals but never christenings or weddings.

GOMEZ

It was a living nightmare and one I couldn't wake from. I'd always have good intentions of going to pick the kids up from school around three o'clock, but by then I would be pissed, so I'd stay out of the way. I'd at least retained the good sense to not embarrass them or Alison in front of others. Instead I'd end up all over the place for days and nights on end. Nameless faces. Stranger's gaffs, council houses, flats, tower blocks, anywhere there was booze and hopefully cocaine. Once people had wanted to drink and snort with the legend that was Gomez. Not anymore. All those sombreros that once flew high in the sky when I won were now being pissed and trampled on.

It was the same self-destruct button that I'd pressed time and again. I'd already lost boxing for good and Alison and the kids would surely not be far behind but I carried on until wasted beyond words and then I'd go home. Dishevelled and destroyed. I had no self-respect. I hated my life. I'd become the bum I never wanted to be. The nightmare had finally come true. No more rounds and the final bell sounded long ago. The truth being I was using the cocaine and booze as a replacement for the boxing and in my mind if I kept going, then the hope remained in some dark, drunken dream that maybe I could once more be somebody. I'd become a lost soul trying desperately to stay afloat but the reality was I was drowning and going under fast.

Alison confronted me one night when I'd returned in such a state, I simply sat on the sofa and started to cry.

'Michael you've got me and the kids. Why are you looking for something you'll never find?'

Life started to get even darker. The depression, the booze and cocaine made me paranoid. I started talking crazy of killing, stabbing and shooting people. Something was going on in the head and I couldn't stop it.

My sister Tina, who is a mental health nurse, came round to the house. She sat and listened and knew the signs.

'Mike you need help.'

ENLIGHTENMENT

But I argued with her. It was simply all the guilt of fuckin' up my career. I didn't need help, I was just angry with myself. But Tina was insistent and I was admitted into Park House mental health care. The doctors took one look and I was sectioned. It was a move that saved my life because undoubtedly without it I'd have killed myself or somebody else. For six weeks they watched me like a hawk. I wasn't allowed to take a bath without supervision. Still, I was looking around for somebody to blame but I couldn't find anyone and it was killing me inside. I just kept repeating the same words. 'I've fucked up my career. I fucked everything up....I fu...'

And then one day I thought to myself, this is getting boring, Mike.

Without realising it at first, the medication and talking to specialists was kicking in. They were bringing me back from the brink until finally I woke up one morning and it was like a huge weight had been lifted from my mind. I could see light once more at the end of a long dark tunnel. The decision was taken that I was no longer a threat to myself or anyone else and I was allowed to go home.

I came out into the light and today, please God, I'm in a better place.

I've piled on a bit of weight but I'm running every day and being back in the gym with my mate, Robert Macdonald, I owe him a lot. Rob hasn't so much kept me from temptation, he's been like a brother. I'm off the booze and cocaine. I go to AA. I'm learning to read and write. More so that I can actually understand what I've said about you all! The film of my life is once more set for lift off. Most importantly, I've finally come to terms with the fact that the boxing and more recently my marriage is definitely over.

Alison finally left but who could blame her? We still talk and are so proud of our kids. Not forgetting that at the grand old age of thirty-eight, I'm now a grandad. Grandad Gomez! He's a little beauty called Oscar, after Oscar De la Hoya. No doubt he'll have a cracking left hook and I've already bought him a mini sombrero.

And then there's our Mikey.

The Gomez boxing legacy is alive and well and in safe hands with my boy.

Michael Gomez jnr: 26 July 2014. The shouts of 'Gomez, Gomez' echoed loud across the *Phones 4u* Arena, formerly the *MEN*. I watched with tears in my eyes and no little fear in my heart as young Mikey took his first tender steps as a professional. There we were in our sombreros. All the old faces and new ones also; the next generation. Ours was some legacy to carry on but they were giving it large and doing my son proud. Many had hardly been born when I was raising hell and tearing the roof off this place. The original crowd were now a lot greyer and balder. With age they were supposed to be slightly more sensible, although looking round at the faces, I doubt that.

In all my years, during the battles and wars fought both in and out of the ring, I'd never felt terror like this. Sheer blind panic. A part of me wanted to run off. Another to go and drag Mikey out of the ring. Then there was another side.

The pride.

The sheer unadulterated pleasure at seeing my boy in his sombrero and being cheered to the rafters, a warrior like his father. Heavy lies the crown went the saying, well not with Mikey as he put away his experienced opponent in the third round with great style and looked the part. The sombreros flew into the air. We hugged and danced and sang the name.

'There's only two Michael Gomez!'

I just couldn't stop crying. Finally, after all these years, the penny dropped and I suddenly realised. It was enlightenment.

It isn't all about me.

Mikey in the ring. My other kids, my sisters and Bones hugging me tight. Even he had tears in his eye, although Bones would later claim it was just dust. In that moment I'd been handed the greatest win of my life. Beating Alex Arthur in Edinburgh didn't compare. Never even came close. By some miracle God had allowed me to stay around and experience this and for that I would always be truly grateful. God knows, I'd pushed my luck and surely tested the Almighty's patience many times over the years. Once I almost shook his hand.

But I'm still around. Like after a storm on a summer's day. You look to the sky and see the colours. Refusing to fade until they're good and ready.

That's me, the traveller's son. Michael Armstrong Gomez.

I'm the rainbow man.

THE END

MICHAEL GOMEZ - THE PROFESSIONAL RECORD

FIGHT NO.	DATE	OPPONENT	RECORD	VENUE	DECISION	
48	27/03/2009	Ricky Burns	25 2 0	Bellahouston Leisure Centre, Glasgow, Scotland, United Kingdom	L	TKO
				COMMONWEALTH (BRITISH EMPIRE) SUPER FEATHERWEIGHT TITLE		
47	21/12/2008	Chris Long	9 21 3	Dalziel Park Hotel & Conference Centre, Motherwell, Scotland, United Kingdom	W	PTS
46	10/10/2008	Baz Carey	11 37 4	Dalziel Park Hotel & Conference Centre, Motherwell, Scotland, United Kingdom	W	PTS
45	28/09/2008	Chris Brophy	3 22 2	Municipal Hall, Colne, Lancashire, United Kingdom	W	TKO
44	21/06/2008	Amir Khan	17 0 0	National Indoor Arena, Birmingham, West Midlands, United Kingdom	L	TKO
				COMMONWEALTH (BRITISH EMPIRE) LIGHTWEIGHT TITLE		
43	29/03/2008	Baz Carey	11 28 4	Scottish Exhibition Centre, Glasgow, Scotland, United Kingdom	W	PTS
42	19/10/2007	Carl Johanneson	26 3 0	Doncaster Dome, Doncaster, Yorkshire, United Kingdom	L	TKO
				BBBOFC BRITISH SUPER FEATHERWEIGHT TITLE		
41	24/06/2007	Youssef Al Hamidi	2 3 1	Robin Park Centre, Wigan, Lancashire, United Kingdom	W	TKO
40	06/05/2007	Daniel Thorpe	21 60 3	WLeisure Centre, Altrincham, Cheshire, United Kingdom	W	TKO
39	28/01/2006	Peter McDonagh	7 11 0	National Stadium, Dublin, Ireland	L	TKO
				VACANT IRISH LIGHTWEIGHT TITLE		
38	11/02/2005	Javier Osvaldo Alvarez	31 4 1	M.E.N. Arena, Manchester, Lancashire, United Kingdom	L	TKO
				WORLD BOXING UNION SUPER FEATHERWEIGHT TITLE		
37	01/10/2004	Levan Kirakosyan	14 3 0	M.E.N. Arena, Manchester, Lancashire, United Kingdom	W	TKO
				WORLD BOXING UNION SUPER FEATHERWEIGHT TITLE		
36	22/05/2004	Justin Juuko	39 7 1	Kingsway Leisure Centre, Widnes, Cheshire, United Kingdom	W	TKO
				WORLD BOXING UNION SUPER FEATHERWEIGHT TITLE		
35	03/04/2004	Ben Odamattey	10 2 2	M.E.N. Arena, Manchester, Lancashire, United Kingdom	W	TKO
				VACANT WORLD BOXING UNION SUPER FEATHERWEIGHT TITLE		
34	25/10/2003	Alex Arthur	16 0 0	Meadowbank Sports Centre, Edinburgh, Scotland, United Kingdom	W	TKO
				BBBOFC BRITISH SUPER FEATHERWEIGHT TITLE & WBA INTER-CONTINENTAL SUPER FEATHERWEIGHT TITLE		
33	05/04/2003	Wladimir Borov	15 15 1	M.E.N. Arena, Manchester, Lancashire, United Kingdom	W	TKO
32	18/01/2003	Rakhim Mingaleyev	25 31 0	Guild Hall, Preston, Lancashire, United Kingdom	W	RTD
31	28/09/2002	Jimmy Beech	8 4 0	M.E.N. Arena, Manchester, Lancashire, United Kingdom	W	TKO
30	01/06/2002	Kevin Lear	12 0 0	M.E.N. Arena, Manchester, Lancashire, United Kingdom	L	RTD
				VACANT WORLD BOXING UNION SUPER FEATHERWEIGHT TITLE		
29	27/10/2001	Craig Docherty	12 0 1	M.E.N. Arena, Manchester, Lancashire, United Kingdom	W	TKO
				BBBOFC BRITISH SUPER FEATHERWEIGHT TITLE		
28	07/07/2001	Laszlo Bognar	26 3 2	Velodrome, Manchester, Lancashire, United Kingdom	W	TKO
				WBO INTER-CONTINENTAL SUPER FEATHERWEIGHT TITLE		

27	10/02/2001	Laszlo Bognar	25 3 2	Kingsway Leisure Centre, Widnes, Cheshire, United Kingdom	L	TKO	23-4
				WBO INTER-CONTINENTAL SUPER FEATHERWEIGHT TITLE			
26	11/12/2000	Ian McLeod	11 11	Kingsway Leisure Centre, Widnes, Cheshire, United Kingdom	W	PTS	23-3
				BBBOFC BRITISH SUPER FEATHERWEIGHT TITLE			
25	19/10/2000	Awel Abdulai	8 11 1	Zembo Shrine, Harrisburg, Pennsylvania, USA	W	UD	22-3
24	08/07/2000	Carl Greaves	20 4 0	Kingsway Leisure Centre, Widnes, Cheshire, United Kingdom	W	KO	21-3
				BBBOFC BRITISH SUPER FEATHERWEIGHT TITLE			
23	24/06/2000	Carl Allen	13 22 2	Hampden Park, Glasgow, Scotland, United Kingdom	W	KO	20-3
22	29/02/2000	Dean Pithie	19 2 1	Kingsway Leisure Centre, Widnes, Cheshire, United Kingdom	W	PTS	19-3
				BBBOFC BRITISH SUPER FEATHERWEIGHT TITLE			
21	29/01/2000	Chris Jickells	13 29 0	M.E.N. Arena, Manchester, Lancashire, United Kingdom	W	TKO	18-3
20	11/12/1999	Oscar Galindo	11 6 1	Everton Park Sports Centre, Liverpool, Merseyside, United Kingdom	W	TKO	17-3
				WBO INTER-CONTINENTAL SUPER FEATHERWEIGHT TITLE			
19	06/11/1999	Jose Manjarrez	13 20 4	Kingsway Leisure Centre, Widnes, Cheshire, United Kingdom	W	UD	16-3
				WBO INTER-CONTINENTAL SUPER FEATHERWEIGHT TITLE			
18	04/09/1999	Gary Thornhill	16 1 1	York Hall, Bethnal Green, London, United Kingdom	W	TKO	15-3
				VACANT BBBOFC BRITISH SUPER FEATHERWEIGHT TITLE			
17	07/08/1999	William Alverzo	15 4 0	Taj Majal Hotel & Casino, Atlantic City, New Jersey, USA	W	PTS	14-3
16	29/05/1999	Nigel Leake	5 4 0	North Bridge Leisure Centre, Halifax, Yorkshire, United Kingdom	W	TKO	13-3
				IBF INTER-CONTINENTAL FEATHERWEIGHT TITLE			
15	27/02/1999	Chris Jickells	11 22 0	Sports Centre, Lord Street, Oldham, Lancashire, United Kingdom	W	TKO	12-3
				VACANT BBBOFC CENTRAL AREA FEATHERWEIGHT TITLE			
14	13/02/1999	Dave Hinds	4 12 0	Telewest Arena, Newcastle, Tyne and Wear, United Kingdom	W	PTS	11-3
13	19/12/1998	Kevin Sheil	1 10 2	Everton Park Sports Centre, Liverpool, Merseyside, United Kingdom	W	TKO	10-3
12	14/11/1998	David Jeffrey	3 8 0	Grundy Park Leisure Centre, Cheshunt, Hertfordshire, United Kingdom	W	TKO	9-3
11	05/09/1998	Peter Buckley	25 88 6	Ice Rink, Telford, Shropshire, United Kingdom	W	PTS	8-3
10	16/05/1998	Craig Spacie	2 0 0	York Hall, Bethnal Green, London, United Kingdom	W	TKO	7-3
9	18/04/1998	Benny Jones	4 12 0	Nynex Arena, Manchester, Lancashire, United Kingdom	W	PTS	6-3
8	11/09/1997	Wayne Jones	6 21 2	Kingsway Leisure Centre, Widnes, Cheshire, United Kingdom	W	TKO	5-3
7	03/05/1997	Chris Williams	0 1 0	Nynex Arena, Manchester, Lancashire, United Kingdom	L	PTS	4-3
6	22/03/1997	John Farrell	debut	Wythenshawe Forum, Manchester, Lancashire, United Kingdom	W	TKO	4-2
5	09/11/1996	David Morris	2 0 0	Nynex Arena, Manchester, Lancashire, United Kingdom	W	PTS	3-2
4	19/09/1996	Martin Evans	3 12 0	Bowlers Exhibition Centre, Manchester, Lancashire, United Kingdom	W	TKO	2-2
3	24/11/1995	Danny Ruegg	2 8 0	Bowlers Exhibition Centre, Manchester, Lancashire, United Kingdom	L	PTS	1-2
2	15/09/1995	Greg Upton	7 6 1	Leisure Centre, Mansfield, Nottinghamshire, United Kingdom	L	PTS	1-1
1	10/06/1995	Danny Ruegg	2 6 0	G-Mex Centre, Manchester, Lancashire, United Kingdom	W	PTS	1-0

INDEX

Arthur, Alex 162, 163, 164, 167, 170, 174, **176-189**, 193, 194, 201, 202, 207, 222, 252, 257, 264, 276, 291

Barnes, David 35

Barrera, Marco Antonio 74, 75

Barrett, Pat 31, 34, 54, 67, 94, 111, 135, 211

Barton, Michael 283

Beattie, Eddie 251

Beech, Jimmy 157, 158, 159

Bell, Stephen 168, 169

Bez 84, 86

Blair, Tony 199

Bognar, Laszlo 114, 115, 116, 117, 118, 119, 120, 122, 132, 133, 134, 137, 143, 214

Borov, Wladimir 161

Botha, Francis 74

Botile, Mbuto 120

Boxing Union of Ireland (BUI) 226, 228

Boylesports 227, 228

Brennan, Stuart 108

Brian Hughes – Bognar fight 121

Briggs, Shannon 74

British Boxing Board of Control (BBBC) 115

Brodie, Michael 44

Brophy, Chris 265, 266

Buchanan, Ken 35

Buckley, George 35

Buckley, Peter 62, 63, 64

Burns, Ricky 269, 271, 272, 273, 274, 276

Calzaghe, Joe 66, 92, 213

Cantona, Eric 38

Carey, Baz 251, 267

Carter, Jimmy (39th President of the USA) 5

Cayton, Bill 76

Cheetham Hill gang 54

Cleary, Mike vii

Collins, Steve 225, 230

Collyhurst and Moston Boys Club 29, 32, 72, 121, 148

Corrales, Diego 202, 203, 204, 263

Cotto, Miguel 203

Coyle, Darren 283

Coyle, John (referee) 134, 181

Creed, Apollo 107

Darke, Ian 70, 83, 182, 207

Davies, Richie 111

De la Hoya, Oscar 290

Derby 84, 109, 118

Dermody, Craig 33, 34

Diaz, Juan Antonio 60

Docherty, Craig 139, 140, 276

Donnelly, Anthony 198

Donnelly brothers, The 198

Donnelly, Christopher 198

Duran, Roberto 230, 280

Edwards, Phil (referee) 68

INDEX

INDEX